MERLIN
AND THE DISCOVERY OF
AVALON
IN THE
NEW WORLD

Also by Graham Phillips

Alexander the Great: Murder in Babylon

Atlantis and the Ten Plagues of Egypt: The Secret History Hidden in the Valley of the Kings

The Chalice of Magdalene: The Search for the Cup That Held the Blood of Christ

The Moses Legacy: The Evidence of History

The Templars and the Ark of the Covenant: The Discovery of the Treasure of Solomon

12 Tribes, 10 Plagues and the 2 Men Who Were Moses

The Virgin Mary Conspiracy: The True Father of Christ and the Tomb of the Virgin

MERLIN
AND THE DISCOVERY OF
AVALON
IN THE
NEW WORLD

GRAHAM PHILLIPS

Bear & Company
Rochester, Vermont

Bear & Company
One Park Street
Rochester, Vermont 05767
www.InnerTraditions.com

Bear & Company is a division of Inner Traditions International

Library of Congress Cataloging-in-Publication Data
Phillips, Graham.
  Merlin and the discovery of Avalon in the New World / by Graham Phillips.
    p. cm.
  Summary: "The first book to present the true identity of the mythic figure Merlin"—
Provided by publisher.
  Includes bibliographical references (p.   ) and index.
  ISBN 1-59143-047-X
  1. America—Discovery and exploration—Welsh. 2. Merlin (Legendary character)
3. Avalon (Legendary place) 4. Towers—New England. 5. Tombs—New England.
6. New England—Antiquities. 7. Newport (R.I.)—Antiquities. 8. Manana Island
(Me.)—Antiquities. I. Title.

E109.W4P48 2005
001.94—dc22

                                                                2005014437

Printed and bound in the United States by Lake Book Manufacturing, Inc.

10 9 8 7 6 5 4 3 2 1

Text design and layout by Jon Desautels
This book was typeset in Caslon with Charlemagne as a display font

To send correspondence to the author of this book send a first class letter to the
author c/o Inner Traditions • Bear & Company, One Park Street, Rochester, VT
05767, and we will forward the communication to the author.

CONTENTS

ACKNOWLEDGMENTS

The author would like to thank the following people for their invaluable help:

Glynn Davis, without whom this book would not have been possible; Sally Evans for all her hard work; my historical researchers Louise Simkiss and Kellie Knights; and everyone who helped me in the United States, including Graham and Jodi Russell, Mat Walker, and Sam and Kerri Brewster. I also want to thank, at Inner Traditions: Jon Graham, Anne Dillon, Jeanie Levitan, Peri Champine, Rob Meadows, Jamaica Burns, Patricia Rydle, and Kelly Bowen. I would also like to offer a very special thank-you to Debbie Benstead and Yvan Cartwright for believing in me all along.

For more information about Graham Phillips, his books, and his research, please visit his Web site at grahamphillips.net.

1

TWO MERLINS

The Arctic wind howled around the cramped cabin of the tiny fishing boat, tossing us mercilessly on the deadly winter seas. Outside, icy spray had frozen to the safety rails and to the ropes that fixed tackle immovably to the deck. Once more, a huge wave rocked the vessel almost onto its side as the gray waters swirled and foamed, seeming to breathe, as if about to finally embrace us in their ocean grave of bitter cold.

"Hang on!" screamed the skipper. Too late! I was slammed against the chart wall, only to be hurled to the floor as the boat somehow managed to right itself.

The roar of the storm powering down from Canadian tundra did hold one macabre blessing: it drowned out the menacing sound of the waves that crashed over the deadly jagged rocks that loomed from the water just a few terrifying feet from the starboard bow.

"If we can make it round the point, we'll have a chance of making land," the skipper shouted.

I looked ahead of him at the cliffs of the snow-covered headland that occasionally appeared between the relentless sheets of the driving blizzard. But just as I thought there was hope, my stomach leaped as the boat dropped suddenly deeper into the violent sea. For a few seconds there was an icy calm. The howl of the wind became a dull moan and the freezing torrent no longer pounded the windows. Then the terror hit me. The vessel had sunk into the trough of an enormous wave. Its dark crest towering before us momentarily shielded the boat from the relentless storm and shrouded us in a cold shadow of impending doom. We were directly in the wave's path and the wave was heading right for the rocks! As the dreadful wall of water drew closer and the vessel began to rise, the captain spun the wheel furiously in an attempt to turn the bow into it.

One of the crew shouted something and we braced ourselves for the assault. In an instant that freezes into memory, my mind flashed back to how it all began. The quest that had led me to face what now seemed a certain death in the bitter waters of the North Atlantic had started as an innocent search for the origins of the Merlin legend, one hazy summer afternoon, six months earlier in a sleepy British town.

The sun's rays fell in bright shafts through the leafy trees that grew around the beer garden of the old country inn. On one of the tables Glynn Davis had spread out a map of Britain, held down by glasses to prevent it from being blown away by the occasional summer breeze. Glynn was an amateur historian in his late sixties who had spent many years investigating the King Arthur legend, and had written me asking to meet up and discuss his theories on the mystery of Merlin. Having written a couple of books on the Arthurian mystery, I was happy to oblige.[1] The pub was an appropriate place for the meeting, as it was in Carmarthen, in Wales, on the western side of Britain. It was here that legend said Merlin was born.

"You say very little about Merlin in your books," said Glynn, looking around thoughtfully at the drinkers at the table next to us, whose children were climbing in the branches of the trees.

"I couldn't find anything to show that he was a historical figure," I replied.

I had found evidence that King Arthur existed, however. Not, though, in the way most people imagine. The story of King Arthur, as we now know it, comes from the work of the English writer Thomas Malory, who wrote in the mid-1400s.[2] This is the Arthur who becomes king by drawing the sword from the stone, founds the fabulous city of Camelot and its Knights of the Round Table, and rules Britain with his beautiful queen Guinevere. This story, in turn, had been taken from older, medieval tales known as the Arthurian romances that were written in the twelfth and thirteenth centuries, in which King Arthur and his knights fight dragons, rescue damsels in distress, and search for the Holy Grail. These were clearly romantic inventions but there was much earlier evidence that this King Arthur figure was based on a real warrior who had lived centuries before.

According to the Arthurian romances, Arthur ruled Britain around 500 A.D., and the work of a ninth-century British monk named Nennius records a warrior called Arthur fighting in Britain at that time. In Nennius's surviving work, in the British Library in London, Arthur is recorded as one of the last native British leaders to make a successful stand against the Anglo-Saxons, who invaded the country from their homeland in Denmark and northern Germany in the late fifth and early sixth centuries A.D.[3] This was during the British Dark Ages: an era of feuding and warfare that followed the collapse of the Roman Empire in the fifth century and lasted for some four hundred years, until the Saxon king Athelstan became ruler of all England in 927. It is appropriately called the Dark Ages, not only because it was a time when civilization collapsed, but also because it is an era from which very few records survive. (It is for this reason that so little is known about the period in which Arthur is said to have lived and why there is such debate concerning his historical existence.)

Unfortunately, Nennius says little about Arthur, nor does he reveal where he originated, but he does list twelve of his battles, and the last of them, the battle of Badon, is datable from a separate historical source: the work of another British monk, named Gildas, who wrote within living memory of the event. In his *On the Ruin and Conquest of Britain*, dating from the mid-sixth century, Gildas makes reference to the battle of Badon occurring around 500 A.D.[4] There does, therefore, appear to have been a historical British leader named Arthur who lived at the time the king Arthur of the Arthurian romances is said to have lived.

However, if Arthur lived in the late fifth or early sixth century as Nennius records, he would not have been a king in shining armor, living in a huge Gothic castle, but instead a Dark Age warlord with Roman-style armor, and his fortifications would have been wooden stockades. The reason that Arthur is now portrayed as a medieval-style king of many centuries later is that writers of the Middle Ages (the period from Athelstan in the ninth century until the Renaissance in the fifteenth century) tended to set ancient stories, such as the legends of Greece and Rome, in their own historical context—a context of knighthood and chivalry.

I was satisfied that Arthur was a historical figure during these early post-Roman Dark Ages, but I had found no similar evidence for the existence of Merlin. In the Arthurian romances, Merlin is a mysterious figure who was once a warrior himself, but eventually became a magician and King Arthur's adviser. In fact, he is portrayed as the real influence behind the throne. Arthur's success and the prosperity of his kingdom are deliberately contrived and orchestrated by Merlin with the magical and prophetic abilities he is said to possess.

When Merlin is young, Britain is a divided country, beset by squabbling between rival warlords who each desire the kingdom for themselves. Knowing there are two chief families with royal claims to the empty throne—the Pendragons and the Amlawdds—Merlin decides to bring them together with the birth of a son, who will be the unifying king of all Britain. The problem is that the Amlawdd heir, the princess Igraine, is already married to Gorlois, the duke of Cornwall, in the far southwest of Britain. With a magic potion, Merlin turns the Pendragon heir Uther into the likeness of Gorlois so that he can make love to Igraine, and thus Arthur is conceived. When the child is born, Merlin takes him from his mother and raises him in secret until he is old enough to become king. At the time, the symbol of British kingship is a splendid sword, which Merlin thrusts into a rock, announcing that anyone who can remove it will become king. Over the years, many try and fail, as Merlin has cast a spell so that only the true Pendragon-Amlawdd heir can pull out the sword. Eventually, of course, it is Arthur who succeeds and who is accepted as king.

In the first year of his reign, Arthur gathers knights from around his kingdom to keep the peace, and Merlin makes a round conference table as a symbol of equality so that no man can sit at its head. The magician then continues to advise Arthur on the running of his prosperous kingdom until barbarians from across the sea begin to raid and pillage the land. To defeat the barbarians, Merlin gives Arthur a second, far more important sword than the one he drew from the stone—one with the power to render its wielder invincible in battle. This is Excalibur, the magical sword that Merlin has acquired from a faraway land, made by a mysterious water nymph called the Lady of the Lake. With the sword, Arthur triumphs and peace returns, and Merlin sets sail for a mystical and secret island called Avalon. Here he remains for many years, living alone except for nine mysterious maidens.

During Merlin's absence, everything falls apart. Arthur's favorite knight, Lancelot, has an adulterous affair with Arthur's queen, Guinevere, and the land is drawn into civil war. When Merlin returns, he is distraught to find the kingdom in ruin and beset by plague and famine, while Arthur himself is sick and weak. To put matters right, Merlin gathers the Knights of the Round Table and tells them to go in search of the Holy Grail. This is the sacred chalice that once held the blood of Christ and is said to cure all ills. Eventually the Grail is found. Arthur is restored to health and leads his army against the chief rebel, his nephew Modred. Although Modred is defeated and killed, Arthur receives a mortal wound. As he lies dying on the field of battle, he orders one of his knights to throw Excalibur, the source of all his power, into a lake, where the hand of the Lady of the Lake rises from the surface to catch the weapon and take it down into the watery depths. When the knight returns to where Arthur had been lying, he discovers that three mysterious maidens have taken Arthur aboard a boat to sail him away to the isle of Avalon.

Like Arthur, Merlin could have been a historical figure upon whom later, fanciful legends were based. He could have been a wise court adviser who was later credited with magical powers. However, I had found no contemporary evidence referring to anyone of this name.

"The name Merlin comes from the Welsh name Myrddin, and there is historical evidence that he existed in Wales," said Glynn, after I explained my reservations. This I knew, but I had reason to doubt that the Welsh Myrddin had anything to do with the period in which the historical Arthur seems to have lived.

When the Anglo-Saxons eventually conquered much of Britain in the sixth and seventh centuries, the native Britons were driven into the mountainous country in the west of the British Isles. The east ultimately came to be called Angle-land, or England, after the Anglo-Saxons, while the west became known as Wales. Two distinct languages also developed in Britain: English, which came from the tongue of the Germanic Anglo-Saxons, and Welsh, which developed from the original British language

Brythonic. As the historical Arthur was one of the native Britons, it was in Wales that the stories of his exploits survived and in the Welsh language that they were preserved.

The Britons had a tradition of composing poems about their battles, and many survive from the Dark Ages; these are collectively known as war poems. I knew of seven such works, dating from before the Arthurian romances, which are thought to refer to Merlin under the Welsh name Myrddin. Three of these are in a collection of early Welsh poems known as *The Black Book of Carmarthen,* so called because of the color of its binding and because it refers to a priory in Carmarthen in which the manuscript was once housed.[5] Although the surviving manuscript was copied around 1250, linguistic analysis dates much of the poetry to the seventh century.

One of the *Black Book* poems mentions Myrddin by name: "The Conversation of Myrddin and Taliesin," in which Myrddin and a poet named Taliesin discuss the battle of Arfderydd, a historical event that took place in 573 in northern Britain on the border of what is now Scotland and England. In the poem, following the battle, Myrddin has retired to a nearby forest to live a solitary existence, having been driven mad by the slaughter he has witnessed. Two other poems in the manuscript, "The Greetings" and "The Apple Trees," refer to the aftermath of this same battle in which an unnamed speaker is living a similar, reclusive life. The inference, therefore, is that all three works relate to Myrddin.

Four other poems relating to Myrddin are found in a manuscript known as *The Red Book of Hergest,* so called because of its red leather binding and the area of Hergest in the county of Herefordshire in southeast England where it was kept for many years.[6] Like the *Black Book,* it is a collection of early Welsh works compiled into one manuscript during the Middle Ages, but it contains poems and prose compositions dating from the earlier Dark Ages.

"The Conversation of Myrddin and Gwenddydd" is a poem about Myrddin's talk with his sister Gwenddydd following the battle of Arfderydd after he has retired to the northern forest. "The Lament of Myrddin in His Grave" purports to be the last words of the dying Myrddin, recalling the fate of the Britons at the hands of the Anglo-Saxons. It too appears to refer to a time after the battle Arfderydd, and the words are spoken by the same figure who is leading a solitary existence in a forest. A poem called "Commanding Youth" refers to the mad Myrddin living in northern Britain after the battle of Arfderydd, as does a poem called "The Prophecy of the Eagle," in which although Myrddin is not mentioned by name, the speaker appears to be the same forest-dwelling recluse from the other works.

The historical existence of this figure seems to be supported by a manuscript known as the *Welsh Annals*.[7] Now in the British Library in London, the *Welsh Annals* were written down around the 950s and are a compilation of earlier records concerning Britain as a whole. An entry for the year 575 says: "The battle of Arfderydd between the sons of Eliffer and Gwenddolau son of Ceidio; in which battle Gwenddolau fell and Myrddin went mad."

However, although this Myrddin may have been a historical figure, he cannot have been the Myrddin associated with King Arthur. In the Arthurian romances, Merlin is already quite old when Arthur becomes king around 500 A.D., which means that he cannot have been alive seventy-five years later when the Myrddin referred to in these war poems appears to have lived. I had, like many historians, tried to work out who this particular Myrddin really was.

It was not only in Wales that Dark Age war poems were preserved, but also in the far north of Britain, in Scotland. Here, too, Dark Age poetry (recorded in a manuscript cataloged as the *Cotton Titus A. XIX* in the British Library) includes a mystic who went mad after the battle of Arfderydd and fled into a forest, where he gained the ability to tell the future. These tales are preserved in detail in *The Life of Kentigern* by a monk named Joceline, from Furness Abbey in Scotland, who wrote during the mid-1100s. Kentigern was the first bishop of Glasgow in the late sixth century and died in 603, so the dating of this reclusive prophet also tallies with the Myrddin mentioned in the *Welsh Annals*. Joceline's account of the bishop's life includes his associations with the mad recluse, although he does not call him Myrddin but rather Lailoken. Two of the Scottish works also refer to this reclusive prophet by the name Lailoken, and in the final lines of one of these poems, "Meldred and Lailoken," the author actually refers to Lailoken by the additional name of Myrddin.

Pierced by a spear, crushed by a stone,
And drowned in the stream's waters,
Myrddin died a triple death.

The reason why Lailoken is also called Myrddin seems to be that the name is some sort of epithet or title. The precise origin of the name Myrddin is a mystery but it appears to have derived from Brythonic words meaning something like "voice of the Eagle"—the eagle being a bird that was associated with foresight in ancient British tradition. This can be gathered from the poem "The Prophecy of the Eagle," in *The Red Book of Hergest,* in which the speaker, Myrddin, is the Eagle in question.

"I know all about Lailoken: a historical Myrddin who was attributed with the gift of prophecy," I informed Glynn. "But he lived three quarters of a century after Arthur is said to have lived."

Glynn smiled and shook his head. "I don't mean *that* Merlin," he said. "You know the name Myrddin appears to have been a title meaning the Eagle, or something along those lines. Well, there seems to have been another important figure credited with prophetic powers who lived in the late four hundreds, a century before Lailoken, who also bore the name. There survives a Dark Age reference to a Myrddin who was alive at the very time of Arthur."

I listened with interest to Glynn's argument that there were two Merlins, both said to have had the ability to foresee the future. He explained how the theory was supported by a work entitled *The Great Prophecy of Britain.* Dating from around 930, it is a war poem preserved in a manuscript cataloged as *MS Peniarth 2* in the National Library of Wales in the town of Aberystwyth. The poem concerns a period some five centuries earlier, around the year 450, when the Anglo-Saxons first began arriving, and includes a British king named Vortigern who ruled shortly before the time of Arthur's reign. "The prophet in the poem is a Myrddin of the Arthurian period, so cannot have been Lailoken, who lived well over a century later," Glynn said. He went on to say he believed that these two Merlins had been confused as one in the Arthurian romances, which began with the works of a Welsh bishop named Geoffrey of Monmouth in the mid-1100s. In 1135, Geoffrey wrote a book entitled *The History of the Kings of Britain,* in which the story of King Arthur and his adviser Merlin was first popularized.[8]

In this book, Merlin seems to be the same character as the Myrddin in *The Great Prophecy of Britain*, as it includes an episode in which Merlin as a young man comes face-to-face with the British king Vortigern (as he does in the poem). In Geoffrey's *History*, Merlin makes his first appearance when he is captured as a boy by Vortigern, who intends to use him as a sacrifice. (This Merlin also goes by another name, Ambrose, the significance of which we will explore in greater depth a bit later in this book.)

Merlin manages to save himself when he impresses the king by revealing his prophetic powers. Below Vortigern's fort there is said to be a pool in which two dragons dwell, one white, the other red. Merlin not only knows the story of the dragons but also explains its symbolic meaning: They represent the Britons and Saxons, who will soon be drawn into a devastating conflict. The Merlin depicted in Geoffrey's *History of the Kings of Britain* is clearly associated with characters such as Arthur and Vortigern, who lived in the late 400s.

However, about fifteen years after he wrote his *History of the Kings of Britain*, Geoffrey composed a work concentrating on Merlin's life after Arthur's death. In his *Life of Merlin* (circa 1150), Geoffrey includes episodes from the Lailoken story, depicting Merlin as a wild man who has lost his reason in battle and subsequently lives in a forest in the north of Britain. [9] Thus, there could have been two prophetic figures who held the same title, Myrddin, and Geoffrey of Monmouth may have confused them as one.

"Interesting, but one reference written in the tenth century associating Merlin with the fifth does not prove he actually existed," I said.

"Alone, it shows that Geoffrey of Monmouth didn't invent him, as many historians believe," said Glynn. "However, this is just one of a number of references to the same character that date from well before Geoffrey's time."

"You've found others?" I asked with interest.

"Dig deeper and you'll find them," he answered, obviously not wanting to reveal his research to a rival. Conversely, however, Glynn appeared to have no such problem trying to get information out of *me*.

"Would you show me the sword?" he asked, abruptly changing the subject. Glynn had asked me to bring along the replica of Excalibur that had been made for me a few years before.

In the Arthurian romances, Excalibur is often depicted as a medieval broadsword. However, if Arthur lived around 500 A.D., then his sword would have been of a very different design. Military leaders of this era used the *spatha,* a cavalry sword originally designed by the Romans. It would have been around two feet long, with a stunted cross guard. In 1993, with coauthor Martin Keatman, I wrote *King Arthur: The True Story,* in which we examined the history behind the Arthurian legend. As part of the research, we wanted to re-create what the historical Arthur's sword might really have looked like.

We consequently approached one of Britain's leading authorities on the weaponry of the period, the author and Dark Age military expert Dan Shadrake, and asked him to design a genuine fifth-century sword. Dan's overall pattern was based on archaeological finds from the period, but the hilt design took into account the oldest surviving description of Excalibur, in a medieval Welsh war poem called "The Dream of Rhonabwy."[10] In the poem, Arthur's sword is described as decorated with "two serpents upon its golden hilt."

When Dan's drawings were complete, we decided that the most appropriate people to make the replica would be Wilkinson Sword, the company that presently makes ceremonial swords for the British military. Excalibur had been made for a British monarch and Wilkinson's Sword still makes ceremonial swords for the British queen. Although the company is now more famous for making razors, it has been in the sword-forging business since the eighteenth century, and its designers came up with truly spectacular re-creation. Its shining steel blade was decorated with Celtic scrolling of the period and the gold hilt was created from two gold serpents coiled around one another, their bodies forming the hand grip and their heads, with teeth exposed, forming the cross guard.

I handed the Excalibur replica to Glynn, who examined it closely for a few moments before speaking. "The serpents: where did you get the exact design?" he asked.

"They were copied from an illustration in a fifth-century Roman military manual called the *Notitia Dignitatum,*" I said.[11] "Evidently, they were the insignia of a Roman legion garrisoned in Britain earlier in the same century that Arthur lived. The twin-serpent motif may have been adopted from them by the post-Roman British kings."

Glynn shook his head but said nothing. We sat in silence as he held up the sword by the blade and examined the hilt from various angles. "You're wrong about the Roman legion," he said eventually. "But the design fits the period. Do you know what the double serpents really mean?"

"Tell me," I said, but once again he changed the subject.

"What I wanted to ask you was if you had discovered anything linking Merlin with Shakespeare," he said.

"Shakespeare! But he was born in the sixteenth century . . ."

"I don't mean that Shakespeare knew him," Glynn interrupted. "Have you found anything that Shakespeare wrote about him?"

I had researched the life of William Shakespeare some years earlier for a book in which I examined his private life, but knew of nothing he had written about Merlin.

"Not that I can think of," I said. "Why do you ask?"

It was then that Glynn hit me with his bombshell. "I believe Shakespeare was killed because of what he knew about Merlin and the two serpents on Excalibur's hilt—serpents exactly like those," he said, tapping the hilt. I didn't quite know how to handle that one. As far as I knew, Glynn was a sensible and respected historian, but this sounded not only off the point but decidedly odd as well. "You *do* think that Shakespeare was murdered," he said, when I looked at him bemused. In my book I had suggested that Shakespeare was killed because of what he knew about an antigovernment conspiracy.[12]

"There are mysterious circumstances surrounding Shakespeare's death, which might imply that someone murdered him, but I can't see how that could have anything to do with Merlin," I said.

"I think you were right about Shakespeare's death. You said you thought Shakespeare knew about plots against the English government but the whole thing was bigger, much bigger than you ever considered." Glynn's easygoing and cheerful expression dropped from his face and he looked positively concerned. He even glanced around at the drinkers at the other tables as if to make sure they couldn't hear what he was saying. "There are still people today who would kill to find out what Shakespeare knew."

"Sorry, I'm not with you," I said.

Glynn looked down to the map of Britain he had been using to point out various locations associated with the Merlin legend and stabbed his finger in the area of Stratford-upon-Avon, in central England, where Shakespeare had lived. It seemed he was about to say something that referred to this area on the map but then decided against it.

"I thought someone like you might have arrived at the same conclusions, independently," he said.

"Someone like me?"

"A person who's researched both the Arthurian legend and the life of Shakespeare."

"Sorry," I said, now having difficulty disguising the fact that I thought Glynn was acting a bit weird. "I don't know what you mean. Not unless you explain."

But it seemed that Glynn had decided he'd said enough. Apparently, he had assumed that I must have known what he was talking about and as I had no idea what he meant, it was best I didn't know. He changed the subject back to the literary evidence for a historical Merlin and returned to his usual easygoing behavior.

When we parted company that afternoon, I had not changed my opinion of Glynn as a knowledgeable historian who had some interesting ideas about Merlin, but I did decide that he was somewhat eccentric and even paranoid about his theories. I didn't give his notions about Shakespeare and Excalibur a second thought at the time, but I was impressed by his theory that there was a historical Merlin during the Arthurian period. I knew of Myrddin's mention in *The Great Prophecy of Britain* but had always assumed this to be yet another reference to Lailoken. Perhaps Glynn was on to something. He had mentioned that there was other evidence for an Arthurian Merlin and I decided to take his advice and dig deeper. I could never have predicted where the investigation would lead me and how dangerous it would eventually turn out to be.

2

A BOY WITH NO FATHER

Carmarthen seemed the obvious place to begin investigating the Merlin legend, as it was here that Merlin was said to have been born. However, most historians thought Merlin's association with the Welsh town was based on a mistake made by Geoffrey of Monmouth in the 1130s. As its title suggests, Geoffrey of Monmouth claimed that his *History of the Kings of Britain* was a factual history book. He introduced the work by saying that it was based on "a certain very ancient book written in the British language [presumably Welsh]" that was given to him by the archdeacon of Oxford to translate. Whether this was true will probably never be known, but even if it was, it had been put together from various accounts to which Geoffrey added sources and possibly what were his own suppositions. One such probable supposition concerned Carmarthen.

According to Geoffrey, Merlin was the son of a princess of a kingdom in southwest Wales called Demetia. This was one of the many small kingdoms into which Britain had fragmented after the Roman legions left the country in 410 A.D. For three and a half centuries before that, the Romans had ruled all of mainland Britain except Scotland. The island had enjoyed an era of peace and stability and had adopted a Roman style of existence. However, once the Roman army was forced to depart to help fight the

Germanic tribes that had sacked Rome itself, law and order quickly broke down.

The country broke apart along ancient tribal divisions, and the strongest tribes established their individual kingdoms. Before the Romans began their conquest of Britain in 43 A.D., the native inhabitants were the Celts—an ancient people who also inhabited other parts of northwest Europe, includ-

Map 1. Britain: key sites

ing Ireland, France, and the Netherlands. As elsewhere, although they had the same or similar beliefs and practices, the Celts were divided into numerous tribes. In Britain, the largest tribes were the Iceni in the east, the Cornovii in the center, the Brigantes in the north, the Trinovates in the south, and the Demeatae in what is now South Wales. After the Romans left, many of these became separate kingdoms again, each with its own king. It was the tribe of Demeatae in southern Wales that founded the kingdom of Demetia, which remained independent for many centuries. Thus, there was indeed a kingdom of Demetia in the historical Arthurian period around 500 A.D.; there were queens of it; and Carmarthen was a part of it—so Geoffrey's story of Merlin's birth is possible.

Nevertheless, Geoffrey seems to have linked Merlin with the town simply because he thought its Welsh name implied that it was named after him. In Geoffrey's day, Carmarthen translated to the Welsh Caerfyrddin, meaning Fort Fyrddin, and the word Fyrddin could have been an early rendering of Myrddin, as Geoffrey believed. However, before Geoffrey's time, in the fifth and sixth centuries, when both Myrddins appear to have lived, the town was called Caer (Fort) Moriddyn, after Moridunum—meaning "Sea Fortress"—the name the Romans used for the fortified town they had established there, on the estuary of the river Tywi.

Given all this, Geoffrey may still have been right about Merlin being the son of a Demetian princess, but where should I begin my search? In Geoffrey's *History of the Kings of Britain*, Merlin makes his first appearance when he is captured as a boy by the British king Vortigern, who intends to use him as a sacrifice. It is in this episode that there may lie clues to Merlin's origins. In the account, Vortigern is attempting to build a mountain fortress on a hill in North Wales, but the foundations keep collapsing and his camp is beset by troubles of various kinds. In the end, the king's magicians tell him that he has to sacrifice a boy and mix his blood with the mortar. However, no ordinary child will do: The victim must be a boy with no earthly father.

> Hereupon messengers were dispatched away over all the provinces, to inquire about such a boy. In their travels they came to a city, called afterwards Carmarthen, where they saw some young men

playing before the gate, and went up to them; but being weary with their journey, they sat down in the ring, to see if they could meet with what they were in quest of. Toward evening, they happened on a sudden quarrel between two of the young men, whose names were Merlin and Dabutius. In the dispute, Dabutius said to Merlin: "You fool, do you presume to quarrel with me? Is their any equality in our birth? I am descended of royal race, both by my father and mother's side. As for you, nobody knows what you are, for you never had a father." At that word the messengers looked earnestly upon Merlin, and asked the bystanders who he was. They told him, it was not known who was his father; but that his mother was daughter to the king of Demetia and that she lived in St. Peter's church among the nuns of the city.[1]

The king's men then visit Merlin's mother, who is living as a nun, and ask about the boy's father. She tells them her own father is the king of Demetia and the reason she has retired to the nunnery and renounced her life as a royal princess is that she gave birth to Merlin without ever having sex with a man. Instead, she had apparently been visited one night by an incubus—a supernatural being—who made love to her and sired the child. Satisfied they have found a boy with no earthly father, the men take Merlin and his mother back to Vortigern.

Merlin in the meantime was attentive to all that had passed, and then approached the king, and said to him,

"For what reason am I and my mother introduced into your presence?"

"My magicians," answered Vortigern, "advised me to seek out a man that had no father, with whose blood my building is to be sprinkled, in order to make it stand."

"Order your magicians," said Merlin, "to come before me, and I will convict them of a lie." The king was surprised at his words, and presently ordered the magicians to come, and sit down before Merlin, who spoke to them after this manner: "Because you are ignorant what it is that hinders the foundation of the tower, you have recommended the shedding of my blood for cement to it, as if that would presently make it stand. But tell me now, what is there under the foundation? For something there is that will not suffer it to stand."[2]

The magicians are unable to answer, and Merlin then tells Vortigern what he should do.

"I entreat your majesty would command your workmen to dig into the ground, and you will find a pond which causes the foundations to sink." This accordingly was done, and then presently they found a pond deep under ground, which had made it give way. Merlin after this went again to the magicians, and said, "Tell me ye false sycophants, what is there under the pond." But they were silent. Then said he again to the king, "Command the pond to be drained, and at the bottom you will see two hollow stones, and in them two dragons asleep." The king made no scruple of believing him, since he had found true what he said of the pond, and therefore ordered it to be drained: which done, he found as Merlin had said; and now was possessed with the greatest admiration of him. Nor were the rest that were present less amazed at his wisdom, thinking it to be no less than divine inspiration.[3]

Once the pond is drained, the two dragons, one red, the other white, break free from the stones and begin fighting one another before flying away. Vortigern is convinced this is an omen, and Merlin reveals its meaning. The white dragon, Merlin tells Vortigern, represents the Anglo-Saxons and the red one the Britons: the peoples who will soon fight in a bloody war to rule Britain. Merlin then relates a series of prophecies that so impress Vortigern that he spares his life.

According to Geoffrey of Monmouth, Merlin was the son of a supernatural entity; he was born with prophetic powers and lived in a world where dragons roamed. I would be forgiven for concluding that Merlin was a myth and that there was no reason to search any further for a man behind the legend. Nonetheless, Geoffrey may have simply confused fact and fiction. He lived in a time when books were rare, superstitions were believed, and true historians were almost nonexistent. The British king Vortigern, however, certainly existed, as he is recorded in a number of Dark Age historical manuscripts as an important British king in the mid-fifth century.

Because of the collapse of society in Britain after the Romans left in the early 400s, hardly any written records of the following few centuries survive. Of those that do, the most important are *The Ecclesiastical History of the English People*, compiled around 731 A.D. by a monk named Bede,[4] and the *Anglo-Saxon Chronicle*, compiled on behalf of the English king Alfred the Great in the late 800s.[5] Neither of these works refers to King Arthur, which is one of the main reasons why some historians doubt his historical existence.

However, Bede may not have mentioned Arthur for the simple reason that he was writing an ecclesiastical history of the Anglo-Saxons and, as such, had no reason to include him. As for the *Chronicle*, since this was King Alfred's attempt to promote the successful exploits of his own Anglo-Saxon ancestors, it is reasonable to assume that he would not have wished to draw attention to the accomplishments of the native British opposition. However, although these works do not mention Arthur or Merlin, they do refer to Vortigern. From these sources it can be gathered that Vortigern was the most powerful of the British kings around 450 A.D., and he seems to have ruled a large part of the country. Although none of the historical sources specifically says which kingdom he ruled, it is fairly certain that his territory stretched into North Wales, where Vortigern was building his fort according to Geoffrey's account. A Dark Age monument in the region, near the town of Llangollen—a column called the Pillar of Eliseg—is inscribed with the names of kings of the area and bears Vortigern's name.

Vortigern, therefore, was no invention of Geoffrey of Monmouth, nor was the site where Geoffrey locates the fort that Vortigern was attempting to build—on a mountain in North Wales now called Dinas Emrys. Significantly, this is less than forty miles to the west of Llangollen, to where the Pillar of Eliseg shows that Vortigern's area of influence stretched. It is quite possible, then, that the historical king Vortigern built, or attempted to build, a fort here to protect his borders. This, I decided, was where I should start my search.

Dinas Emrys stands in the heart of Snowdonia. In this mountain range of North Wales are nestled some of the most scenic little valleys to be found anywhere. Unlike many barren mountainous regions elsewhere in the world, their grassy slopes are scattered with deciduous woods, groves of rowan trees, and copses of twisting, stunted oaks. Here, the lush green hillsides echo with the sound of bleating sheep and the babble of trickling streams, and the rush of tiny waterfalls can be heard as one rambles through the district. The mountains may not be nearly high enough to qualify as true mountains—the highest is only thirty-five hundred feet tall—but they are beautiful.

They are divided here and there by ancient drystone walls, and fields of soft grass, waving ferns, and rainbow-colored brackens grow to the top of all but the highest of them. It seldom snows here, even in wintertime, but it does rain—and rain a lot. Those who are unfamiliar with England may have heard that its weather is usually rain, but while it certainly has a wet climate, it would rain far more in England were it not for the mountains of Wales. This highland area forces the water-laden air that is blown in from the Atlantic to rise and cool, thus causing the clouds to unleash their loads well before crossing over low-lying England to the east. And they were doing just that on the day I arrived.

Accompanied by Sally Evans, an archaeologist who had been involved in an excavation at Dinas Emrys some years earlier, I made my way along a muddy forested ridge toward the top of the mountain. Although it is called a mountain, Dinas Emrys is actually a knoll: a rounded, tree-lined hill with occasional areas of bare, gray rock that stands in a bowl-shaped valley created by a ring of higher mountains around it. Reaching a natural turf-covered terrace near the summit, Sally paused next to a ring of mossy stones about three feet high, between which a number of small silver-barked trees had managed to find root.

"The Romans built a wooden stockade here to keep the local Deceangli tribe in check. Sometime later these stone-walled circular huts were erected," said Sally, as she pointed to the stones and then to other, similar stone rings that dotted the terrace. "They appear to have been dwellings that surrounded a much larger structure."

She led the way up the hillside, where, close to the summit, we stopped next to a row of much larger stones, piled up into a rampart approximately ten feet thick. Although it was now only some three or four feet high, it was believed to be the remains of a defensive wall, Sally explained. In the 1950s, the archaeologist Dr. Hubert Savory conducted a two-year excavation of the area and determined that what we were now gazing upon were the remains of a post-Roman fortification built sometime in the mid- to late 400s.[6] The dating was made possible from pottery, bearing Christian symbols of that time, which is now on display at the National Museum of Wales in Cardiff, where Savory worked.

"These walls, mostly buried now, surrounded an area of about two acres," said Sally. "When we dug here in the 1980s, we found gaps in the walls that served no obvious purpose. We concluded that the fortification was abandoned before it was completed. It dates from approximately Vortigern's time and the fact that it seems to have remained unfinished suggests that it could have been the tower or fort mentioned by Geoffrey of Monmouth."

"You think Geoffrey's story could be true?" I asked.

"Based on truth possibly. There may have been difficulties building any kind of large structure up here, as the ground is too boggy. The walls may have continued to subside, the attempt to fortify the summit abandoned, and the legend arose about the pool with the dragons in it." Sally moved on to a shallow depression a few feet down the hillside. "Dr. Savory excavated this and concluded that it was originally a water-filled pond that acted as a cistern to supply water to the settlement," she told me. "It might have been the pool of the legend. It's not beneath the fortification, but it is below it."

Sally rummaged through her bag and produced a bowl-shaped piece of pottery about six inches across. "This is one of a number of similar ceramic fragments we found here in the eighties. The pool was probably used as a garbage dump by the builders. It's the broken end of a basin and looks like a shell fragment of a giant egg," she said, handing me the artifact. "I may be wrong, but I think when people later found such items here, they thought they were just that—perhaps the remains of dragon eggs."

"So you think that dragon legends developed about Dinas Emrys, and Geoffrey of Monmouth included them in his account?"

"It makes sense," she replied. "A fortification that keeps collapsing for some unknown reason, stories of dragons: Geoffrey must have loved it."

"So the story of Merlin being here is just a myth woven together by Geoffrey of Monmouth in the 1100s?" I asked.

"Not by Geoffrey," said Sally, shaking her head. "Almost exactly the same account is given by Nennius three centuries earlier, around the year 830."

Nennius was the monk who wrote the oldest surviving account of King Arthur's battles, and he also wrote about Vortigern. In his *Latin Historia Brittonum*—"History of Britain"—he includes an account of Vortigern inviting Anglo-Saxon mercenaries to help him defeat his rival British kingdoms, but the Anglo-Saxons ultimately rebel and turn on Vortigern himself. According to Nennius:

> But soon after, calling together his twelve wise men, to consult what was to be done, they said to him [Vortigern], "Retire to the remote boundaries of your kingdom; there build and fortify a city to defend yourself, for the people you havereceived are treacherous; they are seeking to subdue you bystratagem, and, even during your life, to seize upon all the countries subject to your power, how much more will they attempt, after your death!"

> The king, pleased with this advice, departed with his wise men, and traveled through many parts of his territories, in search of a place convenient for the purpose of building a citadel. Having, to no purpose, traveled far and wide, they came at length to a province called Guenet [North Wales]; and having surveyed the mountains of Heremus [the old name for Snowdonia], they discovered, on the summit of one of them, a situation, adapted to the construction of a citadel.

> Upon this, the wise men said to the king, "Build here a city; for, in this place, it will ever be secure against the barbarians."

> Then the king sent for artificers, carpenters, stone-masons, and collected all the materials requisite to building; but the whole of these disappeared in one night, so that nothing remained of what had been provided for the constructing of the citadel.

Materials were, therefore, from all parts, procured a second and third time, and again vanished as before, leaving and rendering every effort ineffectual. Vortigern inquired of his wise men the cause of this opposition to his undertaking, and of so much useless expense of labor? They replied, "You must find a child born without a father, put him to death, and sprinkle with his blood the ground on which the citadel is to be built, or you willnever accomplish your purpose."[7]

Sally was right; Nennius's account is almost exactly that later given by Geoffrey of Monmouth: the building of the fortress in North Wales, the need for a human sacrifice. Nennius even goes on to include the story of the boy with no earthly father and the mysterious pool beneath the foundations of the fort.

In consequence of this reply, the king sent messengers throughout Britain, in search of a child born without a father. After having inquired in all the provinces, they came to the field of Electi, in the district of Glevesing, where a party of boys were playing at ball. And two of them quarreling, one said to the other, "O boy without a father, no good will ever happen to you."

Upon this, the messengers diligently inquired of the mother and the other boys, whether he had had a father?

Which his mother denied, saying, "In what manner he was conceived I know not, for I have never had intercourse with any man"; and then she solemnly affirmed that he had no mortal father. The boy was, therefore, led away, and conducted before Vortigern the king.

A meeting took place the next day for the purpose of putting him to death. Then the boy said to the king, "Why have your servants brought me hither?"

"That you may be put to death," replied the king, "and that the ground on which my citadel is to stand, may be sprinkled with your blood, without which I shall be unable to build it."

"Who," said the boy, "instructed you to do this?"

"My wise men," answered the king.

"Order them hither," returned the boy; this being complied with, he thus questioned them: "By what means was it revealed to you that this citadel could not be built, unless the spot were previously sprinkled with my blood? Speak without disguise, and declare who discovered me to you"; then turning to the king, "I will soon," said he, "unfold to you every thing; but I desire to question your wise men, and wish them to disclose to you what is hidden under this pavement": they acknowledging their ignorance, "there is," said he, "a pool; come and dig": they did so, and found the pool.[8]

In Geoffrey's narrative there are two dragons in the pool, and Nennius includes an almost identical account of two serpents or giant snakes:

The boy, going on with his questions, asked the wise men what was in it? But they not knowing what to reply, "There are," said he, "two serpents, one white and the other red; unfold the tent"; they obeyed, and two sleeping serpents were discovered; "consider attentively," said the boy, "what they are doing." The serpents began to struggle with each other.[9]

As in Geoffrey's account, the serpents fight each other, and when they leave, the boy reveals to Vortigern the meaning of the spectacle:

"The red serpent is your dragon, but the white serpent is the dragon of the people who occupy several provinces and districts of Britain [the Anglo-Saxons], even almost from sea to sea: at length, however, our people shall rise and drive away the Saxon race from beyond the sea, whence they originally came; but do you depart from this place, where you are not permitted to erect a citadel."[10]

One thing was certain—Geoffrey of Monmouth did not invent the tale. In fact, his account is worded so similarly to Nennius's that he probably took it directly from the *Historia Brittonum*. However, Nennius's version of events was less fanciful than Geoffrey's. The serpents in Nennius's account appear to be more of a symbolic vision than an actual event.

To Sally, the Nennius account was evidence that Vortigern was the builder of the Dinas Emrys fortifications she had excavated. For me, however, it was far more interesting. Here there was an account of the boy whom Geoffrey identifies as Merlin, later to become Arthur's royal adviser. Glynn Davis had told me of "The Great Prophecy of Britain" poem, which refers to the Arthurian Merlin two centuries before Geoffrey of Monmouth's time. That poem was written around 930, but Nennius's work has been dated to around 830—a century earlier. That was still more than three and a half centuries after Merlin is said to have lived, but it appeared to place belief in the figure's historical existence back to three centuries before Geoffrey is thought, by some scholars, to have invented him.

The next day, in the public library in the nearby town of Mold, which boasts one of the most comprehensive collections of Arthurian books in Britain, I read through a copy of Nennius's work. Sally considered the account of Vortigern's fortress less fanciful than Geoffrey's, yet it still seemed somewhat imaginary, as the boy was supposed to have no earthly father. However, like the two serpents, this appears to be symbolic or metaphorical. At the end of his account of Vortigern's fortress, Nennius writes that the king asks the boy who he is: "In answer to the king's question, 'What is your origin?' he replied, 'A Roman consul was my father.' "[11]

Roman consuls were originally co-rulers of Rome, appointed annually by the senate in republican times. When Augustus became the first Roman emperor in 27 B.C., the Roman senate continued to exist and, although subordinate to the emperor, it retained political power. Each year two men were appointed joint leaders of the senate; usually they were high-ranking military officers or even the emperor himself. These people were the most powerful in the empire (apart from the emperor) and, like emperors, they were considered godlike. The Roman Empire adopted Christianity as the state religion after 327 A.D., but even then consuls were often accorded a sort of saintly status following their deaths. It seemed to me that what Nennius was saying was that the boy had no earthly father because his father was thought to be semidivine.

Was the historical Merlin really the son of a Roman consul? Although by Vortigern's time the Roman legions had left Britain, the Roman Empire still existed. In fact, after Rome was sacked by the Germanic tribe the Visigoths in 410 A.D., the emperor Honorius resecured the city, and the last Roman emperor, Romulus Augustulus, was not defeated by the Germanic tribes until 476 A.D. Around 450, when the Vortigern fortress episode appears to be set, the empire still struggled on in mainland Europe, where consuls were still appointed. Was the son of one such consul the real figure behind the Merlin legend? On first reading what Nennius wrote at the end of his Vortigern fortress account, it seemed that the enigmatic boy had nothing to do with Merlin. In answer to Vortigern's question "What is your name?" the boy answers, "I am called Ambrosius."

In Geoffrey's account of the dragon pool beneath Vortigern's fortress he, like Nennius, says Merlin had another name: "Then said Merlin, who was also called Ambrose . . ."[12] Ambrose is a shortening of the Roman name Ambrosius. Geoffrey's Merlin, or at least the part of his composite character that was a young man during Vortigern's time, and hence could have lived in Arthur's time a few decades later, was clearly the same figure as Nennius's Ambrosius, son of a Roman consul. Geoffrey might have been right: Merlin's real name could actually have been Ambrosius.

As Glynn Davis had pointed out, the original Welsh rendering of the name Myrddin seems to derive from Brythonic words meaning "voice of the Eagle" and is therefore presumably a title concerning the man's supposed prophetic powers. If Myrddin or Merlin *was* a title, then the man would also have another name. And if Merlin's real name was Ambrosius, it would certainly explain why there were no contemporary, or close contemporary, records concerning a Merlin at the time of the historical Arthur.

In his work, Nennius recounts that Ambrosius eventually became a warrior in his own right and went on to rule the western half of Britain. If this was the historical Merlin, then he is indeed mentioned in the writings of someone who wrote within living memory of the historical

Arthurian period. In his *On the Ruin and Conquest of Britain,* dating from around 545 A.D., the monk Gildas makes reference to a British leader who, for a while, turned the tide of warfare against the Anglo-Saxons. He says he was the son of high-ranking Roman parents and that his name was Ambrosius Aurelinus. This man could well have been the central historical figure behind the Merlin legend. I had to find out more about him.

3

THE NOTABLE STORM

As noted at the end of the last chapter, according to the monk Gildas, sometime in the mid-400s the Britons united under a single ruler. In his *On the Ruin and Conquest of Britain,* he writes: "Their leader was Ambrosius Aurelianus, a gentleman who, perhaps alone of the Romans, had survived the shock of this notable storm."[1]

Who is this Ambrosius who seems to be the same man Geoffrey of Monmouth identifies as Merlin? To begin with, when was he born and when did he come to power? To determine this, I needed to examine the violent end of the Roman Empire in western Europe: Gildas's "notable storm" from which Ambrosius was to emerge as the last Roman officer in Britain.

From 47 A.D. until 410 A.D., southern Britain was a part of the Roman Empire. This province the Romans called Britannia included all of what is now England and Wales and was divided from Scotland by a huge defense called Hadrian's Wall. (The Romans attempted to conquer Scotland, but found it difficult to do because of its mountainous terrain.) In Britannia, rule under a Roman governor and policing by the imperial army meant that for three and a half centuries, the province enjoyed peace and stability.

Most people's idea of the Romans comes from the Hollywood portrayals of the first century or movies like *Gladiator*, which tend to depict the Romans as a race of warmongering soldiers, autocratic overlords, and bloodthirsty arena-going civilians. Although by today's standards the Romans were brutal, and gladiatorial contests were a common form of entertainment, most people in occupied countries like Britain led relatively peaceful and prosperous lives. The towns had water supplies and bathhouses, stores and marketplaces, libraries and theaters. They had workshops that manufactured everything from household accessories to military hardware. There was, in effect, full employment and life was orderly and civilized.

The Roman Empire covered much of Europe and all the countries surrounding the Mediterranean. As well as Britain, the empire included Spain, France, the Netherlands, Italy, Greece, Turkey, Syria, Palestine, Egypt, and the north coast of Africa, and more besides. By the time Britain was conquered, only a small percentage of those in the Roman administration and the army were actually Romans. Those who surrendered to Roman rule became part of the system and were ultimately made Roman citizens, benefiting from the same rights as trueborn citizens of Rome.

By the later years of the Roman Empire, even the emperors seldom were true Romans. The last two emperors to directly rule Britain, for instance, Theodosius and his son Honorius, were actually Spanish. Slaves existed, of course, and although they were usually convicted criminals or those captured in battle and their descendants, they in no way comprised the bulk of the population. Roman law may have been harsh for those who transgressed it, and life may have been difficult for the slaves, but the majority of Britons were freeborn Roman citizens who led ordinary lives, more affluent than anything they had known before or would enjoy again for more than a thousand years. In 410 A.D., however, all this was to change, virtually overnight.

The Germanic tribes east of the Rhine River had never been conquered by the Romans. They and other tribes from Russia, all collectively called barbarians by the Romans, ultimately proved to be the undoing of an empire that had lasted for centuries. The most significant Germanic tribes were the Goths—divided into the Visigoths (western Goths), from what is now Germany, and the Ostrogoths (eastern Goths), from what is now Austria. The most significant Russian tribe was the Huns. It was these people, for so long dismissed as uncultured savages, who eventually brought about the end of the Roman Empire in the West.

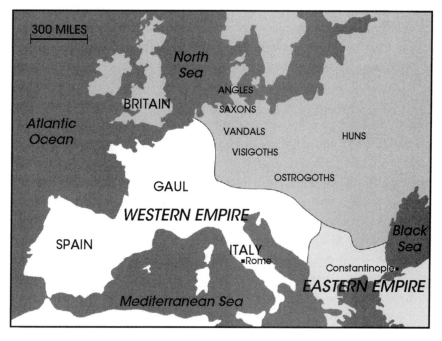

Map 2. The Roman Empire and its enemies during the fifth century

It began in the early years of the fifth century, with a hotbed of trouble brewing among the Huns of central Asia. Driven at first by a series of disastrous crop failures, these fierce and warlike barbarians surged toward the Goths, who were, in turn, driven from their own lands. Consequently, the vanquished Goths crossed the Danube River and the Rhine. With Rome on the defensive, the barbarian hordes across Europe began to break through the frontiers of the empire. One barbarian chief, Alaric, king of the Visigoths, reached Italy in 401, and by 408 was laying siege to Rome itself. To meet this challenge, the Romans were compelled to withdraw troops from the colonial outpost of Britain. Finally, in 410, the Visigoths sacked Rome and the last Roman troops were withdrawn from Britain to help resecure the capital.

Britain had not yet been directly affected by this barbarian onslaught, but when the Roman legions departed, almost immediately the country began to suffer. When the army left Britain, the Roman civil administration remained intact. The courts, the town councils, and the district bureaucracy were all left as they had been for years. The problem was that there was no longer an army to keep order.

By this time, the Roman army in Britain had become more of a police force than a fighting machine. Imagine what would happen in the United States if the Army, the police, the sheriff's departments, the F.B.I., and all law enforcement institutions disappeared overnight? The government and city halls would remain—but how long would anyone continue to take notice of them? It would not be long before local vigilantes, street gangs, and various survivalist groups took over. This is pretty much what happened in many parts of Britain in the first few decades of the fifth century, except it was the leaders of the old Celtic tribes who seized control.

With the breakdown of law and order and the virtual collapse of civilization in Britain, hardly any records were kept for the next few centuries, until the southern part of the island was united into the country of England under one king in the year 927. Reconstructing the history of these so-called Dark Ages is often a matter of historical detective work based on archaeology and the scant writings that survive. In fact, there are only five historical sources providing any real detail that remain from Britain during this time:

1. *On the Ruin and Conquest of Britain,* written by Gildas around the year 445. Reputedly the son of a British aristocrat, Gildas appears to have attended a school in Wales and eventually became a monk, spending some time at the monastery in Glastonbury in southwestern England. Gildas's work was never intended as a straightforward textbook of history; indeed, it is essentially a tirade. As the title suggests, it is primarily a criticism of the author's countrymen, leveled at their petty squabbles that caused the collapse of Britain.[2]

2. Around the year 830, the British monk Nennius, apparently from a monastery in the town of Bangor in North Wales, compiled his *Historia Brit-*

tonum (History of Britain). In this work, Nennius claims to have compiled his information by making "a heap" of what he could find among old documents at his disposal. He tells us: "I have heaped together all that I found, from the annals of the Romans, the chronicles of the Holy Fathers, the writings of the Irish and the Saxons and the traditions of our own wise men." The result is somewhat disorderly, but certainly appears to be a genuine attempt by the writer to reconstruct a history of Britain from what documents were available to him.[3]

3. In 731, *The Ecclesiastical History of the English People* was written by the monk Bede from the monastery of Jarrow in northeast England. It is the first British work that can genuinely be termed historical writing since the departure of the Roman legions, and it transformed the rough framework of existing material into an actual history book. Bede's work established the style for historians that followed; among other developments, he was the first to employ the A.D. system of dating for historical purposes. (A.D. is the abbreviation for Anno Domini, Latin for "in the year of the Lord." In other words, it links Christ's birth with the year 1 and dates it as such.) Bede's sources were primarily ecclesiastical documents from the region of Kent (in southeast England), together with the works of Gildas and a wide variety of oral accounts.[4]

4. Between 871 and 899, *The Anglo-Saxon Chronicle* was compiled, of which a number of versions survive. Although it appears to be based on early West Saxon monastic records, the surviving *Chronicle* was not compiled until the reign of the Anglo-Saxon king Alfred the Great (871–900), perhaps under Alfred's personal supervision.[5]

5. *The Welsh Annals* is a calendar of events dating back to the fifth century that were brought together into one document around the year 950. Compiled on behalf of the kings of South Wales, they are fundamentally of Welsh interest but were also an attempt to catalog events throughout Britain as a whole. Regrettably, the *Annals* are little more than an incomplete chronology of dates, coupled with brief notations on important incidents.[6]

Other records survive only in the form of Dark Age sagas such as war poems, most of which include as much mythology as they do history, and the biographies of a few Christian missionaries, referred to as saints, that concern mainly religious issues. For all intents and purposes, this is all of the written history of the Dark Ages that survives from Britain itself (and it's for this reason that so little is known about the time in which Ambrosius apparently lived).

From these various sources we can gather that, soon after the Romans left Britain, the Scottish tribes whom the Romans called the Picts (meaning "painted people" because of their tattooed skin) began crossing Hadrian's Wall to ravish northern England, while the Irish, whom the Romans had never conquered, began sailing across from Ireland to raid the western coast of Britain. The greatest threat, however, came from Scandinavia and northern Germany, where the Germanic Anglo-Saxons lived. These were actually three closely related tribes: the Angles, the Saxons, and the Jutes. The Angles and Saxons came from the coast of northern Germany, around the estuary of the Elbe River and what is now Schleswig, and the Jutes came from what is now southern Denmark.

In many ways the Jutes, Angles, and Saxons were so closely related that the term Anglo-Saxon can safely be applied to the entire culture. These were the people who eventually conquered most of Britain and founded the kingdom of England; they ultimately founded colonies all over the world, made their indelible mark on North America, and created the language spoken by half the people on earth. And it all began in an area of northern Germany and southern Denmark not much bigger than modern Rhode Island, the smallest state in the United States.

Like the other Germanic peoples, the Anglo-Saxons had never been part of the Roman Empire but rather had been driven to cross the sea to Britain by their neighbors the Visigoths, who had moved north to escape the Huns. At first the Anglo-Saxons began settling in colonies in parts of eastern Britain, where it seems they traded with and were made welcome by the Britons. However, problems between the two peoples were inevitable. Many Britons, having been Roman citizens, were practicing Christians, whereas the Anglo-Saxons were still pagan and had their own gods and religious practices that the Britons clearly found abhorrent. According to Nennius, it was the threat of these Anglo-Saxons that eventually forced Vortigern to retreat to the west of

Britain and the reason why he was attempting to build a fortification there.

But who was Vortigern exactly?

There is only one written piece of evidence to determine when Vortigern's reign began, and that is found in the *Welsh Annals*, which record that "Vortigern held rule over Britain in the consulship of Theodosius and Valentinian." The joint consulship is recorded by the Romans in the year 425. The *Welsh Annals* seems to be implying that this was Vortigern's first year as ruler, as the document goes on to record how, in the fourth year of Vortigern's reign, "the Saxons came to Britain in the consulship of Felix and Taurus." Again, this fits with the Roman records that date the term of these two consuls to 428.

The Britain over which Vortigern ruled was a divided nation. Much of the country had fragmented into various Celtic kingdoms, and although the east of Britain was ostensibly still being run by the old Roman administrators, Vortigern was in overall command.

According to the various sources, Vortigern maintained power with the help of Anglo-Saxon mercenaries whom he had invited into the country and allowed to settle in parts of southeast Britain. This, as it turned out, was a big mistake. As we know, it was this formidable Anglo-Saxon army that led the revolt and forced Vortigern and his armies to retreat progressively toward the west. Vortigern's first defeat was in the county of Kent, in the far southeast of England, but within a couple of years London fell, as did East Anglia. Vortigern appears to have retained his control over the British forces for another year or two, until he died in 447.

There is no specific reference in any of the historical sources concerning exactly how far west the Anglo-Saxon onslaught pushed, but it must have been close to Wales, as it was here, and at this time, that Nennius's account of Vortigern's building the fortification at Dinas Emrys is set.

> But soon after, calling together his twelve wise men to consult what was to be done, they said to him, "Retire to the remote boundaries of your kingdom; there build a fortification to defend yourself."[7]

Dinas Emrys is in North Wales, but this does not appear to have been Vortigern's actual homeland, as Nennius later records that, following Vortigern's defeat by the Anglo-Saxons, he ultimately lost the support of the Britons and it was at this point that: "Vortigern withdrew in disgrace to the fortress of Vortigern, which is in the country of the Demetians."[8] This is exactly where we find the young Merlin in Geoffrey of Monmouth's *History of the Kings of Britain*. It is at Carmarthen, the chief port of Demetia, where Vortigern's men find the boy.[9]

This fortress of Vortigern must have been Vortigern's seat of power. In other words, Vortigern had finally been forced to return home to his tribal kingdom of Demetia—in southwest Wales.

> Vortigern withdrew in disgrace to the fortress of Vortigern, which is in the country of the Demetians, on the river Teibi. Saint Germanus followed him, as before, and stayed there fasting with all his clergy for three days and as many nights to achieve his end, and on the fourth night about midnight, the whole fortress was suddenly destroyed by fire . . . Vortigern was destroyed with all who were with him . . .[10]

Vortigern, it appears, died in some natural catastrophe that was perceived as an act of divine vengeance. Nennius provides no dates, but the event can be dated by the presence of Germanus.

Germanus was a rich and powerful bishop of Auxerre (in what is now northern France) who visited Britain on two occasions, the first recorded by the contemporary Roman writer Prosper of Aquitaine as occurring in 429.[11] This is much too early to have been when Vortigern died, as the Anglo-Saxons had only just begun arriving in the country and were not yet present in numbers large enough to cause the kind of problems Vortigern faced at the end of his life. Germanus's second visit is recorded by Bede, who gives the year as 447.[12] When compared to Roman records, which do survive from this period, Bede is usually found to be accurate concerning the movement of Church officials.

The year 447, therefore, is a reasonable date for Vortigern's death—meaning that Nennius's account of the Dinas Emrys incident, when

Vortigern and Ambrosius met, was set somewhere around 445 A.D. From this we can guess when Ambrosius was born. He is described as a boy when he first meets Vortigern, although he is old enough to speak eloquently on his own behalf. Presumably he is in his early to mid-teens, meaning he was born about the year 430, give or take a year.

Having a rough date for Ambrosius's birth, I needed to determine when he assumed command of the Britons. According to Nennius, Vortigern was succeeded by a man named Vitalinus, possibly his son, and for the next ten years the Britons continued to suffer defeats by the Anglo-Saxons, until Vitalinus was defeated by Ambrosius in battle. In fact, according to Nennius, this occurred twelve years after Vortigern's death: "From the reign of Vortigern to the strife between Vitalinus and Ambrosius are twelve years."[13] It was then, according to Gildas, that Ambrosius not only took over command of the British forces, but somehow managed to halt the Anglo-Saxon advance as well.

This is the same Ambrosius who Nennius tells us was brought before Vortigern as a youth just over a decade earlier. At that time, he was a boy who was thought to have prophetic powers, the same figure who Geoffrey of Monmouth later tells us became the Merlin of Arthurian fame. Although Ambrosius is mentioned by Gildas, Bede, and Nennius, regrettably none of them directly tells us much about him, although as we have seen, Gildas refers to him as the last of the Romans and both Gildas and Bede go on to say that Ambrosius's parents were high-ranking Romans.

The name Ambrosius was of Roman origin, but the family name Aurelianus, which Gildas uses, appears to have been a mistake. Bede, who provides almost the same account as Gildas, calls him Ambrosius Aurelius: "They had at that time for their leader, Ambrosius Aurelius, a modest man, who alone, by chance, of the Roman nation had survived the storm."[14]

From this passage, it is clear Bede was copying Gildas, or at least a common source. Why, then, does he use a different name? The answer might be that the oldest surviving Gildas manuscript is an eleventh-century copy in which the writer may have wrongly copied the name. Whatever the reason, the name Aurelius was a Roman family name, and an important and royal one at that.

This royal race was not the family of some minor Celtic kings of Demetia in southeast Wales, as Geoffrey of Monmouth depicts Merlin's kin, but instead of the emperors of Rome itself. Aurelius was indeed the name of a family whose ancestor had been one of the most popular Roman emperors there had ever been: Marcus Aurelius, who ruled from 161 to 180 A.D. Marcus Aurelius had been not only a great military strategist; he was also a philosophical writer and advocate of civil rights. This was the so-called good emperor; (the character played by the actor Richard Harris, who dies at the beginning of the movie *Gladiator*). Ambrosius, it would seem, was the historical Marcus Aurelius's descendant.

Historians have long been fascinated by Ambrosius as a genuine and significant historical figure in the period just before the legends of King Arthur are set, but as so little is written about him in the few Dark Age sources that do exist, he has remained almost as mysterious as Arthur himself. In fact, historians who attempted to discover more about Ambrosius were disappointed to find no contemporary references from Rome, or any archaeological evidence from Britain, to show that the Aurelius family was ever in Britain at all.

That is, until 1992.

On a November day in 1992, Eric Lawes, a retired gardener, was metal detecting in a field outside the tiny town of Hoxne in Suffolk in eastern England. He had been detecting for about three hours when he received a signal. He dug down to find a silver Roman coin. This was exciting, but nothing unusual: Roman coins are found all the time in England. However, when he dug deeper, Lawes was elated to discover dozens of Roman coins, all made from gold. But this was by no means the end of it. Excavating further, he unearthed many other artifacts, including precious stones, bracelets, chains, pendants, and statuettes.

Luckily for historians, Lawes was an honest man and notified the landowners and local police. When archaeologists were called in to make a proper examination of the discovery, it was found to include an astonishing array of treasure: precious figurines, decorative tableware, jewelry, and more than fourteen thousand gold and silver coins. It was the greatest archaeological treasure ever found in Britain, and Lawes received the equivalent of approximately three million dollars as a reward. This, however, was a mere fraction of the true cost of the hoard in material value alone. In historical terms, the discovery was priceless.

Some of the treasure, a set of silver spoons, was inscribed with the name of the owner—one Ursicinus Aurelius. Not only did this show that an important and wealthy Roman of the Aurelius family was in Britain during the time of the Roman Empire, but also the treasure could be dated to the fifth century, when Ambrosius had lived. How does Ambrosius fit in to this discovery and what precisely was his relationship, if any, with this branch of the Aurelius family in Britain?

The last date to be found on any of the coins was the year 408, proving that the hoard dated from after this time. The question was When?

When archaeologists examined the find and excavated the surrounding soil, they discovered the metal clasps, hinges, and fittings of what had once been wooden chests that originally contained the treasure, together with some smaller silver boxes that had survived intact. In no way could the hoard have gotten there accidentally. It had been packaged, ready to be moved, or was already being carried away when something forced its owners to bury it. Whoever hid the treasure must have been fleeing from an enemy who overwhelmed them by surprise. At what point after 408 could a wealthy Roman family have met with such a fate?

The county of Suffolk, where the discovery was made, is in a part of eastern England called East Anglia, named after the Anglo-Saxons who invaded and settled there in the fifth century. For the first few decades of the 400s, the region was firmly under the control of the Britons, and a Roman way of life continued virtually unchanged. This is demonstrated not only by archaeology that has discovered no Anglo-Saxon burials there at the time (only Romanized, Christian ones), but also by one of the rare descriptions of life in Britain at the time, provided by a monk known as Constantius of Lyon, from France. Around the year 480, Constantius wrote a biography of Bishop Germanus and records his first visit to Britain, which, as we have already established, was made in 429.[15] Although he offers frustratingly few details, Constantius paints a broad picture of life in Britain at this time.

From this work, it can be gathered that even though much of northern, central, and western Britain had broken up into tribal kingdoms, the south and east of the country were still relatively prosperous. Here law and order was maintained by the old Roman aristocracy, presumably by their own private militia or auxiliary forces hired from mainland Europe. If the *Welsh Annals* are right, the Anglo-Saxons did not start arriving until the time of this visit by Germanus, and it would have taken some years before they were large enough in number to have rebelled (seemingly during Vortigern's time in the 440s). Gildas gives us some idea of the dreadful fate of the Britons and of their towns in the east of England in a graphic account of the Anglo-Saxon onslaught:

> All the columns were leveled with the ground by the frequent strokes of the battering ram, all the husbandmen routed, together with their bishops, priests, and people, whilst the sword gleamed, and the flames crackled around them on every side. Lamentable to behold, in the midst of the streets lay the tops of lofty towers, tumbled to the ground, stones of high walls, holy altars, fragments of human bodies, covered with livid clots of coagulated blood, looking as if they had been squeezed together in a press; and with no chance of being buried, save in the ruins of the houses, or in the ravening bellies of wild beasts and birds . . .[16]

Those not killed in the original attacks on the towns were to suffer cruelly at the hands of the enemy. Many "were murdered in great numbers; others, constrained by famine, came and yielded themselves to be slaves for ever to their foes, running the risk of being instantly slain, which truly was the greatest favor that could be offered them."[17] A few lucky ones, however, managed to escape to the west. The Aurelius family of Suffolk seem to have been attempting to do just that when marauders caught up with them.

In fact, it seems that they had fled from the coastal port of Caister and were attempting to make for the British garrison in the Roman fort of Sitomagus, some forty-five miles to the southwest. The Roman town of Caister—what is now Caister-on-Sea near the seaside resort of Great Yarmouth—was not only the largest Roman settlement in Suffolk; it seems also to have been the home of the Aurelius family in Britain.

The presence of the Aurelius family in Suffolk should have been realized before the Hoxne treasure was discovered. A bronze plaque inscribed
with an Aurelius name was unearthed during excavations at Caister in
the 1950s, but its significance remained unappreciated until after the
discovery at Hoxne.[18] The plaque, which appears to date from the early
fourth century, bore a dedication to the Roman god Mercury. It reads:
ATTICIANUS AURELIUS WILLINGLY AND DESERVEDLY FULFILS HIS VOW
TO MERCURY.[19]

The nature of this vow is unknown, but the plaque, which would
probably have been set in a temple, reveals two important things: first,
that Mercury was the Aurelius family god. In pre-Christian times, the
Romans had many gods, but individual families tended to have a favorite
god whom they venerated and to whom they attributed their fate and
fortune. Atticianus had obviously done something he had hoped would
win favor with this deity. More important, the plaque showed not only
that the Aurelius family had been living in Britain in the century before
the legions departed, but also that they had been in East Anglia for
many years before the time the Hoxne treasure was buried. In other
words, they were no brief visitors to the country, but rather had an
established presence there.

If the Aurelius family had lived in Caister, then whoever hid the
hoard at Hoxne had probably fled the town that the Anglo-Saxons had
attacked from the sea. According to Nennius, about this time:

> The Saxons now dispatched deputies to Germany to solicit large re-
> inforcements, and an additional number of ships with many men: and
> after he obtained these, they fought against the kings of our peoples
> and princes of Britain.[20]

Hoxne, where the treasure was buried, is on a direct route between
Caister and the Roman fort of Sitomagus, which stood near the modern Suffolk village of Ixworth. If the Aurelius family were heading here,
they had another fifteen miles to travel. Had they made it to safety? The
chances are they did; otherwise, they would probably have revealed the
whereabouts of the hoard to their Saxon pursuers in an attempt to buy
their lives.

All this was happening not long before Vortigern's men found the young Ambrosius playing in a field somewhere in western Britain. Could Ambrosius, Geoffrey's Merlin, have been one of the Aurelius children who had managed to escape? Evidence to help answer this question might still survive in the area where Ambrosius had been living when Vortigern's men found him. In order to answer this question satisfactorily, I needed to find out more about the Aurelius family and about Ambrosius's place in it.

4

AMBROSIUS EMRYS

The Aurelius family—the Aurelians, as they are known—had been important Roman aristocrats since the time of the Roman emperor Marcus Aurelius in the second century, and in the fifth century they were still immensely rich and wielded considerable political influence in the empire. Judging by the hoard of treasure found at Hoxne, those living in East Anglia were no exception. They had presumably enjoyed a life of luxury in one of the Roman villas that still existed in that part of Britain at that time.

These villas were more than just homes: They were the country estates of the Roman elite. They were also working ranches with a cluster of outbuildings such as barns, smithies, and dwellings for laborers. Most villas were built of stone with tiled roofs and provided the kind of amenities that would not be seen in Britain again for more than a thousand years. They had plastered walls, marble floors, and stylish wooden furniture; they even had an ingenious form of under-floor central heating and glass in the windows. There were bathroom facilities with running water supplied by clay- or sometimes lead-pipe plumbing. Accessories included razors for shaving and soap for washing, and women had makeup and perfume. As well as bedrooms graced with feather beds and woven blankets, cleaned by servants and kept sweet-smelling with incense, there would be an office for the master of the house, with desks and writing equipment, complete with a private library of handwritten books and scrolls.

The main house was usually built around a courtyard surrounded by cloistered walkways where statuary, flowering shrubs, and fountains stood and which echoed with the sound of exotic birds perched in gilded cages. The main room of the house was the dining hall, its ceiling supported by ornamental pillars and the aisles decorated with plinths holding marble busts, statuettes, and Grecian urns. The walls were painted with scenes from nature and family portraits, and the mosaic floor typically was covered with lavish, intricate patterns. Here, food, flavored with herbs from the Mediterranean and spices from the East, would be served to the family and guests, who dined reclining on cushioned couches around a low central table, the meal accompanied by minstrels playing harps and flutes.

These grand villas were usually built near Roman towns that offered all the benefits of imperial life. For entertainment, most towns had an open-air theater, where plays and recitals would be performed, and an arena where games and gladiatorial events were staged. Many towns even had a track for horse and chariot racing, complete with bookmakers and betting stalls. The main streets were flanked by stores selling goods from all around the empire, and there were inns and even cafés that sold take-out food. Many urban centers had a public swimming pool—heated, of course—and a basilica, an indoor hall for sport and physical recreation.

This was the kind of life the Roman Empire had brought to Britain, and it was still being enjoyed in East Anglia by the Aurelius family in the mid-fifth century. In many places, however, the law and order required to maintain such an opulent lifestyle had broken down and town life had disintegrated. Difficult to protect from thieves and vandals, the villas had been abandoned and regional chieftains now ruled with their private armies of hired thugs from the more easily defended hill forts. Here, even the ruling elite lived in cold, damp wooden structures with few amenities. Gone were the creature comforts of bathhouses and plumbing; central heating was nonexistent and buildings were warmed by open fires that filled the air with smoke. Most people lived in what were little more than mud-brick hovels with simple thatched roofs, in a single room they shared with their livestock. There were no toilets, no feather beds, and almost nothing with which to keep clean. Life was dirty, smelly, and hard. As for entertainment, there was none, other than whatever one could devise for oneself.

The young Ambrosius obviously enjoyed a pampered Roman life-style before the Anglo-Saxons invaded, plundered, and pillaged East Anglia. This much was clear. However, I needed to find out exactly who Ambrosius was. Who were his parents?

Gildas provides us with another tantalizing clue. When referring to the "notable storm"—the collapse of the Roman Empire of which the waves of Anglo-Saxon revolts and invasions in England were a large part—he says that Ambrosius's "parents who had worn purple, were slain in it."[1] Purple was the color reserved for imperial families—relatives and descendants of emperors—which is exactly what Bede tells us when he says Ambrosius's parents "were of the royal race."[2]

The name found engraved on some of the Roman treasures discovered at Hoxne is Ursicinus Aurelius. Was Ursicinus Aurelius Ambrosius's father? There was no way of knowing from the hoard itself. Ursicinus was obviously an important member of the family, but he could have been Ambrosius's brother, uncle, grandfather, or any other male relative. To find out more about the family, I visited the British Museum in London, where some of the treasure is now on display.

The first thing I discovered was that the owners of the Hoxne hoard were practicing Christians, as Christian emblems were inscribed on a number of the artifacts. Although Christianity was the state religion of the empire, and had been since 325, being a Christian was not mandatory. In the early fifth century, the Roman aristocracy was still divided between Christians and pagans, those who continued to venerate the old gods of Rome. The fourth-century bronze plaque found at Caister bearing the name of Atticianus Aurelius shows that the family had previously venerated the god Mercury, which means their conversion probably occurred only after Christianity became the official state religion. Specifically, they appear to have been members of a Christian sect that venerated the Roman saint Helena.

One of the household items found at Hoxne, a spice or pepper jar, had been made in the likeness of the saint. This would not be particularly unusual today, when many Catholic homes have decorations made in the images of church figures. However, at the time it was a rare practice, particularly in the case of Saint Helena. She was not even considered a saint outside the city of Milan. It was there that a bishop, now known as Saint Ambrose, originated her veneration just over half a century before.

St. Ambrose, or Ambrosius, to use his full Roman name, had been bishop of Milan from 374 to 397. Apart from being one of the most important and influential Christians of the time, he began what has been referred to as the cult of Saint Helena. Helena was the mother of the first Christian emperor, Constantine the Great, and in the 320s her influence was decisive in persuading her son to adopt Christianity as the state religion of the empire. However, her role was not officially recognized until St. Ambrose insisted she be revered as a saint. The Catholic Church did indeed do this later on, but in the fifth century her veneration did not really catch on outside of Milan.

There were many branches of the Aurelius family in various locations in the Roman Empire, but the fact that the Aurelians living in Suffolk seemed to have ties with a sect uniquely centered in Milan would suggest they had some connection with that city. Indeed, as Ambrosius bore the same name as the onetime bishop of the city, he may have been named after him. In fact, as I soon discovered, St. Ambrose himself had been a member of the Aurelius family—his Roman name was also Ambrosius Aurelius.

St. Ambrose's father, yet another man called Ambrosius Aurelius, had been governor of Gaul in the 440s. When his father died in 354, Ambrose moved to Rome, where he was educated for ten years before entering the army. In 371, at the approximate age of thirty, he was appointed governor in northern Italy, where he was made *dux*, or duke, of the city of Milan. Then, three years later, the emperor Valentinian unexpectedly appointed him bishop of that city. The appointment, which was for political rather than religious motives, came as a shock to Ambrose, who had not even been baptized! He hurriedly had himself confirmed and reluctantly accepted the office.

Despite his original ambivalence toward Christianity, Ambrose soon became a fervent Christian and one of the leading Church figures of his day. He was also a senator, and it was in this capacity that he was led into conflict with his cousin Quintus Aurelius Symmachus, the leader of a group of pagan senators in Rome. (In the fourth century, through marriage, two branches of the family emerged—the Aurelius family proper and the Aurelius Symmachus line.) Although the emperor held absolute authority in theory, the senate still enjoyed considerable power, particularly in religious matters, which few emperors had the inclination to be bothered with. At that time, the senate was hotly debating the abolition of the official powers the pagan religion still retained and, more than anyone else, it was Ambrose who won the case for Christianity.[3]

Although Ambrose died in 397 and Quintus died in 405, the Aurelius family continued to be divided along religious lines: St. Ambrose's immediate relatives were committed Christians, whereas the Symmachus side of the family remained pagan. This is clear from the fact that Quintus's son collected all his father's official letters and pagan writings and had them copied for posterity. Thanks to him, Quintus's works survive today. I expected that Ambrosius would turn out to have been from the St. Ambrose side of the family, as the Aurelians in East Anglia appear to have been Christians. It seems, however, that I was wrong.

While both Gildas and Bede imply that Ambrosius's father was a high-ranking Roman official, the only historical source to specifically identify Ambrosius's father's position is Nennius, who, as discussed in chapter 2, records that he was a Roman consul. According to Nennius, Vortigern decided to let Ambrosius live once he learned who he was:

"What is your name?" asked the king. "I am called Ambrosius," returned the boy; and in answer to the king's question, "What is your origin?" he replied, "A Roman consul was my father."[4]

As noted, consul was the highest office in the Roman Empire, apart from emperor, and two consuls were appointed each year: one in Rome itself and the other in the eastern empire's capital at Constantinople (now Istanbul). So important were they that the years of the Roman calendar were named after them. Unlike today, when in the West each year is the number of the year since the birth of Christ, the Roman years were identified by the joint consuls who ruled in that particular year.

The year 432, for instance, was known as the year of Aetius and Valerius. If a consul was appointed more than once, such as in the case of Aetius, the year would include that distinction. For example, 437 was the year of Aetius II (second consulship) and Sigisvultus. Such was the honor of having the year named after oneself that often the emperor would overrule the senate and appoint himself consul, sometimes year after year, as in the case of Honorius (the emperor who withdrew the troops from Britain), who appointed himself consul thirteen times. For this reason, many surviving Roman writings record all the consuls by name.

If Nennius was right about Ambrosius's father, then his name should appear in the list of consuls. Was there anyone on the consulate list who bore the name Aurelius? As expected with such an important family, there were many. However, there was only one who could have been Ambrosius's father. According to Nennius, Ambrosius is no older than his mid-teens around the mid-440s, when the Dinas Emrys encounter with Vortigern occurrs. He was, therefore, born somewhere around 430, give or take a few years. There was only one Roman consul of the first half of the fifth century with the name Aurelius, and that was Quintus Aurelius Symmachus, the grandson of the senator of the same name who opposed St. Ambrose. Quintus was consul for one year in A.D. 446, which is precisely around the time that the Dinas Emrys incident is set.

Nennius says Vortigern died during Saint Germanus's second visit to Britain, which Bede tells us was during the year 447. From what can be gathered from Nennius's account, Ambrosius's encounter with Vortigern at Dinas Emrys occurred shortly before this, within, at the most, a couple of years. Quintus Aurelius Symmachus must have been the consul that Nennius, or at least his source, had in mind as Ambrosius's father. (The previous Aurelian to have been a consul was Quintus's grandfather in the 390s, but he died in 405, well before Ambrosius could have been conceived.)

However, this discovery left me with something of a historical dilemma: Ambrosius did not appear to be directly related to the Aurelius family of East Anglia, as Quintus Aurelius not only seems to have been a pagan, but he was also from the Symmachus side of the family. These did not seem to be the Aurelians living in East Anglia; they were Christians with apparent connections with the St. Ambrose line. Beside which, while he was consul, Quintus Aurelius had been living in Rome. So if Quintus Aurelius really was Ambrosius's father, what happened to put Ambrosius in Carmarthen, where he is discovered by Vortigern?

It was all guesswork, of course, but one scenario as to the real set of circumstances might have gone something like this: Ambrosius's father, as Roman consul, lived in Rome together with his wife and son. When the Anglo-Saxon onslaught occurred (which may or may not have been the same one that precipitated the burying of the treasure at Hoxne), Ambrosius and his mother were visiting a branch of the Aurelius family—their relatives—in East Anglia. To save themselves, they, together with other family members, fled to the west of Britain, where they came under the protection of Vortigern, who, as we have established, had retreated westward toward Wales after his army was defeated.

Although at that time the western half of Britain was still in British hands, no one knew then how far the Anglo-Saxons would push: According to the *Anglo-Saxon Chronicle,* the Britons "fled before them as they would flee from fire." It makes sense, therefore, that surviving members of the Aurelius family would seek protection well behind Vortigern's front lines, probably in the safety of Vortigern's heartland.

If this was so, how, then, do we factor in Gildas's account, which tells us that vis-á-vis the notable storm, "Ambrosius's parents who had worn purple were slain in it." As we know, the "notable storm" refers to the fall of the Roman Empire, not merely its decline in England. The foregoing scenario and the above-referenced account by Gildas are not mutually exclusive; Ambrosius's parents *could* have been killed (together if they had reunited, or separately) anywhere within the empire, at any time during the ongoing barbarian invasions that were bringing the Roman Empire to its knees.

Knowing who Ambrosius's father was helped me to put a precise date on the Dinas Emrys incident. Nennius does not reveal exactly how long before Vortigern's death Ambrosius was brought before him. Nevertheless, he tells us that Ambrosius informed Vortigern that the consul *was* his father, which might imply the man was dead.

Almost nothing is known about Quintus. However, we do know that he had another son named Quintus Aurelius Memmius Symmachus who fled to the city of Constantinople when the western Roman Empire and

Rome itself were finally overrun by the Germanic tribes in the 460s and '70s. Here, this Quintus converted to Christianity and became consul himself in the empire's new capital in 485. From what is known of this son, Quintus cannot have died until a good few years after he was consul in 446. Gildas and Bede do not introduce Ambrosius into their narratives until the time he had become the British leader a decade or so later.

Ambrosius's words "a Roman consul was my father" might not mean that he was dead. The word *was* might relate to his father's position as consul: He was—had been—a Roman consul. If this was so, it meant the Vortigern/Ambrosius encounter would have to be set after Quintus's term as consul in 446 ended but before Vortigern's death. As Vortigern died in 447, it has to have been sometime during this same year of 447 that the Dinas Emrys incident occurred.

So there was a consul who could well have been Ambrosius's father, as Nennius says, but how could I find out more about Ambrosius himself? Perhaps a visit to "the fortress of Vortigern," where the king ultimately retreated and died, would shed more light on this question.

Nennius does not provide an exact location for Vortigern's fortress, but he does say that it was "on the river Teibi." No river in Britain still has that name, but there is the similar sounding Teifi, which runs along the northern coast of the Dyfed Peninsula in southwest Wales, once part of Demetia. It was here that Sally Evans was convinced she had located Vortigern's fort.

Since Sally's involvement with the excavations on Dinas Emrys, she had become fascinated by Vortigern and had attempted to trace his origins. Many of her colleagues assumed that he came from central England, as Nennius refers to one of Vortigern's ancestors coming from the Midland city of Gloucester. Archaeological evidence indicates he had refortified the Roman city of Viriconium, in the county of Shropshire, again in central England. However, none of this, according to Sally, proved that this part of England had actually been Vortigern's homeland, merely that one of his ancestors had lived there and had spent time there during his period as British overlord. When I again contacted Sally and asked for her opinion regarding the viability of Demetia as Vortigern's homeland, she offered to take me to a location that she was certain was Vortigern's seat of power.

The early-morning sun had burned off the fog from most of the countryside, leaving only the low-lying mist now hanging over the course of the Teifi River. It looked like a giant vaporous serpent winding its way through the valley some three hundred feet below us. Sally and I were standing on the edge of a wood that grew around the top of a hill overlooking the small town of Llandysul, some twelve miles to the north of Carmarthen. Both within the trees and circling the fields around us was a ring of grassy banks and ditches encompassing an area of approximately four acres. These, Sally told me, were the rampart remains of a huge hilltop fortification that once would have been surmounted by stonewalls and a timber stockade. On the maps it is marked simply FORT, as all that's known of the place is that it had been the site of an ancient citadel built somewhere between fifteen hundred and two thousand years ago. Who built it is a mystery, as no archaeological work has been properly carried out. However, the Welsh name for the hill is Craig Gwrtheyrn— Gwrtheyrn's Rock—and it was this that had led Sally to the area.

Sally's research was based on a number of Dark Age poems, such as those in *The Red Book of Hergest* and *The Black Book of Carmarthen*, that mention Vortigern. "They add little to what we already know of him," said Sally as she guided me around the site, "but they refer to him by the Welsh version of his name, Gwrtheyrn. Craig Gwrtheyrn seems to have been named after Vortigern, which suggests to me that this was his fort."

The chieftains of pre-Roman Britain built such hill forts from which to control their territories. Inside, there would have been a small town surrounding the tribal chief's residence. Such defenses were effective for centuries, but the Roman military had little difficulty breaking down their walls with siege catapults. For three and a half centuries, such hill forts were abandoned as civilization became centered in the Roman towns that grew up in the valleys and on the plains, usually beside rivers and newly built roads, which were the arterial trade routes of the empire. However, once the legions departed, these towns were difficult to defend and the sites of the old hill forts were often reoccupied. From the few archaeological finds that had been made on Craig Gwrtheyrn, it was known that this was one such fort.

"Nennius says Vortigern had finally withdrawn to a fortress on what has to have been the river Teifi," said Sally. "This is a fort beside that river which bears his name. It has to be the Fortress of Vortigern—the overlord's seat of power—referred to in the account."

As we walked around the remains of the defensive embankments, now about ten feet high, Sally explained that they would originally have been at least three times higher. Reaching a twenty-or-so-foot gap in the ramparts to the south of the hill, she halted. "This would have been the entrance," she said. "From what we know of other, similar forts, there would have been defensive wooden towers, one on either side of a huge double gate that could be closed in time of attack. Without the technology employed by the Roman military, these fortifications were pretty effective. However, they were vulnerable to fire, and Nennius says Vortigern died when his fortress burned to the ground. Nennius reckoned that it was fire from heaven, but it may have been lightning, an accident, or perhaps an act of sabotage."

"Do you think it was somewhere here that Vortigern's men found the young Ambrosius?" I asked.

"Somewhere in the area, perhaps," she said, walking through the gap where the gates would have stood.

As I followed, I told her how I was persuaded that the Nennius account of the Dinas Emrys incident fit into a historical context. However, the part about Ambrosius being selected as a human sacrifice seemed fictional.

"Not necessarily," Sally said. "The story could have arisen because Ambrosius was really used as a hostage. Although Nennius originally tells us Vortigern required a boy with no earthly father, he later says Ambrosius was the son of a Roman consul. The Aurelius family was extremely wealthy and influential. Perhaps the truth behind what had obviously become a legend by Nennius's time, four centuries later, may be that Vortigern intended to ransom Ambrosius back to the Romans in mainland Europe."

I pondered this for a moment. "If you're right, what do you think happened next?" I asked.

Sally shrugged. "None of the historical sources tells us what happened to Ambrosius for the next ten years or so. All we know is that Ambrosius was a clever young man and appears to have been quite capable of making the best out of whatever happened to him. Nennius tells us that he greatly impressed Vortigern with his intellect."

"You mean his prophecies?" I asked.

"Nennius refers to only one prophecy, and that concerned the ongoing war with the Anglo-Saxons. It's Geoffrey of Monmouth who depicts the boy in the incident at Dinas Emrys as a fledgling prophet. But there he's confusing the historical Ambrosius with the legendary Merlin."

"But not if Myrddin is a title and not an actual name," I said. When Sally didn't answer, I prompted her again.

"You don't think that Geoffrey's Merlin was based on Ambrosius?" I continued. Sally smiled. "Certainly he is concerning the incident at Dinas Emrys. Sadly, as so little is known about Ambrosius, there's no way of knowing whether the rest was invention. Excalibur, the Holy Grail, Avalon, Merlin's gift of prophecy: We would have to know more about Arthur's time a few decades later. It would help if we knew what happened to Ambrosius between the Dinas Emrys episode and his emergence as the British leader twelve years after Vortigern's death."

I changed the subject back to Ambrosius's childhood and the possibility that he had fled to the kingdom of Demetia during the Anglo-Saxon revolt. "Geoffrey says that Merlin was found playing in a field at Carmarthen, only twelve miles over there," I said, pointing to the countryside to the south. "Could that have been where the historical Ambrosius was living?"

"It's possible. The Roman town there was still occupied and being used as a seaport at the time. In fact, it was probably the kingdom of Demetia's main trading center. If any of the Aurelius family made it to Demetia as refugees, they would presumably prefer to live in what was still a relatively prosperous and civilized town rather than be stuck up here in a hill fort."

Sally went on to explain that although she doubted the bulk of Geoffrey's Merlin story had anything to do with the historical Ambrosius, she considered that the details of his account concerning Vortigern's men finding Merlin could have related to Ambrosius. This was because Geoffrey referred to Merlin's mother as a Demetian princess and, in Sally's opinion, the historical Ambrosius's mother could actually have been such a woman.

"Nennius says that Germanus preached against Vortigern because he married his own daughter," she said. "He does not name her or explain why, but the inscription on the Pillar of Eliseg in northern Wales tells us that Vortigern's wife was a Roman woman named Severa, the daughter of Maximus, a Roman emperor in the 380s whose family lived in Britain.[5] She would have been in her sixties in the 440s, but she previously bore Vortigern a daughter, whom, presumably on his wife's death, he decided to marry. It seems that Vortigern was attempting to found a Roman dynasty in Britain and the sin of incest wasn't going to stand in his way."

She paused for a moment and then continued. "Given Vortigern's ambitious political proclivities, it's likely that, as Ambrosius's mother was a high-status Roman, living within his purview in the south of Wales, Vortigern seized an opportunity to take advantage of her elite status and marry her off to one of his sons. I realize that Geoffrey says Merlin's mother was the daughter of a Demetian king, but this may have been due to confusion over a princess as the daughter of king and a princess as the wife of a prince."

"Why does Geoffrey also say that Merlin's mother became a nun, or at least was living in a nunnery in Carmarthen?" I asked. "Perhaps she was there seeking sanctuary from the marauding Anglo-Saxons."

"Not necessarily," Sally said. "Remember, in Carmarthen she was presumably under Vortigern's protection, and thus would have been safe from the barbarian invaders. Perhaps, if she had been forced to marry Vortigern's son, she sought sanctuary with the nuns in order to escape her unwanted husband. It's all a guess, of course."

"Any idea which of Vortigern's sons she married?"

"The most likely is Vitalinus, the person who appears to have taken over after Vortigern's death."

As Vitalinus was the man from whom Ambrosius later usurped command of the Britons, Sally offered to take me to see what was thought to be his gravestone in the churchyard at Nevern, some twelve miles to the west.

The tiny village of Nevern lies amid spectacular scenery near the northern coast of the Dyfed Peninsular, in the shadow of the Preseli Mountains. By mid-morning a misty rain had begun to fall, but by the time we reached the church, the sun had come out again. The old parish church of St. Brynach, with its gray stone tower, traces its origins to the earliest Christian times in Britain, and inside and around the church there are a number of fifth- and sixth-century gravestones.

Sally wanted to take me inside the church, but it was locked and there was no sign of the rector. In fact, the entire village seemed deserted. The only person we could find was a small, thin, middle-aged man with wiry gray hair who was examining one of the gravestones behind the church. Even he seemed reluctant to talk; he quickly walked away and left the churchyard the moment he saw us approaching. Left alone, Sally took me over to the gravestone she wanted to show me. Clearly ancient, and much taller than the rest, it stood to the east of the church porch. About six feet tall, it was inscribed in Latin: VITALIANI EMERETO.

"Vitaliani means 'of Vitalinus'—in other words, 'in memory of Vitalinus,'" said Sally, as she pointed out the weathered inscription on the old monument. Wet with the morning drizzle, it sparkled in the sunlight.

"How do you know this was the same Vitalinus that Ambrosius overthrew?" I asked.

"Vitalinus was a rare name in the Roman world, and he is the only one we know of in Britain in the late fifth century, from when the inscription dates."

"But there's no date, is there?" I asked.

"The gravestone can be dated by this additional inscription here," Sally said, showing me a series of lines and notches cut down the side along one edge of the stone. She explained that this was a unique but wonderfully simple form of writing developed in Ireland.

In Roman times, both the Britons and the Irish were Celts, their name coming from the word Keltoi, the Greek name for a common people who dominated northwestern Europe from around 700 B.C. Although they had a remarkable culture, the Celts lacked the kind of civilization and technology the Romans and Greeks enjoyed and consequently never developed paper and accordingly a form of writing. After the Roman invasion, the Britons adopted the Latin alphabet, but in Ireland, which the Romans never conquered, the Irish Celts continued on as before. Then, around 400 A.D., inspired by the Latin alphabet, the Irish came up with their own form of writing, in which Roman letters were replaced by symbols that were far easier to engrave on wood or stone. Known as Ogham script, named after a Celtic god of language, it employed a series of simple parallel lines to represent the same sounds as the individual Roman letters.

"After the Roman army left, Irish raiders began to plunder the western coast of Britain," said Sally, "but from the time of Vortigern, when the west was more organized, the raids ceased and the Irish began to trade and settle peacefully in parts of Wales. From around 450, the Irish settlers sometimes inscribed Latin monuments with additional Ogham words so that their own people could read them. Consequently, both Latin and Ogham inscriptions are often found on the same stone, as they are here. It is from slight variations in Ogham script that inscriptions can be dated."

The Romans called the Celts the Gauls and referred to their common language as Gaelic, Sally explained. Between 58 and 51 B.C., Julius Caesar conquered the Celts in France, Switzerland, the Netherlands, Belgium, and Luxembourg, and established the Roman province of Gaul throughout this huge area. For the next century, the inhabitants of the British Isles remained free from the Romans and continued to speak Gaelic. However, in the three centuries after the Roman invasion of mainland Britain, the language of the natives here became a cross between Gaelic and Latin known as Brythonic, which eventually developed into Welsh.

In unconquered Ireland, however, the language remained Gaelic. Problematically, the Gaelic language employed sounds that were unlike anything in the Latin language, especially the vowels, and so Ogham script used a series of dots or notches to represent them. The Gaelic and Brythonic languages were still similar enough for the Irish and Britons to understand each other, but there were differences that made writing difficult.

"When the Irish first settled in Wales, their Ogham inscriptions continued to use these dots, but by the sixth century, when their language became more Brythonic, they dropped the dots in favor of the parallel lines representing the Latin vowels," said Sally. She ran her finger along the edge of the stone. "Here we can see that the dots are still being used, which means the inscription must date from between 450 and 500 A.D."

"The inscription reads 'Vitalinus Emerito.' What does *emerito* mean?" I asked.

"Some scholars suggest that it was a British dialect variation of the Latin word *emeritus*, referring to a person who had retired but was still holding an honorary title: a king, for instance, who had abdicated in favor of a younger man. However, this makes no sense on a gravestone; such titles were used in old age but not employed on memorial stones. He would have been remembered as the ruler he once was. It should read Vitaliani Rex—'king'—or something like that. Personally, I doubt it was a grave marker at all."

Sally explained that in the 1800s, the stone was moved into the graveyard from another location. "There are a number of fifth- and sixth-century gravestones in and around the church, showing that it was being used as a Christian burial site during Vitalinus's time. As the stone bore his name, it was probably thought to be a more fitting place to reerect it. Today, because it's in a graveyard, scholars automatically assume that it is a grave marker and consequently attempt to translate the word Emerito in the context of an epitaph. I think it means something very different that makes sense only when you realize where the stone was originally." Sally told me how in 1873 the Welsh historian John Rhys recorded that it had originally stood beside a road, two miles to the east, in a valley called Cwm Gloyne.[6] "I'll take you there," she said.

That afternoon we drove along the A487 road, following the course of the river Nyfer, which wound its way through sheep-covered mountains, until we crossed an old humpback bridge and turned into a narrow lane that ran beside a wooded escarpment.

"The stone originally stood somewhere beside this lane," Sally said, as she stopped the car. She pointed up at the thick trees that covered the slope. "Up there, there's a hill fort similar to the one at Craig Gwrtheyrn. It's been partially excavated and artifacts found there date it to the post-Roman era, meaning it was occupied during Vitalinus's time.[7] If Vitalinus died in this area, then he would indeed have been buried in the contemporary graveyard at Nevern. He probably had a grave marker there, but the stone that stands there now is not it. It originally stood here, which means it has to have been something else—a stone commemorating a particular event that occurred where we are now."

Sally reminded me of the words of Nennius: "From the reign of Vortigern to the strife between Vitalinus and Ambrosius are twelve years."[8]

"This strife appears to have been when Ambrosius overthrew Vitalinus, and it may have been here, at this hill fort, that this event occurred. If so, then the word Emerito makes sense. It would be a version of the name Emrys—the Brythonic rendering of the name Ambrosius."

Sally explained that the Brythonic and the later Welsh language had their own local renderings of Roman names, in much the same way as, these days, the French name André becomes the English Andrew, or Pierre becomes Peter. The Romans themselves shortened the name Ambrosius to Ambrose, as Marcus was shortened to Mark, and the Britons went one further and rendered Ambrose as Emrys, which was easier for them to pronounce. "Early British writings refer to various people named Ambrosius in the Roman Empire as Emrys. As such, Emerito might have been an attempt to re-Latinize the name. It's possible that the inscription should be translated as: 'In memory of Vitalinus and Ambrosius.' It might be a memorial stone to commemorate the battle fought between them here."

Latin, Gaelic, Welsh, Brythonic! I was getting a bit confused. I had no idea whether Sally was right and this was the place where Ambrosius took command of the Britons, but she had got me thinking along new lines. I already knew Emrys was the Welsh name for Ambrosius and that Dinas Emrys in North Wales was named after him. However, I had not considered researching references to the name Emrys regarding my investigation into a historical Merlin. If Merlin was Ambrosius Aurelius, then his activities may also have been recorded under the name Emrys.

5

THE LADY OF THE LAKE

The next day, at the National Library of Wales in Aberystwyth, about fifty miles up the coast, I made a computer search of the archives concerning Dark Age Welsh literature. There were in fact two references to Ambrosius Aurelius as Emrys in a series of unusual Welsh poems known as the Triads due to the fact that their characters or themes are grouped into sets of three. These Triads have names such as "The Three Fair Princes," "The Three Defilements," and "The Three Harmful Blows." They are not actually poems in the true sense of the word, but rather seem to be listings of what would once have been full poems or stories. The ones including Emrys are found in *The Red Book of Hergest,* which dates from the Middle Ages, but linguists date the original period of composition to sometime in the eighth or ninth century and believe them to be an attempt to preserve a Welsh oral tradition that was quickly becoming lost.[1]

The first was in a Triad called "The Three Skilful Bards." Emrys is one of the three most important bards, or venerated poets, in Dark Age Britain. The Triad simply listed them:

Myrddin, son of Morfryn,
Myrddin Emrys,
and Taliesin.[2]

Although the Triad offered no more information, it provided me with a surprising insight into how Ambrosius was perceived. First, his name was unequivocally associated with Merlin under the Welsh rendering Myrddin. Second, it showed that there were indeed two Merlins: Myrddin, son of Morfryn (presumably Lailoken), and Myrddin Emrys— Merlin Ambrosius. This was exciting enough, but the fact that he was referred to as one of the chief bards was more significant than it might appear initially. Bards were much more than mere poets.

As the Celts originally had no form of writing, their history, religion, even their skills had to be committed to memory. For this reason, certain members of a tribe were chosen when young to be trained in remarkable memory techniques, which included rhyming and poetry as mnemonic devices. These special individuals were not only the librarians of Celtic culture, but they were also the libraries. The poems and sagas they kept in their heads were the archives of the civilization's knowledge and history. When the Romans brought writing to the Celts, these people soon became obsolete. However, poetry and storytelling retained their prestige in Celtic society and the most revered poets were known as bards. But the bards were credited with far more than the skills of poetry composition and storytelling; they were thought to have inherited the knowledge of the ancient Druids.

In simple terms, the Druids were the pre-Roman Celtic priesthood. There are a number of groups in Britain today who call themselves Druids, such as those who perform ceremonies at Stonehenge on midsummer's day, but they can be traced only to the eighteenth century, when it became fashionable to re-form ancient mystical societies. Unfortunately, little is know of the original Druids, other than that they were said to possess astonishing powers of the mind. In the first century B.C., Julius Caesar encountered the Druids in Gaul and in his writings he refers to them:

> Of the two classes above mentioned one consists of Druids, the other of warriors. The former are concerned with divine worship . . . a great number of young men gather about them for the sake of instruction and hold them in great honor. In fact, it is they who decide in almost all disputes, public and private; and if any crime has been committed, or murder done, or there is any dispute about succession or boundar-

ies, they also decide it, determining awards and penalties . . . All men move out of their path and shun their approach and conversation, for fear they may get some harm from their contact, and no justice is done if they seek it, no distinction falls to their share. Of all these Druids, one is chief, who has the highest authority among them. At his death, either any other that is pre-eminent in position succeeds, or, if there be several of equal standing, they strive for the primacy by the vote of the Druids, or sometimes even with armed force . . . It is believed that their rule of life was discovered in Britain and trans-ferred hence to Gaul; and to-day those who would study the subject more accurately journey, as a rule, to Britain to learn it.[3]

According to Caesar, it was in Britain that Druidism began and where its heartland still lay. Caesar also provides a tantalizing insight into their practices—for instance, how long it took them to master the same memory techniques later employed by the bards. He tells us: "They learn by heart a great number of verses, and therefore some persons remain twenty years in training."[4] Caesar also records Druidic beliefs:

The cardinal doctrine which they seek to teach is that souls do not die, but after death pass from one to another; and this belief, as the fear of death is thereby cast aside, they hold to be the greatest incentive to valor. Besides this, they have many discussions as touching [interpreting] the stars and their movement, the size of the universe and of the earth, the order of nature, the strength and the powers of the immortal gods, and hand down their lore to the young men.[5]

The Druids were astrologers, philosophers, and nature-lovers, and, as discussed, believed in reincarnation. Caesar's contemporary, the Roman writer Cicero, recorded additionally that they were skilled in herbal medicine and were credited with the gift of prophecy.[6] In many ways, Druidic practices were similar to those of Japanese Zen or Tibetan Buddhism, except the Romans accused the Druids of performing human sacrifices. However, most historians consider this an invention of propaganda, as the Romans were intent on eradicating the Druids. Because the Druids maintained Celtic law, they were viewed as enemies of Rome, and the Romans wasted no time in wiping out their influence. However, if Dark Age Celtic poetry is to be believed, individual Druids survived in secret as the bards—from a Gaelic word meaning "sacred speaker." Once the Romans left Britain, these shamanlike bards reemerged as both tribal court poets, to record the exploits of kings, and advisers on spiritual affairs. Like the Druids, they were even credited with the gift of prophecy and magical powers and were often referred to as wizards. To me, the Triad of "The Three Skilful Bards" was something of a revelation. It not only confirmed that Emrys—Ambrosius—was also called Merlin, but it also showed that he was seen as something of a magician, just as Merlin is depicted in the Arthurian romances.

Like Glynn Davis, I was beginning to accept that there was enough evidence for Merlin's existence in something like the way he was later portrayed by Geoffrey of Monmouth and the medieval romancers. Parts of the Merlin legend were clearly based on Ambrosius Aurelius, who was a genuine historical figure who lived at the right time, a man who was actually known by the Welsh epithet Myrddin. Like Merlin, Ambrosius could well have spent time in Demetia as a boy and, again like Merlin, he seems to have been considered something of a magician. None of this was actual historical proof, but it was now a reasonable conjecture that the seemingly fanciful stories of Merlin were embellished accounts of the life of a real man.

If I was to discover more, I needed to address not only the mystery of how Ambrosius became such a successful warrior, but also how he might have become a bard. How—and, more important, where—did the boy who was raised as a pampered colonial Roman learn to become a war leader and, if he was indeed the historical Merlin, the most famous wizard in history? As Sally had rightly said, someone needed to find out where Ambrosius spent those mysterious twelve years from 447 to 459 B.C.: between the time when he was brought before Vortigern at Dinas Emrys and the time when he led the Britons to victory against the Anglo-Saxons.

It was the second reference to Emrys in the Triads that gave me the vital clue I needed. In a Triad called the "Three Dishonored Men," one of the characters is Vortigern, who is accused of exiling "Emrys Wledig [the noble Emrys] . . . from this island [Britain] to Armorica."[7] Armorica was a Roman district in the province of Gaul, around what is now Brittany in modern France. If the Triad was right, Sally was probably correct when she guessed that Vortigern ransomed Ambrosius to the Romans in mainland Europe after the Dinas Emrys incident.

And indeed, historically, in the year 447, it does appears that a British delegation was sent to the province in northwest Gaul. According to Gildas, the British dispatched a message to the senior Roman general in Gaul asking for help.

> The miserable remnant [the British] therefore sent a letter to Agitius, the Roman commander, speaking as follows: "To Agitius, thrice consul, answer the groans [pleas] of the Britons." Further on came the complaint: "The barbarians drive us to the sea, the sea pushes us back to the barbarians; by one or other of these two modes of death we are either drowned or slaughtered." But they got no help in return.[8]

Gildas does not provide a date for the letter, but the year 447 can be derived because of the activities of the Roman commander in question. Gildas refers to him as Agitus, but he has to have been a man named Flavius Aetius. Not only is the name Aetius similar to Agitus, but Gildas refers to him as "thrice consul" as well. Aetius was the only man in a span of three hundred years, other than an emperor, to serve three consulships. As his third consulship was shared with Quintus Aurelius in 446, the letter was obviously sent after this, when Aetius was no longer consul and had been sent by the emperor Valentinian to command the armies in Gaul. This new commission was in response to a direct threat by the Huns, and this indicated a more precise date for the letter.

By the mid-440s the Huns, who started the barbarian invasions by moving west from the steppes of Russia, pushed through the Goth regions of Austria and Germany and crossed the Rhine into Gaul. Led by their infamous, fearsome leader Attila, the Huns devastated everything in their path. (Their savagery was such that the name Hun became synonymous with the word *barbarian*. This is why the Allies derisively, and incorrectly, referred to the Germans as Huns in the First World War.)

The Goths had already brought the western Roman empire close to collapse a few decades earlier, but the Huns were a far more formidable enemy.

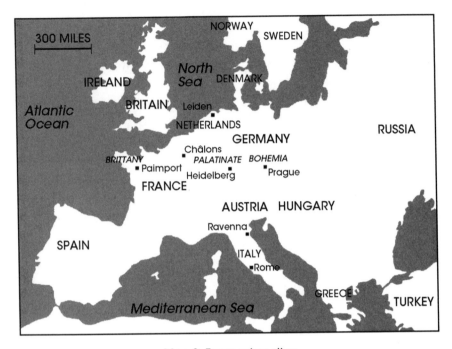

Map 3. Europe: key sites

They may have lacked the kind of military expertise employed by the Romans, but they vastly outnumbered the imperial forces and were expert horsemen. It was to meet this threat that Aetius was sent to command the Roman armies in Gaul.[9] Gildas recounts that the commander was unable to send help to the Britons, the implication being that he was preoccupied with the Huns. In 448 the Romans secured a peace with the Huns, who then retreated beyond the Rhine. If the letter was sent after this time, the chances are that some kind of aid could have been sent in reply to the Briton's plea for help. It seems, then, that the letter was sent between 446 and 448—presumably in 447. As this is the year that Vortigern evidently sent Ambrosius to Armorica, it is possible that the letter was sent along with him.

Armorica is the most likely place for any delegation from the Britons to have been sent, as it was on the northwest tip of France and the closest point on the European continent to the coast of mainland Britain still free from Anglo-Saxon control. As the Triad referred to Ambrosius's *exile* in Armorica, it seemed to imply that he had spent some time there, rather than having moved directly on to Rome. Indeed, the trouble with the Huns may have prevented Ambrosius from traveling farther, at least for a while. In fact, Rome itself might not have been considered safe.

Armorica, on the other hand, was far from the front lines and thus a secure place to be. Many Britons were known to have fled to this area during the Anglo-Saxon conquest of Britain, which is why it later became known as Brittany, or Little Britain. Here they remained, free from barbarian incursions for years. If I was to discover any clues as to what became of Ambrosius for the next twelve, formative years, it was to Brittany that I would have to go.

If Ambrosius arrived in Brittany in 447, the most likely place for him to have journeyed to was the Roman city of Sulis, the regional capital, situated in a forested area known as Broceliande. The forest of Broceliande still survives, although as a much smaller wooden district around the French town of Paimpont, some forty miles southwest of Rennes. Although I could find no historical references to Ambrosius in that area, remarkably there were legends concerning the young Merlin.

Merlin was said to have been the court adviser to King Arthur, king of the Britons, and so it is understandable that there are sites in Britain around which legends of Merlin have developed. It is surprising, though, that any such folklore exists in France. Many of the medieval Arthurian romances were written in French, but this is because the language was spoken by the English aristocracy after the Normans (from Normandy, in northern France) invaded England in 1066.

However, an Arthurian romance actually written in France around 1220, known as the *Estoire de Merlin* (The Story of Merlin), concentrates on Merlin's life until the enthronement of King Arthur.[10] Most of the story is similar to Geoffrey of Monmouth's works written a century earlier, but it includes an account of Merlin's early life in Brittany—in the forest of Broceliande.

In the story, Merlin travels to Brittany and goes to the forest to meditate. While there, he encounters the Lady of the Lake: a beautiful and mysterious water nymph who gives him the magical sword Excalibur. This is the first time the Lady of the Lake appears in any of the Arthurian romances, and, according to the anonymous author, the sources of the legend were earlier sagas from Brittany. None of these original stories survives, but the legends they inspired live on in local folklore around the French town of Paimpont, in the heart of what remains of the Broceliande forest.

I had assumed that this Merlin legend in Brittany was preserved in rather obscure and little known folklore. In fact, I expected the local population to scoff at the idea that Merlin could possibly have had any connection with their district. Far from it: I was astonished to find that the small town of Paimpont had developed something of a tourist industry around the Merlin legend. There was even a Legend Center to sell books, DVDs, and other Arthurian memorabilia. Apparently the Paimpont townsfolk not only accepted that Merlin had genuine associations with the area, but they were proud of it as well.

Just outside the town there is a tranquil lake surrounded by overhanging trees. The lake is called l'Etang de Comper and, according to local folklore, this had been the home of the Lady of the Lake. The people of the area insist that this is the lake into which Excalibur was eventually thrown by one of Arthur's knights, although in the medieval romances this episode takes place near the site of Arthur's last battle in Britain. The locals also say that Excalibur was forged nearby, at a natural spring called la Fontaine de Barenton. This part of the legend *is* included in the *Estoire de Merlin:* Here the Lady of the Lake makes Excalibur for Merlin so he will be invulnerable, but the magician later decides Arthur should have it.

I was taken to la Fontaine de Barenton by George Candy, a retired English lawyer who now lived in the area. I had been introduced to him at the Arthurian Legend Center, as he was something of an authority on the local folklore, which was his passion since moving to Brittany five years earlier. As my French was virtually nonexistent, the locals thought he would be my best guide. George drove me to the tiny hamlet of Folle-Pensée, to the north of Paimpont, and led me down a forest track until we reached a clearing among thick pine trees. Here, surrounded by ferns and gorse bushes, the spring bubbled out from between a pile of boulders into a shallow well.

"This is where Excalibur was supposedly made by the Lady of the Lake," said George, as he leaned over the little wall that surrounded the pond and ran his hand through its clear, cold water. Although he considered the *Estoire de Merlin* story a romantic invention, he believed the

Fontaine de Barenton episode was based on a historical tradition associated with the spring.

"The story may have been rooted in an ancient practice of consecrating swords to a water goddess," he continued. "In pre-Christian times, the Celts considered springs like this to be sacred to female deities. During forging, a sword has to be immersed in water, and this was often done in such springs in the belief that a water goddess would protect the owner in battle."

I had previously reasoned that the story of Excalibur being thrown to the Lady of the Lake when Arthur lay dying might have derived from an early Celtic custom. As part of their funeral rites, the ancient Britons threw a warrior's treasured possessions into a lake as an offering to the gods to grant him safe passage to the afterlife. Archaeological excavations have unearthed many precious artifacts, including swords, that long ago were thrown into sacred lakes and pools by the Celts as offerings to water deities.

One such dig, at Anglesey in North Wales in 1942, recovered no fewer than 144 items that had been preserved for almost two thousand years in the mud of the dried-up lake of Llyn Cerrig Bach. The theme of Excalibur being thrown to the Lady of the Lake could well have come from the ancient Celtic practice of making a sacred offering to a water goddess.[11] However, I had not previously considered that the story of the Lady of the Lake forging Excalibur derived from a similar custom.

"The Lady of the Lake could have been based on a real woman who represented the goddess," said George. "Women enjoyed equal status to men in Celtic society, and there were many female warriors and also female Druids. Druid priestesses, in the role of the goddess, probably consecrated the warriors' weapons, and one particular Druidess may have been the original Lady of the Lake."[12]

George's theory would have fit nicely before the Roman invasion of Gaul in the first century B.C. The Merlin story, however, was set in mid-fifth century A.D. "Celtic religion would have been eclipsed by Roman religion by the time the Merlin legend is set," I said. "Would the people of this area have still continued with such customs?"

George explained that the Celts of Gaul, particularly in the remote area of Brittany, had carried on with their pre-Roman practices. "Julius

Caesar says the chief god of the area was Mercury.[13] Obviously the Celts had not called their god by that name, but the Romans usually equated local deities with their own. There was obviously something similar to the Gaul's god that reminded them of Mercury. They may have gotten rid of official Druid power, but they allowed the Celts to continue with their religion as long as they accepted that the god being venerated was their own Mercury. This seemed to have worked, as archaeology has unearthed many statues and inscriptions to Mercury from the Roman sites in north-west France."

As a party of Spanish tourists arrived and excitedly began throwing coins into the well to make wishes, we continued to discuss the continuation of Celtic religion in the area during Roman times. Mercury was the messenger of the gods; he was also the god of writing, learning, and magic. The Druids were the guardians of learning; they committed Celtic lore and knowledge to memory. Their chief god presumably reflected this sacred tradition, so the Romans regarded him in the same way as they did their own Mercury. Something similar probably happened with the Celtic water goddess and patron of weapons, George suggested.

"The Arthurian Romances refer to the Lady of the Lake as Nimue," said George. "Here in Brittany she is called Mneme, which has to have been a version of the Roman water goddess Minerva, whom Caesar tells us was the principal goddess of the Gauls.[14] The Romans took many of their gods from earlier Greek mythology and Minerva came from the Greek Mnemosyne, the mythical water nymph who made weapons for the hero Perseus. Mneme is such a similar name to Mnemosyne that they have to share a common origin."

I agreed that George was probably right. The Roman capital of Armorica was at Sulis, just a few miles to the west of where we were. The town had actually been named after Minerva, her full Roman title being Sulis Minerva. Minerva was not only a water deity, but she was a goddess of war and patron of soldiers as well. Although the Romans were great conquerors, the success and longevity of their empire often came down to the fact that the Roman occupiers allowed local religion to remain, and frequently adopted the local deities themselves. That they named their regional capital after Minerva suggests the area was already the center for an equivalent Celtic goddess.

"So you think the original Celtic water goddess associated with this spring was still being venerated here at the time the Merlin story is set, in the mid-fifth century?" I said.

"Yes, and swords were most likely still being consecrated to her by Celtic priestesses."

"Hadn't this area become Christian by then?"

"Interestingly enough, no." George explained that in the 1980s, French archaeologists excavated a Roman cemetery near the village of Trehorenteuc, on the southwest edge Broceliande forest, and uncovered burials dating from the mid- to late 400s. Although there were some Christian texts found on the gravestones, most were carved with distinctly pagan symbols.[15] "The Roman Church did not record a bishop of Armorica until the first, Mansuetus, was appointed in 461," said George. "Christianity does not appear to have established itself in the area until after 450, and it was brought here by the Britons who fled from the Anglo-Saxons."

"So Druidism, or at least some form of original Celtic religion, could have survived here?"

"It still does, in a way." George pointed to the coins that lay at the bottom of the little well. "People still throw money into springs like this for good luck. The entire custom of wishing wells worldwide probably derived from the Celtic tradition of making offerings to a water goddess. The Romans adopted it, and our modern ancestors took it from the Romans."

George was right; the custom is known the world over. In less than half an hour, more than fifty tourists had gathered at the well and all of them had eagerly thrown coins into the water. All but one, that is: a short, thin guy with wiry gray hair who just stood there alone, listening to one of the tour guides. I was also sure that he was trying to listen in on *our* conversation and could have sworn he was the same man from the churchyard at Nevern! I was about to talk to him when he moved away and merged into the crowd. I was trying to pick him out among the tourists when George told me he needed to get back home. I decided that I had to be mistaken and followed him back down the forest path, mulling over the significance of what George had told me.

It seemed too much of a coincidence that the story of the young Merlin was associated with precisely the area that the young Ambrosius seems to have come to. There was no way of knowing for sure, but it was a reasonable guess that stories associated with the man who was later to achieve fame as Merlin the magician had survived in Brittany to give rise to the legend of his encounter with the Lady of the Lake. Merlin was said to have been a magician, and the Triad of "The Three Skilful Bards" asserted that Emrys (Ambrosius) was Merlin and that he had been a bard—a spiritual descendant of the Druids, themselves regarded as magicians.

It had been a mystery as to how Ambrosius, a highborn Roman, might have become such a bard. It now seemed that it could well have been in Brittany, in the forest of Broceliande, that Ambrosius became acquainted with Druidism, or at least the Celtic lore that survived in that region at that time. Perhaps he had even been initiated into its mysteries—just as Merlin is portrayed as developing his skills as a magician in this very area in Breton folklore and the *Estoire de Merlin*.

But there was more. I could not help but feel that it was significant that the emblem of Mercury, the chief god of the area in the hybrid Romano-Celtic religion, figured in the Excalibur legend. The hilt of Excalibur was said to have been decorated with two golden serpents, and the twin-serpent motif was the symbol for the god Mercury. In Roman statues, Mercury is usually represented holding a winged wand with the emblem of two serpents intertwined around the shaft. As Ambrosius was the son of an important Roman official, had the Celts of Brittany given him a sword that was not only consecrated to their water goddess, but also decorated with the twin serpents of their chief god?

I had previously thought that the twin-serpent motif on Excalibur had originated with the insignia of a Roman legion stationed in Britain. However, the Mercury connection now seemed more feasible: It fit with the origins of the Excalibur story in Brittany. It was when I was discussing the idea with George at a Paimpont café after we had returned from the spring that I suddenly remembered that Glynn Davis had told me I was wrong about Excalibur's double-serpent hilt coming from a Roman military emblem.

"Do you know what the double serpents really mean?" he had asked me. I had not given it another thought since he had told me something about Shakespeare being killed because of the sword and people still willing to kill for its secret today. I had to admit that although Glynn may have had some odd ideas, he appeared to have been right about Merlin being a historical figure. He told me to dig deeper and I would find evidence for Merlin's historicity and I had. I decided that he might have had a genuinely good theory concerning Excalibur and thus I decided to give him a call.

Glynn's wife answered the phone and sounded suspicious when I told her who I was. In fact, she sounded positively concerned. At first she told me that her husband was resting, but then I heard Glynn's voice in the background and he took my call. He sounded out of breath, as if he had been running. He excused himself and explained that he had been unwell.

"You're getting closer," he said when I told him about my idea concerning Mercury and Excalibur. When I asked him if he would tell me more about what he knew, or thought he knew, about Excalibur he was uncharacteristically helpful.

"As the Celts adopted Roman gods, so the Romans had previously adopted Greek gods," he said. "Mercury was borrowed from the Greek god Hermes, who was also depicted with the same double-serpent wand. Like Mercury, Hermes was the god of learning and magic; in fact, the modern word *hermetic,* meaning of a magical or occult tradition, is derived from his name. The double serpent on Excalibur held the secret to what the Druids' hermetic tradition was all about. This is the secret I told you that Shakespeare was murdered for. And believe me, it was, and still is, worth a great deal to certain people."

I felt like Bob Woodward talking to "Deep Throat" during the Watergate affair as Glynn told me to continue digging. When I told him that he had to be more helpful, and at least give me some plausible reason to believe him, he promised that he would mail me a copy of his research notes. After he hung up without revealing more, I had to admit I was intrigued. I still thought he was a bit melodramatic, but I hoped he really did have something worth knowing concerning Excalibur and the Druidic tradition.

While waiting for his research notes to arrive in the mail, I continued my own research and attempted to answer an important question. If Mercury and Minerva were the chief god and goddess of Brittany—at least, this is what the Romans called them—it would make sense for an important sword to be consecrated to the goddess and decorated with the insignia of the god. However, if Ambrosius had been given such a sword, why had it become so famous? In the Arthurian Romances, Merlin returned to Britain with Excalibur, which he made a symbol of British kingship. When I examined what Ambrosius must have done in the latter part of the twelve years between the Dinas Emrys incident and becoming a British leader, Excalibur suddenly fit into a historical context. It may not have had the magical powers it was credited with, but it did have an important religious and political significance.

6

EXCALIBUR

Excalibur was not only credited with the power to render its wielder invincible in battle, but it was also depicted as a sword of kingship. Like a crown, it became the badge of office for the British king. Today Excalibur is known specifically as King Arthur's sword, but in the Arthurian romances it previously belonged to Merlin, for whom it was made. Why, though, should Merlin, the magician and prophet, be associated with a warrior's sword?

Few people now think of Merlin as a warrior; he is instead thought of as the aging magician of King Arthur's court. In the Arthurian romances, however, he was portrayed as having originally been a warlord and a great king in his own right. Geoffrey of Monmouth, for instance, in his *Life of Merlin*, introduces Merlin with the words: "Merlin the Briton was famous throughout the world as prophet and king."[1] Because, as the name suggests, the Arthurian romances concentrate on the time of Arthur, when Merlin was old, they say very little about Merlin's time as king.

Most of the episodes regarding Merlin's younger days concern how he acquired his powers of prophecy and magic. However, it seems the authors took it for granted that their readers were familiar with this part of his life and knew he had once been war leader. Geoffrey, for example, begins his *Life of Merlin* by having Merlin lead an alliance of British kings in battle without any explanation as to how he acquired such status.[2] Evidently,

71

unlike Arthur, who is portrayed as being the sole ruler of Britain, Merlin was regarded as having been some kind of generalissimo, a supreme commander of a military alliance. This is exactly how Ambrosius is described by Gildas, who says he commanded the British forces and led the British kings.

Geoffrey suggests that Merlin had originally been made the king of South Wales, describing him as "law-giver to the proud South Welsh,"[3] which would fit with what Nennius says about Ambrosius usurping Vortigern's successor Vitalinus in what appears to have been the kingdom of Demetia. As noted, this occurred twelve years after Vortigern's death, making it 459, a time from which archaeological evidence confirms a massive British counteroffensive into the east of Britain.

For example, excavations of a series of huge, twenty-foot-high defensive earthworks or banks in East Anglia, which date from precisely this period, have uncovered hundreds of hobnails. These were nails used to fix the soles of Roman-style military boots, which the Anglo-Saxons did not have. Such finds showed that whoever built the entrenchments had to have been using Roman armor: in other words, the British side, which had managed to retake land right across England, areas that had been under Anglo-Saxon control for more than a decade.[4]

So both in the legend of Merlin and in history, Ambrosius was a warrior, but what about his sword? Did it play as great a part in British history as Excalibur did in the Arthurian romances? My discoveries in Brittany suggested the legendary sword *had* actually existed in a historical context. But if it did exist, why should it have become a symbol of kingship across the sea in Britain? When I arrived back in England, I decided to spend a few days in London in order to utilize the massive database of historical manuscripts at the British Library. Hopefully, by piecing together what was known about the period leading up to Ambrosius's time as British leader, I could discover more about the origins of the Excalibur legend.

For Ambrosius to have been so successful in leading the Britons against the Anglo-Saxons, he must have had previous military experience, presumably in the Roman army sometime during or after his stay in Brittany. If Ambrosius was in the Roman army between the years 447 and 459 A.D., then he would almost certainly have seen action fighting one of the most formidable enemies the Roman Empire had ever faced—Attila the Hun. The truce the Romans secured with the Huns in 448 did not last long; it simply played into Attila's hands, giving him time to prepare for a massive assault.

The following year, with an army of over half a million men, he swept into Gaul. Some of the greatest cities of northern Europe were sacked before Attila came up against the man who would finally stop him—the commander Aetius. Aetius was without doubt the leading Roman general of the era and in 451 he eventually defeated the mighty Huns at the battle of Châlons in France, less than four hundred miles to the east of Brittany.

By this time, Ambrosius would have been somewhere around the age of twenty and would almost certainly have seen some kind of military service. Aetius conscripted every man he could find to oppose Attila, and even made an alliance with the old Roman enemies the Visigoths. Unfortunately, there is no way of knowing in exactly what capacity Ambrosius might have served in the Roman army or precisely what action he saw: The last surviving lists of serving military officers in the western empire date from half a century before this time. Nevertheless, it was a fairly safe bet that he was among it somewhere.[5]

It was while I was researching the history of Attila that I found a historical precedent for Excalibur. According to the contemporary Roman historian Priscus, who had actually spent time at Attila's court as a hostage and knew the leader personally, Attila possessed a special sword. Known as the Sword of the Gods, the Huns believed that it made their leader invulnerable.[6] Apparently the psychological power of the myth had united the Huns for years. Evidently, the sword had been broken during the battle of Châlons, an ill-timed event that may have played a part in the Huns' demise.

Although the Huns were defeated at Châlons and retreated from Gaul, Attila remained alive, and in 452, with a sizable army, he crossed the Alps into Italy. This aggressive action caused the emperor to withdraw from Rome, leaving the capital defenseless. However, after their defeat by Aetius, Attila's army had lost the will to fight and began deserting in droves. Attila ultimately retreated from Rome without attacking the city and died shortly afterward—not on the field of battle, but on his wedding night, when a massive and unexplained nosebleed caused him to choke

With Attila dead, the Huns were leaderless and retreated in a
ed rabble back to the steppes of Russia. If the sword really was
broken at the battle of Châlons, then it may have been a contributing factor in demoralizing the Huns.

Whether or not Ambrosius was present on the front lines to witness
the retreat of the Huns, he would certainly have heard of the famous
sword and known of the effect it had over the minds of the men in Attila's
army. For years it had been a visible token of their invincibility and had led
them to victory after victory. It cannot be a coincidence that within a few
years, an identical tradition had become attached to a sword that Merlin
was said to have brought to Britain.

It already seemed feasible that, as the son of an important Roman,
Ambrosius was given a sword by the Celts of Brittany that was considered
sacred, one that had been consecrated to the water goddess and decorated with the twin serpents of the chief Celtic god. After fighting the
Huns, Ambrosius might well have appreciated the psychological power
of the Attila sword myth and contrived a similar lore around his own
sword—just as the Arthurian romances depict Merlin attributing magical
powers to Excalibur. It was an intriguing idea, but would such a concept
have really appealed to the British?

From the accounts of Gildas, Nennius, and Bede it seemed that
Ambrosius returned to Britain about the year 459, when he would have
been in his early thirties. The question was: Why would he want to return?
The only real description we have of Britain at this time is provided by
Gildas, who does not paint a pretty picture of life for the native Britons.
He says that for the past decade they had been constantly assailed by the
Anglo-Saxons, who ravished much of the country:

> Some of the wretched remnant [the Britons] were consequently cap-
> tured on the mountains and killed in heaps. Others, overcome by
> hunger, came and yielded themselves to the enemies, to be their slaves
> for ever, if they were not instantly slain, which was equivalent to the
> highest service. Others repaired to parts beyond the sea . . . Others,
> trusting their lives, always with apprehension of mind, to high hills,
> overhanging, precipitous, and fortified, and to dense forests and rocks
> of the sea, remained in their native land, though with fear.[7]

However, no matter how bleak a place Britain had become, the historical records of the period show quite clearly that it was preferable to mainland Europe. Britain was an island; with strong leadership and a small but well-trained army, the Anglo-Saxons could be contained. The Germanic tribes, by this time ravishing much of western Europe, were, by comparison, an unstoppable horde. Within a few years of Aetius's victory over the Huns, the Roman Empire finally collapsed.

In 454, Aetius was such a successful and popular general that the Roman emperor Valentinian III saw him as a threat to his power and murdered him in a fit of jealousy. The following year, two of Aetius's officers avenged his death and assassinated the emperor. If one single act could be said to have been the death knell for the Roman Empire in the west, it was this. Valentinian had been emperor for thirty years and was just about the only thing holding the empire together. Within days of his death, civil war erupted among various claimants to the imperial throne, leaving the empire totally exposed. Just eleven weeks later, Rome itself fell to a Germanic tribe called the Vandals, who pillaged and sacked the city so brutally that their name has become synonymous with acts of mindless carnage. The emperor's widow, the empress Licinia, and her daughters were raped and dragged away into slavery, and anyone who had not managed to flee the city was butchered in the streets.[8]

Incredibly, even the sacking of the capital did not bring together the warring Roman factions. Throughout Europe, various commanders assumed the title of emperor and fought each other to a standstill while the Goths, Vandals, and other Germanic tribes surged between the last of the Roman legions, plundering towns and cities as they went. The Roman civilization that had dominated western Europe for centuries crumbled to ruins in a matter of months. Italy, where the empire had begun, held together for a few years while a Roman army general named Ricimer tried to save the empire by installing a series of puppet emperors at the new capital of Ravenna on the Adriatic coast 170 miles north of Rome. However, his authority did not extend much outside Italy; northwestern Europe beyond the Alps had collapsed into chaos.

This was the situation in the year 459, when Ambrosius returned to Britain. Anyone with wealth and influence in Italy was fleeing to what had been the eastern Roman Empire in what are now Turkey and the eastern

Mediterranean. This was now a separate empire, known as the Byzantine Empire, which had its own emperor and capital at Constantinople (modern Istanbul). However, anyone unfortunate enough to be north of the Alps would have been marooned in a hellish war zone where regional warlords fought over whatever scraps of civilization still remained. Memmius, the son of the consul Quintus Aurelius, was on the Italian side of the Alps and left the West to start a new and prosperous life in the East, but it seems that Quintus's other son, Ambrosius, had still been in Gaul. Cut off from Italy by the Vandals, Ambrosius may have decided that moving back to Britain was his best option, and he returned with the troops under his command. He must certainly have arrived with a sizable force of trained Roman soldiers, as he managed to defeat the British leader Vitalinus in South Wales and somehow unite the Britons to repel the Anglo-Saxons.

With the collapse of the western empire, few records survive, even from mainland Europe, let alone Britain. All we really know of Ambrosius's return is what Gildas records:

> A remnant of these wretched citizens [the British] flocked from different places on every side . . . and they took up arms and challenged their victors to battle under Ambrosius . . . and to these men, there came victory.[9]

The Anglo-Saxons were not expelled from Britain entirely, but appear to have been confined to a pocket of stiffer resistance in the southeast region of the country. Although Gildas records a series of skirmishes between the two sides, for all intents and purposes the British remained safely in control of most of their country for the next few decades. "This continued until the year of the siege of Badon Hill," Gildas records, which, he tells us, occurred forty-four years before the time of his writing, making it around the year 500[10] (as we have noted in chapter 1). Nennius writes that it was during this same siege—the battle of Badon—that King Arthur emerged as victor.[11]

Apparently, Ambrosius not only returned to Britain to lead the Britons to victory, but he also protected the country for years and prepared the foundations for the triumphant age of Arthur. As my research brought these turbulent times into focus, I could not help but feel that Ambrosius's remarkable achievements would have taken more than just military know-how. Victory in battle is one thing, but the unification of a deeply divided and unruly nation requires a new faith in leadership. Why had the tribal Britons united so effectively behind this aristocratic foreigner? In the Arthurian Romances, it had been the wielder of Excalibur behind whom the Britons had united. Historically, had Ambrosius's sword played a real and significant part in the events?

The twin-serpent design on Excalibur's hilt seems to have been derived from the wand of Mercury. A short rod, entwined by two snakes and topped by a pair of wings, it was known as the caduceus. (This is the same emblem that has become associated with the medical profession, as Mercury was, among other things, the god of medicine.) In Roman mythology, the caduceus wand was used by Mercury as an amulet of invulnerability. In the Arthurian story, Excalibur is a similar talisman, one that made its wielder invincible.

The mythology of Mercury had been adopted by the Celts of Brittany, but what about Britain? Certainly, the dual-serpent motif seems to have had significance to the Britons. In Nennius's account, Ambrosius was already associated with two serpents he discovered at Dinas Emrys, as is Merlin in Geoffrey of Monmouth's account. The two serpents at Dinas Emrys and the two serpents on Excalibur—it seems too coincidental for there not to have been some connection.

Sally Evans thought the story of the Dinas Emrys serpents might have arisen because of the ceramic fragments, which could have been taken for dragons' eggs. However, it seemed to me more likely that these dragons or serpents were some kind of analogy that held symbolic significance for people alive during the Dark Ages. It must have had something to do with the Celtic god the Romans equated with Mercury. I needed to find out more about him.

According to Julius Caesar, the Celts "worship principally the God Mercury; they have many statues of him and consider him to be the inventor of all skills . . ."[12] (Like most other Roman writers, throughout his works Caesar refers to the deities of other cultures by their nearest Roman equivalent. The Greek love goddess Aphrodite, for example, he refers to as the Roman Venus.) What was it about this god that made Caesar and the Romans equate him with Mercury? It would help if I knew what this god looked like. Unfortunately, as the pre-Roman images Caesar referred to were carved from wood, none of them has survived. However, archaeological finds from various sites in northwestern Europe have produced Roman coins and other ornaments inscribed with images of this god in his original Celtic form. He is usually depicted with a head-dress of antlers and holding one or two serpents.

The only pre-Roman depiction of the god survives from decorations on a silver cauldron found in a peat bog near Gundestrup, Denmark, in 1891. The so-called Gundestrup Cauldron is a bowl thought to be used for ceremonial purposes. It is dated to around 120 B.C., made by the Celtic people who had migrated to Denmark from Gaul.[13] A number of mytho-logical images are depicted on the cauldron, but one panel appears to show the chief Celtic god. He is sitting in a kind of half-lotus position with his eyes closed as if meditating. On his head are the antlers and in one hand he holds a huge serpent. The representations of this god make it clear why the Romans associated him with Mercury. Mercury was depicted with a winged helmet, similar to the antler headdress of the Celtic god, and he held the serpent wand similar to the way the Celtic god was depicted holding a serpent.

So who was this god? Apart from equating him with Mercury, Roman writings refer to him only as Cernunnos. As this comes from the Latin meaning simply "the horned one," it cannot have been his actual Celtic name. Although no writings survive from the Roman or pre-Roman period to tell us about this god, fortunately much of Celtic mythology has been preserved in later Irish literature.

Gaul and Britain were conquered by the Romans, but Ireland remained free from direct Roman influence for centuries. Although they had no form of writing until late Roman times, the Irish composed war poems and sagas between the sixth and tenth centuries; these preserved pre-Christian Irish mythology remarkably intact. Committed to writing in the eleventh century, these works survive today in various medieval manu-scripts known collectively as the Invasion Cycle—so called because they refer to periods of mythical Irish history when various tribes of demigods and demonic races were said to have invaded Ireland.[14] Reading the Irish Invasion Cycle, it quickly becomes clear that the deity that the Romans equated with Mercury is a god named Lugh (pronounced Loo).

Like the Roman gods, the Celtic gods were thought to have once lived humanlike existences in another realm. They were, like humans, conceived and born. In the Irish literature, Lugh is depicted as part god, part demon, as his mother was from a demonic race called the Fomorians. She was visited one night by Cian, the god of medicine and healing, who made love to her while she slept; thus was Lugh conceived. No sooner was the child born than Lugh's grandfather, Balor, the king of the Fomorians, discovered what had happened and had the baby thrown into the sea. However, Lugh did not drown, but instead floated and drifted on the tides among the islands of the Otherworld. This was the realm of the gods and other mystical beings: a group of mythical islands that were said to lie across the western sea (the Atlantic, as opposed to the Irish Sea which lies between Ireland and mainland Britain).

In the legend, Lugh is eventually washed up on Manannan Island, named after the sea god Manannan, whose home it is. Manannan rescues the child and raises him in secret with the help of the earth goddess Tailtiu. Here is found Lugh's association with serpents: The goddess often appeared in the guise of a serpent, as did Manannan, in that of a sea serpent. Lugh is therefore raised by two serpent deities, which seems to be why he was represented with these creatures in Celtic art.

When Lugh grows up, he decides to avenge himself and destroy his grandfather and the entire Fomorian race. To aid him, Manannan gives Lugh a magical sword of invincibility and sends him to Avallach, an island named after one of Manannan's sons, who lives there with his nine sisters. Here, Lugh is taught the secrets of magic and trained to be a great warrior. Eventually, he sets sail for the four islands of the Tuatha De Danaan, "the peoples of the goddess Dana," a race of demigods who are the sworn enemies of the Fomorians. Lugh joins the Tuatha in battle against the Fomorians and, although he loses a hand in the fight, ultimately kills his grandfather, the demon king Balor. The Tuatha hail Lugh as a hero, but at first will not allow him to reside with them, as his mother was Fomorian—that is, until his father, Cian, the god of medicine, appears and replaces Lugh's lost hand with a miraculous silver one. Seeing that Lugh is the son of a god, the Tuatha accept him as one of their own. In fact, Lugh eventually becomes their king and chief of all the gods when he steps on a magic stone, which cries out his name. Called the Liá Fail, or Stone of Destiny, it is a rock that is said to cry out when it is trodden on by a true king.

Ultimately, Lugh and some of the Tuatha visit Ireland, where they drive out the Fomorians who have sought refuge there. Here they are said to have first imparted the secret lore of Druidism to the Celts, who later took the knowledge to Britain and Gaul. When they return forever to the islands of the Otherword, the Tuatha leave behind four sacred relics: a cauldron that, when drunk from, can cure all ills; a spear that can kill immortals; the Stone of Destiny; and Lugh's magic sword. The cauldron and spear are eventually lost but the sword is hidden and the stone is given to the Irish kings. In fact, so strong was this myth that for centuries all the historical kings of Ireland were crowned on a real stone kept at Tara, the old Irish capital, that was claimed to be the original Liá Fail.

Archaeological evidence and surviving Roman works suggest that religion and mythology were pervasively consistent throughout most of the Celtic world. The Invasion Cycle of Ireland, therefore, appears to preserve an original version of the mythology surrounding the Celtic god that the Romans equated with Mercury. Like Mercury, Lugh was a god of skills, medicine, magic, and weapons. Like Mercury, he traveled freely between earth and the realms of the gods and, like Mercury, he was associated with serpents.

In fact, there is direct evidence that the Britons had exactly the same god. Although far less ancient Celtic mythology has been preserved from mainland Britain, Welsh myths refer to a godlike hero called Lludd who has to be one and the same as Lugh. (Lludd is pronounced Looth: The *th* is spelled with a double *D* in Welsh.) Not only are the two names remarkably similar, but also Ludd was called Lludd Llaw Ereint, meaning "Lludd the silver-handed," and Lugh had a silver hand. Furthermore, Lludd's father, Beli, was the Britons' god of medicine, as was Lugh's father Cian in the Irish legends.[15]

As I continued to research the mythology of this god the Romans equated with Mercury, it became patently clear that the legend of Excalibur owed much to it. It was not only that the two serpents on Excalibur were this god's emblem, or the fact that Lugh's sword and Excalibur were both swords of invulnerability; the very name Excalibur seems to have been taken from Lugh's sword. The word Excalibur, the name for the sword in the Arthurian romances, derived from the name Geoffrey of Monmouth uses for the weapon: Caliburn, which means "flashing sword." In Irish mythology Lugh's sword is called Fragarach, meaning "the Answerer," as it was said to reveal answers to the mysteries of life, but it is also referred to as Caladbolg, meaning "lightning sword."[16] Caliburn and Caladbolg are so similar that there must have been a link between them.

But there was more. It was not only the legend of Excalibur that had been borrowed from the mythology of Lugh, but other aspects of the medieval Merlin story as well. Like Lugh, Merlin is the son of a supernatural being who made love to his mother while she slept. Also like Lugh, Merlin was depicted as a half-demon. Although Geoffrey of Monmouth simply says that Merlin's father was an incubus, more of a mischievous, oversexed spirit than a demon, one of the first Arthurian Romances to be composed after Geoffrey's work portrays Merlin as the son of a devil. In Robert de Boron's *Le Roman du Graal* (Romance of the Grail), written around 1200, Merlin was supposed to have been Lucifer's plan to create the Antichrist, but Merlin overcomes his evil side and uses his powers for good.[17] When he grows up, Lugh spends time on the island of Avallach, somewhere over the western sea, where he is taught magic by nine unmarried sisters. In the Arthurian romances, Merlin frequently travels to the similar-sounding isle of Avalon, a mystical island also said to lie over the western sea; it too is the home of nine mysterious maidens.

There could be no doubt that much of the Merlin legend—certainly as it existed in the Middle Ages—had been taken from the mythology of Lugh. Merlin was clearly being portrayed as some kind of incarnation of this ancient Celtic deity. But what about the historical Merlin, Ambrosius? Was he regarded as a personification of Lugh during his lifetime? Could this have been how Ambrosius managed to unite the Britons—they thought of him as their ancient god?

Lugh, under his British name Lludd, appears to have been widely venerated in Britain, even at the end of Roman times. Archaeology has unearthed many religious artifacts inscribed with the name of the deity dating from the late Roman period. For instance, excavations of an important Roman temple at Lydney in the English county of Gloucestershire have shown that it was dedicated to Lludd and that offerings were made to the deity here throughout the entire Roman era.[18] This god was clearly far from forgotten, even though Britain was officially a Christian country by the time the Romans left. In fact, it was really only in the Roman towns that Christianity had taken hold.

In the countryside, where most of the native Britons still lived, the populace was practicing pagan religion. This is demonstrated not only by archaeology, which has found little evidence of Christianity outside the cities. The very word *pagan*, meaning "a follower of a non-Christian god," comes from the Latin word *paganus*, which simply means "country-dweller."

The country-dwellers of Britain were still venerating the old Celtic gods, or their hybrid Roman equivalents, to such an extent during the late Roman, Christian era that their very name became synonymous with the old religions. In fact, as town life was largely abandoned by Ambrosius's time, the pagan religion had probably resumed prominence. The chances are that Lludd was an important god, if not the chief god, of the Celts, whom Ambrosius was trying to unite. If Ambrosius was as successful as Gildas says, he could well have been regarded as this god returned. In fact, in the Welsh Triads in *The Red Book of Hergest*, there is a direct link between Ambrosius and Lludd, which suggests just this.

A Triad called the "Three Fortunate Concealments" concerns three sacred relics that had been hidden in Britain. The first relic is the head of a hero named Bran, the second consists of the bones of a hero called Gwerthefyr, and the third comprises the two dragons that Ambrosius discovered in the pool at Dinas Emrys. It is not clear what these dragons really were but they do not appear to be actual creatures. Like the other relics, they are said to be talismans with the magical power to protect Britain from invasion; they had been hidden at some unspecified period by the god Lludd. The Triad describes them: "the second fortunate concealment: the dragons in Dinas Emrys, which Lludd son of Beli concealed."[19] Another story in *The Red Book of Hergest*, "The Tale of Lludd and Llefelys," also refers to Lludd hiding these dragons at Dinas Emrys:

And while he [Lludd] was there, he beheld the dragons fighting. And when they were weary they fell, and came down upon the top of the satin, and drew it with them to the bottom of the cauldron. And when they had drunk the mead they slept. And in their sleep, Lludd folded the covering around them, and in the securest place he had in Snowdon, he hid them in a kistraen [stone coffin]. Now after that this spot was called Dinas Emrys, but before that, Dinas Ffaraon. And thus the fierce outcry ceased in his dominions.[20]

In this story, Lludd has used the dragons to bring peace to Britain. Again, it is difficult to tell what these dragons were thought to be. They were certainly small, as they were put into a cauldron and then buried in a *kistraen,* or stone coffin. Perhaps they were figurines, believed to have been imbued with serpent power. Whatever they were, they were a talisman of protection against foreign aggression, and they were one and the same as the dragons or serpents later said to have been found by Ambrosius.

What originally seemed to have been an odd tale, about mythical beasts and prophecies recorded by Nennius, now made sense. Whether or not Ambrosius historically did discover anything at Dinas Emrys when he was taken before Vortigern, the fact remains that he was credited with rediscovering the talismans of the god Lludd, talismans designed to protect Britain from foreign invasion. When this is coupled with the legends of Merlin, which clearly equate him with the same god, there can be little doubt that Ambrosius was seen as some kind of personification or successor of the deity. Perhaps, in order to unite the Britons, Ambrosius was happy to be regarded as the god personified. He may even have believed it himself. After all, he seems to have come from the pagan side of the Aurelius family and—according to the inscribed plaque found in East Anglia—Mercury, the Roman equivalent of Lludd, was his family god. No wonder, then, that Ambrosius's sword was important. Ambrosius knew how useful the sword of invincibility myth had been to Attila the Hun and may have deliberately pandered to the similar legend of the sword of the Celtic god in order to fulfill the perception that he was this god reincarnate.

The story of Excalibur no longer seemed like a fairy tale; it fit into a historical context. I was now intrigued to know what Glynn Davis knew, or thought he knew, about the Excalibur myth, and was dying to read what he had promised to send. However, when I returned home a week after speaking to him on the phone, I was in for a shock.

At that time, I was living alone in an apartment near the city of Birmingham in central England. My girlfriend Sarah and I had recently separated but we were still friends and she had been looking in on my place while I was away. While I was in London, she had called me to say that she had found the hall window broken, but as nothing had been stolen, damaged, or apparently even moved, she decided that it was due to either an attempted burglary that had been disturbed or a kid's badly aimed ball. When I returned and found nothing missing, I agreed.

That is, until I called Glynn Davis to ask whether he had mailed me his research notes on Excalibur, as they had not yet arrived. The first few times I called there was no answer, but eventually Glynn's wife picked up the phone. Distressed, she told me Glynn was in hospital after suffering a heart attack. Apparently, this was his second in a matter of weeks, which explained why he had sounded unwell the last time we spoke. I apologized for disturbing her, explaining that I had only called to see if her husband had sent me his notes. When she told me that she, personally, had mailed them to me the same day as my earlier call—a week before—I felt the first twinge of anxiety. I had been wondering why a number of letters I was expecting had not yet arrived. Perhaps something had been stolen after all—my mail!

Sarah had discovered the broken window two days after my conversation with Glynn, and all my mail after this time had been delivered. I checked with the local post office and my neighbors to see if there had been any problem with the delivery of their mail during this two-day interval, but no one had anything out of the ordinary to report. I also checked with others from whom I was expecting correspondence and they assured me that their mail had, indeed, been sent to me. Had someone actually broken into my apartment to get at my mail? I realized that people steal bank statements, credit cards, and other such financial information in order to perpetrate identity theft, but when the thieves were in my apartment, why wouldn't they have taken any number of other small but valuable objects, such as my DVD player or my spare laptop?

Nothing of any value to anyone had been in my mail—except, perhaps, Glynn Davis's notes. Glynn was clearly paranoid about his theories and believed there were people who would do anything to know what he knew. I had assumed he was suffering from a case of melodrama. Maybe I was wrong. Perhaps people did consider his research worth stealing. But even if this was true, how would they know he had sent me anything of interest? It had to be coincidence, surely! I wanted to question Glynn's wife to see what she knew about Glynn's theories and discover more about his trepidations, but decided against it. It was the last thing she would want to talk about, with her husband in hospital. I decided to wait until he was better and talk to him myself.

I was intrigued, to say the least. I opened my bedroom closet to take out the replica of the sword and look at it from a fresh perspective. It was gone! Something of value had been taken after all! Were there really people who shared Glynn's belief that Excalibur held a secret, a secret that, by breaking into my apartment, they hoped to learn? Together with the missing mail, the missing Excalibur replica more than answered my question.

7

THE SHAKESPEARE ENIGMA

The break-in of my apartment had to be somehow connected with Glynn Davis. Perhaps he had done it? Maybe he had thought twice about sending me his precious research notes and wanted the Excalibur replica for himself. No, that didn't fit. Glynn's wife had told me he had been taken to hospital the day after I'd last spoken to him; he was in no state to *do* anything. Maybe he had gotten someone to do it for him? He may have been a bit melodramatic—but an elderly historian, bedridden and on the critical list, hiring burglars to break into my apartment? I just couldn't see it—besides which, from everything I knew, Glynn was an honest man.

This left only one reasonable possibility: Glynn was right about others who would do anything to get their hands on what he knew about Excalibur. But how would anyone have known he sent anything to me—except, of course, if he was being bugged? Was he? Surely not! Then again, whoever had broken into my place was prepared to break the law, and electronic surveillance equipment is virtually in the public domain these days. One way or another, it genuinely seemed that an unknown person or persons seriously wanted to know what Glynn knew, or thought he knew, about Merlin and the Excalibur legend.

I would have to wait to find out more from Glynn himself; all I could do in the meantime was try to figure out why anyone would have such an extreme interest in a fifteen-hundred-year-old mystery. However, to be frank, I was now more interested in finding out who had broken into my place than in discovering more about Merlin. The mystery of Merlin was an academic pursuit, but this was personal. When I continued my research, I was not expecting or really looking for any historical revelations about Merlin; rather, I wanted to find out what people might have *thought* they knew about him. Why would Merlin be so important to anyone today? The heart of the mystery seemed to have something to do with William Shakespeare. I remembered Glynn's words the day we met in the beer garden in Carmarthen: "I believe Shakespeare was killed because of what he knew about Merlin and the two serpents on Excalibur's hilt."

Looking across at the boarded-up window in my hallway, I felt a pang in the pit of my stomach. I remembered Glynn's other words: "There are still people today who would kill to find out what Shakespeare knew."

I had studied the life of William Shakespeare in considerable detail, but that had been more than ten years ago. What I had learned was all a bit hazy now, but as far as I could recall, I had never found anything to link Shakespeare with Merlin. I hadn't given Glynn's supposed Shakespeare connection a thought since our meeting. Perhaps I should have at least made a casual search. I sat at my computer and typed two words into the search engine: Shakespeare and Merlin.

The second URL listed: The Birth of Merlin. *A play sometimes attributed to William Shakespeare.*

I wished there had been an Internet when I wrote my book on Shakespeare. I managed to download a copy of the play, which was a five-act comedy. I could probably justifiably be called uncultured, but the only thing that ever made me laugh about Shakespeare's comedies was that category. Perhaps they would have been comical to an Elizabethan audience, but the humor was lost on me. The truth is that I had never voluntarily seen a Shakespeare play in my life, only those I had been forced to watch at school. Because of my unenlightened attitude and unfamiliarity with Shakespeare's plays, many people had asked me how, or, for that matter, why, I had written a book about him. The answer is that I was intrigued by the man himself. I wanted to learn about the personality and life of the most famous writer in history. As far as I was concerned, having no prior prejudice about Shakespeare based on his works, I was in a good position to conduct an unbiased historical investigation of the man's life. Needless to say, most of the critics disagreed.

When I published the book in 1994 with coauthor Martin Keatman, we got more publicity than we could possibly have imagined.[1] Not only in England, but around the world as well, we were described as "the worst kind of Philistines," "literary barbarians," and "enemies of the arts." Apparently, we had desecrated a sacred cow.

Shakespeare has become a kind of patron saint of the English language. Like some holy figure, he is considered almost beyond mortal failings. He is "sweet Mr. Shakespeare": a kind and forgiving soul who abstained from drink, dearly loved his family, and never hurt a fly. However, the historical records we uncovered revealed a *very* different man. He was known to run out on debts and charged exorbitant interest on loans of his own; he had a restraining order issued against him for threatening the life of a colleague; he was frequently drunk and disorderly; and when he died, he left his wife nothing in his will but his "second best bed." Martin and I had impugned the good name of the Bard, and the media were not going to take it lying down. Still, all publicity is good publicity, so they say. Evidently not! I had assumed that the media coverage would make our book a bestseller. In fact, it sold hardly at all.

Obviously, literary enthusiasts would not soil their hands with such filth; the rest of the market probably had had so much Shakespeare rammed down their throats at school that they concluded that anything concerning the English playwright was mind-numbingly dull. However, the first thing I came to realize about William Shakespeare was that his life had been anything but dull. Before reading the Merlin play, I decided it would be a good idea to reacquaint myself with Shakespeare's life and reread my own book. Many mysteries surrounded the man, and there was seemingly a dark side to his activities that may have had some relevance to Glynn Davis's ideas.

In a period of twenty-six years, between 1590 and his death in 1616, Shakespeare wrote at least thirty-six plays and dozens of poems. He not only acted in most of his own plays and those of other playwrights, but he also directed many of his productions all over England. But this was only the thespian side of Shakespeare's life; the rest of it was decidedly weird.

In Stratford-upon-Avon, in central England, where Shakespeare was born, records show that he became an extremely wealthy man who acquired many properties and large tracts of land. However, in London, where he spent much of his time involved with the theater, he seems to have lived on the breadline, dwelling in squalid accommodations and constantly fleeing from debt. This did not reflect the financial ups and downs that might be expected for a writer; it was evidence of a bizarre double life.

For example, in 1597, property deeds in Stratford showed that Shakespeare bought the second largest house in town. At the very same time, in the poor Billingsgate district of London, Shakespeare was being sought by the authorities for failing to pay a debt of five shillings: Even with inflation taken into consideration, that would be a modest one hundred dollars by modern standards. The following year, in the very same month of October, the Billingsgate court issued a warrant against Shakespeare for failing to pay a similar sum in taxes, while in Stratford a surviving letter shows that he lent an acquaintance thirty pounds—more than four thousand dollars in today's money.[2] Perhaps Shakespeare was a miser who simply didn't like paying debts, but this does not explain his incongruous lifestyle.

Throughout the late 1590s and the first decade of the 1600s, Shakespeare acquired more and more real estate in Stratford—fields, cottages, and holdings that he rented out—while in London he is recorded as living in a succession of rented rooms in virtual slums where he could easily have afforded to buy an entire block. Stranger still, he was repeatedly thrown out of these seedy apartments for failing to pay a paltry rent.[3] In fact, this peculiar double life went so far that it appears that although in London Shakespeare was widely known as a playwright and actor, in Stratford there is no evidence that anyone knew he had anything to do with the theater in any way!

In Stratford, tax records show that he made money in the lucrative business of supplying malt and barley to the liquor trade. Surviving documents refer to Shakespeare as a businessman, a moneylender, and a gentleman of means, but not one refers to literary interests of any kind. Indeed, when he died, it seems no one in his hometown had any idea that he was a writer at all.

Every year thousands of tourists visit Shakespeare's grave in Stratford's Holy Trinity Church. The grave is close to the altar, which means that Shakespeare had been a man of importance, and a monument on the wall above the tomb reveals his status in the community. The life-size stone bust of the head and torso of the playwright depicts the famous balding figure with a mustache and goatee. With a feather pen in one hand and the other pressed down upon a parchment, he stares forward into space as if contemplating what he is about to write.

At first glance, everything appears normal enough, but then something seems strange: The parchment is resting on a cushion. Who would try to write on a piece of paper resting on a cushion? "It's a writing cushion," the guide will tell you. But writing cushions were to rest the elbow on, not the parchment. This incongruous image has led to wild speculation. Was it somehow a secret message concerning a sack of buried gold? The theorists are right about it being a sack, all right—but not one containing any treasure. Remarkably, considering the number of books about Shakespeare that have this image of the playwright on their cover, the present monument is little more than a fake.

In the mid-1700s, almost a century and a half after Shakespeare's death, the original monument was badly in need of repair. In response, in 1748 a wealthy theatrical agent named John Hall paid for a complete restoration.[4] Fortunately, a drawing of the original monument survives in an architectural tome called the *Antiquities of Warwickshire*, which was published by the English antiquarian Sir William Dugdale in 1656. It shows the same monument and the same man, except that he has no pen and no parchment; instead, his hands are resting on a sack. John Hall obviously decided that the great playwright should be portrayed as he is remembered, as a writer.

When Shakespeare was buried, in 1616, it was customary for such monuments to depict the deceased in some way associated with his lifetime's trade or profession. Hall placed a pen in one of Shakespeare's hands and had the representation of a parchment carved beneath the other. The problem was that without replacing the entire thing, he could not get rid of the sack. Instead he had it recarved to make it look like a cushion. For any Shakespeare enthusiast who has seen Dugdale's drawing of the original tomb, the cushion is an embarrassing reminder that when the most famous playwright in history died, his nearest and dearest honored him as a successful dealer in bagged commodities. This is, in fact, precisely how the records of Stratford suggest William Shakespeare made his money—selling sacks of malt and barley to the liquor trade.

When Martin Keatman and I discovered this when researching our book, our first thought was that William Shakespeare the London playwright and William Shakespeare the Stratford entrepreneur were actually two different men. However, there was one clear piece of evidence that they were one and the same: The Stratford Shakespeare left money in his will to his "fellow actors" from the theater company in London.[5] The enigma of this bizarre double life has led many writers to speculate that Shakespeare had something to hide and that he may not have been the author of the plays published in his name.

Yet another enigma in Shakespeare's strange life that has helped fuel such speculation is that of his education. He seems to have attended elementary school in Stratford, but there is no record of his having attended the equivalent of high school, nor is there any indication that he had been enrolled at university. He could, of course, have been self-taught, but if he was, he kept this a secret, too.

In fact, there is not a single record to indicate that he ever bought a single book. Shakespeare's will, for instance, meticulously records every one of his possessions but there is no mention of a library, books, works of art, or anything else that suggests intellectual, cultural, or academic interests of any kind. He was a wealthy man and could have surrounded himself with reminders of the philosophy, culture, history, and the classics of which he wrote so knowledgably and eloquently—yet all he owned or was ever recorded as owning were purely functional or household items.[6]

This astonishing paradox has led to the obvious conclusion that William Shakespeare was no writer at all. Various candidates have been proposed as the "real" author of the Shakespearean plays, such as the Elizabethan lawyer Sir Francis Bacon, the Earl of Oxford, and another contemporary playwright, Christopher Marlowe.[7] It is suggested that the "true" author had reasons to keep his identity a secret and hired Shakespeare to front the works. However, all the theories have a common failing. One thing is certain regarding the perplexing life of William Shakespeare: In Stratford, at least, he kept his theatrical activities a closely guarded secret. Surely the purpose of a front man would be to front the works. Why choose a seemingly uneducated, secretive, and, at the very least, modest man to pretend to the world to have written the greatest works of the day? It just didn't make sense.

The most convincing evidence that Shakespeare had indeed written his own plays is that his theatrical colleagues said he did. In 1623, the first compilation of Shakespeare's complete works was published in one volume now known as the First Folio. It was entitled *Mr. William Shakespeare's Comedies, Histories and Tragedies* and on the cover showed a picture of the author who is clearly the same balding figure depicted on Shakespeare's monument at Holy Trinity Church. A preface to the plays includes tributes and obituaries written by contemporary poets, playwrights, and actors from Shakespeare's theater company in London. Presumably these people who had worked closely alongside Shakespeare for years would have been in the position to know whether or not he had penned the great works.[8]

So what was really going on? Did Shakespeare have something else he wanted to hide? When Martin and I studied the records more closely, we realized that he did. His books—financial ones, that is—did not balance.

Shakespeare died a wealthy man. He was one of the richest, if not the richest, men in Stratford-upon-Avon, and he was completely self-made. His father was a relatively successful trader who made a comfortable living making and selling gloves, which was how he managed to send the young Shakespeare to elementary school in the days before state-funded education. However, when Shakespeare was approximately eleven years old, he left school to work for his father manning the glove store at the Stratford market. Sadly, in 1587, when William was twenty-three, his father apparently drank away the profits from the business and ended up bankrupt.

Two years later, William was thrown out of his modest cottage on the outskirts of Stratford when the mortgage went unpaid. The following year, Shakespeare first appears on record in London working as a stagehand at a small theater in the East End district of Shoreditch. Within a few months, he began his writing career by helping to edit other authors' works and soon after his own works began to appear.[9]

At that time, working in the theater was no way to make money. It was not the West End or the Broadway of today. Actors, playwrights, even directors had to double up as scene painters, costume makers, and ticket sellers, and earned little more than a pittance. The records show that Shakespeare and his contemporaries were paid an average of only two pounds a play, which would have taken months of hard work. For a while, Shakespeare had a small shareholding in the theater company for which he worked, but even this appears to have been worthless after the company's home, the Globe Theatre, burned to the ground in 1613. Simple math tells us that Shakespeare could not have earned much more than seventy-two pounds for all the plays he wrote in his entire life. By modern standards, that would be about fifteen thousand dollars for a lifetime's work, and spread over twenty-six years. That is an average of less than three pounds a year, or the modern equivalent of earning a little more than an annual salary of around nine hundred dollars. The property he owned in Stratford alone was worth well over a million dollars by today's standards. Obviously he had some other, lucrative source of income and on the face of it this seems to have been the malt and barley business.

Yet another mystery unfolds in the anything but dull life of William Shakespeare. Although the records of Stratford-upon-Avon show that he was taxed for profits made in the grain trade, there is not a single record of him ever actually growing, buying, or selling the stuff.[10] As far as the people of Stratford were concerned, all this was done in London. At the time of poor communications, who would know differently? Shakespeare spent half his time away in London; why shouldn't he have been making money in this way? Today, however, we know that in London, Shakespeare had been prolifically writing his plays and working hard in the theater. He was lying, but why?

Shakespeare was clearly making a great deal of money in some other way and seems to have invented the grain trade as a cover. No wonder, then, that he could not let the people of Stratford know he was a playwright. It would not have taken much to figure out that such employment could not possibly have made him rich. Equally, he had to make out to his colleagues in London that he was broke. There was no grain business. The real Shakespeare mystery is not whether he wrote the plays; it is how he made his money.

There was one possibility that might fit the picture, but it initially sounded crazier than the idea that Shakespeare hadn't written the plays. Shakespeare may have been paid as a government spy. "Licence to Quill" was the cynical heading to one particular review of our book. However, the notion of Shakespeare as some kind of Elizabethan James Bond, with a bar wench on one arm and a loaded flintlock held across his chest, was not the kind of spy we had in mind. Like other poet-dramatists of his time, Shakespeare could have been a government informer.

In the 1590s and early 1600s, when Shakespeare was writing, Britain was a country deeply divided between Catholics and Protestants. In the 1530s the English king Henry VIII had broken away from the Roman Catholic Church and set up the Protestant Church of England, or the Anglican Church. In the ensuing years, laws were passed against those who refused to convert to the Protestant faith and many were persecuted and killed. When Henry's daughter Mary Tudor came to the throne in 1553, the pendulum of persecution swung the other way. Mary had remained a Catholic, so Protestants now found themselves the victims. Thousands were locked up and had their property seized, and many were burned at the stake. In fact, so savage was this counterreformation that Mary earned herself the nickname "the Bloody Queen."

When Mary died of cancer in 1558 and her younger sister Elizabeth came to the throne, the religious pendulum swung again. Elizabeth was a Protestant and thus leading Anglicans who had survived Mary's reign were recalled to serve as ministers under the new queen. Unlike her sister, however, Elizabeth was no fanatic and refrained from openly persecuting those who remained with the Catholic faith. Nevertheless, there were many in the new court who feared the return of Catholicism and urged the queen to take a firmer stance.

Elizabeth remained unmarried and childless; her legal successor was her cousin, another Mary who happened to be a Catholic. More famously known as Mary Queen of Scots, Mary had been queen of Scotland, but when she was deposed in a civil war in 1568 she fled to England. Unfortunately for her, she fled straight into captivity. Persuaded by her ministers that Mary was a threat to her throne, Elizabeth had her cousin placed under house arrest.

For the next nineteen years, Mary was kept a virtual prisoner on a number of English estates until she was executed on what appears to have been a trumped-up charge of treason in 1587. With Mary dead, the matter of succession was anything but clear. However, Elizabeth's chief minister, Francis Walsingham, decided to make sure that whoever succeeded the queen was not a Catholic. Consequently, he set up the most elaborate spy network ever before devised to maintain a close watch on Catholic aristocrats and keep him informed about any potential plots to undermine the Protestant regime. This Secret Service, as it was called, was the beginning of what would later be known as MI5. It might sound strange, but some of Walsingham's best informants were recruited from the theatrical profession.[11]

At a time when travel was difficult and risky, few people journeyed far from home. One exception was the theatrical companies that performed their plays in the stately homes of the English aristocracy. The lifestyles of poet-dramatists such as William Shakespeare were particularly suited to Walsingham's purpose. They had the perfect cover—traveling widely, in and out of the homes of the nobility all over the country—any role-playing was second nature to them, as many of them were actors. Moreover, the usual social barriers were often dropped for poets, who dined and drank freely with the aristocracy. "A poet and a flagon of ale are worth ten hangmen and as many racks," Walsingham is reported to have quipped. He realized that discretion was usually the first formality to be dropped by a drunken man in a setting of leisure and entertainment.

Playwrights had all the qualifications for joining Walsingham's spy network—not least of which was that most of them were broke. Even a leading playwright earned little more than a few pounds a year, whereas Walsingham's agents received around fifty pounds up front, twenty pounds per month, and as much as one hundred pounds for really useful information. Some of them were earning one thousand pounds a year, and that was real money: more than a quarter of a million dollars by today's standards. A number of Shakespeare's contemporary poet-dramatists are known to have been on the Secret Service payroll and two of its top spies, Christopher Marlowe and Anthony Munday, were not only playwrights, but they were Shakespeare's colleagues as well.[12] In his early writing career Shakespeare helped Marlowe edit his works, and a few years later he collaborated with Munday on a number of plays.

Unfortunately, many of Elizabethan Secret Service records have not survived, so there is no way of proving that Shakespeare was a spy. Nevertheless, like his colleagues Marlowe and Munday, Shakespeare lived well beyond his means, and an income from espionage is a real possibility to account for his mysterious wealth. Eventually, however, such clandestine activities may have cost him his life.

In 1603, Queen Elizabeth I died and her second cousin James I came to the English throne. Like Elizabeth, James was a Protestant, but unlike his predecessor, he passed strict laws against the Catholics, excluding them from politics and making them pay heavy fines for not converting to the Church of England. Consequently, a number of plots were hatched by leading Catholics to assassinate the king and overthrow the Protestant regime. The first of these was uncovered just a few months after James came to the throne. It was a conspiracy called the Bye Plot, devised by a group of Catholic landowners led by Lord Cobham, one of the wealthiest Catholics in the country. The plan was to assassinate the king and his sons and place the king's seven-year-old daughter, the princess Elizabeth, on the throne as a puppet queen while Cobham ruled as regent.

Another person involved in the plot was the famous statesman and explorer Sir Walter Raleigh. Raleigh was the favorite of Elizabeth I and was once the leading figure in the queen's court. He was also an admiral in the navy and had been governor of the American colonies. However, he was not a Catholic. In fact, he seems to have been an atheist. Raleigh may now be remembered as something of a pirate and the man who brought tobacco to Europe, but he was one of the leading intellectuals of his day. He led an influential society known as the School of Night: a group of learned men who advocated free thought, freedom of expression, and religious tolerance. It seems that Lord Cobham had also been a member of this society and had promised a country of religious choice if he succeeded in becoming regent on the British throne.[13]

Unfortunately for the conspirators, someone betrayed the scheme. In 1590, Walsingham died and the new chief minister, Robert Cecil, inherited the Secret Service, which, by the early 1600s, was an extremely efficient and well-established network of spies. One of these agents appears to have been in the School of Night and alerted Cecil to the plan. A large number of people were rounded up and tried for treason, including Raleigh. Most were executed, but the king ordered a stay for Raleigh and instead imprisoned him in the Tower of London. The reason for this apparent act of clemency is unknown but it probably had something to do with Raleigh's naval experience at a time when the French and Spanish were threatening to invade. Raleigh remained in prison for the next thirteen years, until the king decided to release him to lead an expedition to South America in search of Spanish gold.[14]

If Shakespeare had been a government spy, then it may well have been he who betrayed the plot. Not only does he appear to have been a member of the School of Night, but he was related to Raleigh by marriage as well. Raleigh's wife, Elizabeth Throckmorton, was Shakespeare's cousin. However, it was the circumstances surrounding Shakespeare's death that made Martin and me suspect that Shakespeare was responsible for putting Raleigh behind bars.

After the Globe Theatre burned down in 1613, Shakespeare retired to his home in Stratford-upon-Avon. On March 19, 1616, Raleigh was unexpectedly released from prison and given a few months to prepare for his voyage to South America. Six days later, on March 25—for the first time in his life—Shakespeare made a will. The reason for this sudden act is unknown but it can only be assumed that something turned Shakespeare's thoughts to his possible death. There is no evidence that the fifty-one-year-old Shakespeare had been in ill health, but if he was responsible for putting Raleigh in jail, then he would indeed have had good reason to fear for his life, as the man was now free.

As if he had been expecting it, just a month later, on April 23, Shakespeare was dead. After a night out drinking with his friend and fellow playwright Ben Jonson to celebrate his fifty-second birthday, Shakespeare became violently sick and died during the night. Evidently no one else is reported as suffering any ill effects from the food or drink served that night. Shakespeare could have died of alcohol poisoning, but he could have been poisoned by something and someone else. It seemed too much of a coincidence that, at that very time, Walter Raleigh was visiting his wife at her family home of Coughton Court—not ten miles from

Stratford-upon-Avon.[15] Again, nothing could be proved, but Martin and I suggested that Shakespeare had been murdered by Sir Walter Raleigh.

Shakespeare could well have been involved in the shady world of Elizabethan espionage and he may even have died because of it, but I could not see how this tied up with what he might have known about Merlin or of the two serpents on Excalibur's hilt. I was about to read *The Birth of Merlin* in the hope of gaining some insight into Glynn Davis's thinking when I suddenly remembered something. Raleigh's society, the School of Night, had also been referred to as the Dragon Men. This was a derogatory term used by its opponents because its emblem was a caduceus wand—the symbol of the double serpents. Could there have been a connection between this and the double serpents on Excalibur's hilt? For the first time, I began to wonder if Glynn Davis really was on to something about Shakespeare's death.

8

THE ALCHEMICAL WEDDING

Would there be anything in *The Birth of Merlin* to throw new light on the life of Ambrosius, or at least explain Glynn Davis's notion that Shakespeare knew some secret concerning Excalibur and the two serpents on its hilt? From what I could tell, opinion was divided as to whether the play had any genuine associations with William Shakespeare. When it first appeared in print in 1662, the title page declared that it was a play by Shakespeare and another contemporary playwright, William Rowley. Before he died in 1626, Rowley wrote a number of plays, usually in collaboration with more successful writers. However, although Shakespeare did collaborate with others, the first known performance of *The Birth of Merlin* is not recorded until 1622, six years after his death. The work could, of course, have been written earlier, but without anything to specifically date its composition, the argument all came down to style. Critics maintained that it was too crude for Shakespeare; advocates drew attention to similarities with Shakespeare's later works. With the jury still out on the true authorship of the play, I sat down to read it.[1]

At first I was disappointed; there appeared to be nothing revelatory from the historical perspective. The story line basically followed

Geoffrey of Monmouth's account and incorporated other mythological themes taken from the later Arthurian romances. Despite the title, the play concerns not only Merlin's birth but also his life leading up to the birth of King Arthur. Set against a vaguely historical background of the political divisions in Britain in the mid- through late fifth century, the plot centers on the squabbles between the rival British kingdoms and Merlin's attempt to unite them against their common enemy the Anglo-Saxons. Vortigern is included, as is Uther, Arthur's legendary father, and Ambrosius makes an appearance (at least a character called Aurelius), although he is cast as a separate person to Merlin. The authors were obviously aware of Ambrosius's existence as a British leader prior to Arthur's time, but evidently regarded him only as one of Vortigern's rival kings.

There is no mention of Excalibur, although there is something of interest concerning the two serpents. The incident with the dragons at Dinas Emrys is included pretty much as it appears in Geoffrey's account of Merlin's summons before Vortigern; it follows Geoffrey by having Merlin interpret the creatures as representing the warring factions who fought for control of Britain. However, unlike the earlier version of the story, the two dragons appear again toward the end of the play when they unite into a single entity, which becomes a new star in the sky. Merlin interprets this as a sign that the newly born Arthur is destined to unite Britain as its king.

Although there was nothing in *The Birth of Merlin* that I could immediately see as casting any new light on the historical Merlin, there *was* something that associated it with Sir Walter Raleigh and the Dragon Men. Throughout the play, Merlin is accompanied by a clown or jester who acts as a kind of wise fool. The clown is obviously there to add humor, but he also guides Merlin by astute observations, shrewd insights, and clever riddles. Most literary scholars observed that the characters of Merlin and the clown were based on two real-life Elizabethan figures: John Dee, a man who considered himself a genuine magician, and his assistant, Edward Kelly, a strange individual who acted as Dee's spirit medium. Both are recorded as having been involved with the Dragon Men, and John Dee appears to have been one of the society's founding members.

John Dee was born in 1527 in London to a family of reasonable means: His father was a tailor at the court of Henry VIII. Most of Dee's early life was spent as a respected academic, and he was one of the first scientists of the European Renaissance. After studying languages, mathematics, and astronomy at Cambridge University, he traveled widely around Europe, writing two groundbreaking textbooks on cosmology both published in 1550. He ended up in France, where he lectured to crowds of enthusiastic students who flocked from all over the country to hear him talk.

So popular and respected was Dee by the French that he was offered a university professorship in Paris—a rare honor for a foreigner, especially one who was still only twenty five years old. However, Dee declined and returned to England, where he was offered a similar position at Oxford University, which he also turned down. Rather than be confined by the cloistered world of academia, Dee opted to pursue the practical applications of astronomy and mathematics for navigational purposes. The Americas had not long been discovered and the French, Italians, and Spanish were way ahead of the English in exploring the vast American coastline and establishing colonies there. The English were keen to catch up and there was a place in history to be made for those who helped gain a foothold in the New World.

During his travels, Dee had spent most of his money acquiring one of the largest collections of navigational instruments in Europe, and he now needed to make a living. In 1555 he was retained as a consultant by the explorer Sebastian Cabot, who was searching for a northeast passage for trade with Russia. However, Dee's income fell far short of financing his work and in 1558 he accepted an unusual proposal from the new queen, Elizabeth I. She offered to employ him not only as a navigator but also as an astrologer. Although witchcraft was a crime, astrology and even magic (as long as it was white magic) were considered acceptable ancient arts in England, as they were in other Protestant countries. (During the Elizabethan era, the word *witch* was applied to someone who was thought to commune with the devil and witchcraft was regarded as the use of black magic to commit a crime.) Scientific astronomy was a brand-new science and the only interest that most people had in the stars involved fortune-telling.

Elizabeth was a great believer in astrology and Dee, needing the money, applied his astronomical knowledge for this purpose. Until this time there is no evidence that Dee had much interest in magic. However, his work as the queen's astrologer seems to have kindled a passion not only for astrology but also for the occult in general. Over the next few years he assembled a huge library of books on magic, alchemy, and the supernatural and quickly became one of Europe's foremost authorities on occultism.[2]

In 1564, at the age of thirty-seven, Dee produced what he considered to be his finest work: an enigmatic treatise on the occult called the *Monas Hieroglyphica*—The Hieroglyphic Monad. It concerned an esoteric hieroglyph, or symbol, that he claimed held the secrets of creation. The ancient Hebrews believed the universe began with a single four-syllable word—the true name of God—a word so secret, so mysterious, and so powerful that even the *name* for the name, Yahweh (meaning "I am that I am"), could not be spoken aloud.

The later Greeks referred to it as the Tetragrammaton, meaning "a four-part word," but they did not regard it as four spoken syllables or even sounds, but rather as four separate cosmic forces. These were the four elements that were thought to make up matter: earth, air, water, and fire—all that is solid, gaseous, liquid, and volatile. Something had brought these elements into existence, it was believed, and this was a fifth element, which also unified them as one. This equivalent to the Hebrew name of God was imagined as a kind of geometric equation, or glyph, called the Monad, and for centuries philosophers debated what it might be. Now, John Dee believed he had discovered it. This was his *Monas Hieroglyphica:* a symbol comprising a rounded M shape, surmounted by a cross, a circle, and a crescent.[3]

Ironically, the notion of the Monad was not dissimilar to today's ideas of the unified field theory to account for the origins of the universe. Theoretical astrophysics suggests there should be one equation to account for everything: one algebraic formula that brings together the four cosmic forces already known (electromagnetism and gravity and what physicists refer to as the strong and weak nuclear forces within atoms). If these forces could be unified in one theorem, scientists believe they would have the answer to the big bang. However, it has evaded even the greatest minds. Apparently, on his deathbed, even Einstein was still trying to work it out.

The effect that Dee's book had on Europe's academic community in the late 1500s was not unlike the effect that Einstein's theory of relativity had on the scientific world in the early twentieth century. There was, though, one big difference. When Einstein first published his work, hardly anyone understood it; when Dee published his *Monas Hieroglyphica*, no one—including Dee himself—understood it. Apparently, the idea came to him in a series of dreams or visions that he experienced over a period of twelve days and the book was his attempt to interpret their meaning. All the same, it sparked an occult revival in which many leading thinkers of the time became embroiled.[4]

At that time, science was very much in its infancy; it was still a century before the age of Isaac Newton and the foundations of the modern scientific method. There was no real dividing line between what was then regarded as science and what we would now call magic. Many of Dee's contemporaneous scientists would be considered occultists today. The botanist Leonard Fuchs was as intrigued by alchemy as he was by the biology of plants; the mathematician Thomas Hariot was as much a numerologist as he was the father of modern algebra; and the astronomer Johannes Kepler cast as many horoscopes as he made objective planetary observations. As such, Dee's work was not regarded as some crackpot hypothesis, but rather as real food for thought, and one leading intellectual who became captivated by it was Sir Walter Raleigh.

It was while Dee was at Queen Elizabeth's court that he first met Raleigh, a man who was both a personal friend of the monarch and her captain of the royal guard. The men shared an interest in the exploration of the Americas and together they organized a series of expeditions. Raleigh procured the financial backing and planned the voyages, while Dee instructed the crews on the geometry and cosmography necessary for successful navigation before they set sail. A number of English expeditions navigated large sections of the North American coastline and made exploratory landings, although attempts to found permanent colonies in Virginia and North Carolina initially failed.

Nevertheless, Dee and Raleigh's work paved the way for the first successful English colonies in the early 1600s. Indeed, if it was not for Dee and Raleigh, the chances are that the Spanish or the French would have beaten the English to it, and North America would have been very different from what it is today. There would have been no *Mayflower*, no Pilgrim Fathers—the United States would not be the United States we know today. It probably would have been a Catholic nation and its first language would certainly not have been English.[5]

But exploration was not the only interest Dee and Raleigh shared. Given the fascination with the occult that Dee's work had generated, the two of them, together with the wealthy government minister Fulke Greville, established an informal society in which metaphysical concepts could be discussed. It began not as a magical group, practicing sorcery or conjuring spirits, nor even as a secret society, but rather as a meeting of minds where ideas pertaining to mysticism and theoretical occultism were aired. At this stage it seems that the society did not even have a name: The term School of Night was later applied to it by others who were disturbed by the philosophy of free thought and religious tolerance advocated by its members; the name Dragon Men was not coined until the caduceus symbol was adopted as its emblem in the early 1600s.

The group met monthly at Fulke Greville's London home, and a growing number of European luminaries were eager to attend. Over the 1580s and 1590s, membership increased. It included the German theologian Simon Studion, the Italian philosopher Giordano Bruno, the English architect Inigo Jones, and Francis Bacon, widely regarded as England's greatest philosopher. Because Greville was a part-time dramatist with investments in the theater, a number of playwrights, poets, and others with theatrical interests joined its ranks. These included the playwrights Christopher Marlowe and Ben Jonson, the dramatist and politician Sir John Harrington, and Lord Strange, owner of the theatrical company for which Shakespeare originally worked. It was through one of these, Lord Strange, that John Dee met Edward Kelly.[6]

Kelly was one of the most colorful and bizarre characters of the Elizabethan era. He was a small-time criminal, a con man, and something of a lovable rogue, and his interests included heavy drinking, bar girls, and raising the dead. Kelly had served time for a string of petty crimes; he had been lashed on many occasions, fined out of any money he ever acquired, and had his ears chopped off for counterfeiting. None of this deterred him, and in 1580 he was discovered attempting to steal corpses from a churchyard, presumably in the hope of resurrecting them. This was a far more serious offense for which he could have been hanged. However, the body-snatching Kelly was acquitted when a wealthy benefactor bribed the magistrate to set him free. This was Ferdinando Stanley, otherwise known as Lord Strange.

The name Strange was not a description of Stanley's character; it was an oddly named town in northern England of which he was lord. Nonetheless, he did have strange interests and one of them was attempting to communicate with spirits. Kelly was rough, uncultured, and broke, but he appears to have had remarkable charisma. He managed to convince Strange that he possessed a rare gift. Almost unheard of at the time, he claimed to be a spirit medium who could channel the voices of the dead.

Strange proudly introduced Kelly to other members of the School of Night. They were, understandably, skeptical about him, as was John Dee initially, but Dee was soon persuaded that Kelly was just what he needed. Dee had become frustrated with the occult and had been unable to interpret the true meaning of his *Monas Hieroglyphica*. Kelly, he decided, might be key to providing answers: The man claimed he could channel not only spirits but also angels. Perhaps the angels could help Dee understand the secrets of creation and the meaning of life. Unlike the others in the School of Night, who regarded Kelly as a fraud or at best with suspicion, Dee struck up a close friendship with Kelly and together they spent night after night supposedly communicating with angels. However, these angelic entities speaking through Kelly gave only glimpses of the cosmic truth Dee was seeking, and conveyed their secrets in riddles.

Given Kelly's criminal history and his dubious character, historians generally consider him to have been nothing but a fake. Nevertheless, Kelly may genuinely have believed that he was a spirit medium. After all, he was prepared to risk his life snatching bodies to be used in his experiments to raise the dead. In fact, his narrow escape from the gallows didn't stop him, and in 1582 he was at it again, this time with Dee as an accomplice. Although it was said that he was caught red-handed dragging a fresh corpse through a cemetery gate and Dee was implicated in the crime, neither of them was charged. It has been suggested that the queen herself ordered the matter dropped. There is no official record of whether Elizabeth intervened, but if she did, it was going to be the first and last time. Dee was no longer welcome at court and, with allegations of witchcraft hanging in the air, he and Kelly left for France.

Dee no longer had an income and Kelly, typically, was penniless, so the unlikely couple journeyed around Europe performing what must be described as a traveling spiritualist act. Billed as an "Angelic Conference," Dee recited magical incantations while the entranced Kelly offered advice and predicted the future for paying customers. Dee and Kelly were constantly on the move, just one step ahead of the Church and civic authorities. In cities across Europe, warrants were issued for their arrest on charges of witchcraft and deception, and before long their antics became legendary. They would roll into town, nail up posters promoting their event, and set up a stand in the marketplace.

In a small tent painted with bright astrological symbols, Kelly would fall into trance while Dee sold tickets for customers to have their fortunes told. There was merchandise to be had, too. Anyone who paid for an Angelic Conference could also buy a bronze medallion to commemorate the event. After it was over, Dee and Kelly would sell a variety of potions and charms, before being forced to hurriedly close down the operation, bundle everything into the back of their wagon, and hightail it out of town before the militia arrived. John Dee, one of Europe's leading intellectuals, the man whom the French had wanted to honor as a professor of mathematics at the age of twenty five, was now eking out a living performing a two-bit medicine show. He had become the laughingstock of the academic world, and whoever wrote *The Birth of Merlin* a few years later was clearly lampooning him.[7]

Although John Dee, the Elizabethan era's own wizard, provided the character for Merlin, and his sidekick, Kelly, was Merlin's clown, I could find nothing to suggest that the author of the play knew anything concerning the historical Merlin, which could be considered secret knowledge. However, there was something else in the play that indirectly gave me the lead I was looking for. This is the episode where the two serpents unite to become a new star as a portent for King Arthur's reign. In 1604 a new star really had appeared in the sky (or at least one that had previously not been visible to the naked eye). It was what we now call a supernova:

an exploding star that shone brightly for many weeks afterward. The new star in *The Birth of Merlin* play was undoubtedly an allusion to it. To begin with, it was associated with two serpents.

Now known as the Kepler Supernova, after the German astronomer Johannes Kepler, who first recorded it, it appeared in the constellation Ophiuchus—the Serpent Bearer. Once regarded by the ancient Greeks as the thirteenth sign of the zodiac, the stars of Ophiuchus are seen to make up the figure of a man holding two serpents, one in each hand. Supernovae are common throughout the universe, but those close enough to Earth to be seen with the naked eye are very rare; in fact, the Kepler Supernova was the last known such event. Consequently, astrologers in 1604 regarded it as an exceptional omen, heralding a new age, just as the star of Bethlehem had accompanied the birth of Christ. The School of Night considered the event so significant that it adopted the caduceus, the twin-serpent symbol, as its emblem.[8]

By this time, John Dee was living in obscurity and Walter Raleigh had been locked up in the Tower of London. However, despite this and the discovery of the Bye Plot and the implication of some of its members in the conspiracy, the School of Night continued to exist. (King James had been satisfied that the society in general was ignorant of the plot.) In England the society was still small, but in Germany its membership had grown considerably. Led by Simon Studion, the German theologian, it had a number of branches, or lodges, in the cities of Stuttgart, Tübingen, and Heidelberg in southwest Germany. In 1604 Studion published a book called the *Naometria* (Temple Measure) in which he interpreted the star's meaning. Ophiuchus was regarded as a sign of union and for Studion the star's appearance heralded the unification of Protestant Germany.[9]

Protestantism and the new age of enlightenment were inseparable, while the Catholic Church actively discouraged the new sciences and regarded occultism as heresy. It was only in the Protestant countries that the kind of freethinking and the ideas advocated by the School of Night were tolerated. However, Protestant Europe was militarily weak compared to the more powerful Catholic countries, which constantly threatened to invade. At the time, Europe was deeply divided between Protestant and Catholic nations (the largest Catholic powers were France, Spain, and the Hapsburg Empire centered on Austria and Hungary; the Protestant countries included Britain, the Netherlands, and Germany).

The central problem facing Protestantism was that its heartland of Germany was divided into a large number of independent states, each with its own princes and dukes, and it faced imminent invasion by the Catholic Hapsburg Empire. For some years there had been political hopes of uniting Germany into a stronger nation, under a single monarchy, and Studion proclaimed that the new star was a celestial omen that this event would soon occur. Furthermore, he interpreted the two serpents of Ophiuchus as representing Germany and England and believed that the star's appearance implied that these two countries would soon unite in a grand Protestant alliance against the Catholic nations.[10] Like the new star in *The Birth of Merlin*, the supernova not only was associated with two serpents, but it was also regarded as heralding a new, unifying monarchy, just as the star in the play heralded the unifying reign of King Arthur.

In the late first decade of the seventeenth century, another German theologian, Johann Valentin Andreae, became leader of the School of Night and radically restructured the loose amalgamation of new-age thinkers into a single organization called the Rosicrucians—the fraternity of the Rose and Cross. The name came from the new emblem that the society adopted, a rose overlaid on the center of an equal-armed cross. The symbol held a double meaning: The cross symbolized Germany and the rose was the emblem of England, but it also represented the Monad—the arms of the cross were the four elements of earth, air, fire, and water, and the rose was the elusive fifth element. In 1610, Andreae circulated a document called the *Fama Fraternitatis* (The Discovery of the Fraternity) in which he claimed that the Rosicrucian elite had discovered the tomb of an occultist named Christian Rosencreutz who had supposedly lived for one hundred and six years between 1378 and 1484.

According to the *Fama*, this tomb held the secret knowledge of the Monad, and once England and Germany were united and Protestantism was safe, the Rosicrucians would reveal it to the world.[11] Much of the document was written in code and symbolism that remain undeciphered today, while the tomb's discovery, said to have been made in 1604, appears to have been allegorical. Even the name of the tomb's occupant, Christian Rosencreutz, simply means Christian Rose Cross.

Like Studion, Andreae predicted that Germany would soon be united and that a grand alliance with England would be formed. In fact, Andreae went one step further and predicted that the two nations would be united under one monarchy. For a while, things seemed to be going the way the Rosicrucians hoped. Prince Frederick of the Palatinate, a state in southwest Germany with Heidelberg as its capital, was being considered as a possible figurehead for a union of German states, and in 1613 he married Princess Elizabeth, the daughter of King James I of England (the same woman whom the organizers of the Bye Plot had wanted to enthrone). James seems to have arranged the marriage in anticipation of German unity: If the union occurred, the marriage would already have cemented a grand Protestant alliance.[12]

The Birth of Merlin was clearly an analogy for this Rosicrucian ideal of a Protestant union between Germany and England. In the play, Merlin works to unite Britain, as John Dee and his successors hoped to unite Protestant Europe; the supernova in the constellation of the two serpents was seen as heralding a monarchy uniting England and Germany, as the two dragons that fused to become a single star in the play was a portent of the unifying reign of King Arthur.

There was certainly something here that associated Merlin and the twin serpents with supposed mystical knowledge during the time of William Shakespeare. But had Shakespeare himself been involved? He may not actually have written the play, and there was, so far, no proof that he was a member of the School of Night or of its successor, the Rosicrucian movement. Although Shakespeare's involvement with the School of Night seemed likely, as his closest colleagues such as Christopher Marlowe and Lord Strange were leading members and he was related by marriage to Raleigh, there was no indisputable evidence. However, an event in 1613 put William Shakespeare right in the thick of it all.

The Rosicrucians had considerable influence in the German Palatinate. Prince Frederick was a personal friend of Andreae and made no secret of being a member of the society himself. In England, too, the new Rosicrucian order had far more political influence than its predecessor the School of Night. Here, its leading member, Francis Bacon, had now become the attorney general. Interestingly, considering it was called a fraternity, even Princess Elizabeth appears to have been a Rosicrucian. Her guardian and mentor John Harrington certainly was. The seventeen-year-old Elizabeth had not been raised at court; her busy father King James had entrusted her upbringing and education to the wealthy Harrington family, and she had spent most of her childhood at their country home of Coombe Abbey in Warwickshire, central England. (Coombe Abbey was once a monastery but the Harrington family was given the estate after Henry VIII confiscated it from the Catholic Church in the 1530s.) It was here, on May 1, 1613, that one of the most unusual events of the Renaissance was staged.

Frederick and Elizabeth were married in London on February 14, 1613, St. Valentine's Day, but a few weeks later, to coincide with May Day, the marriage ceremony was restaged for a private gathering at Coombe Abbey. Officially, it was supposed to be a delayed reception so that Frederick's German guests, who had been held up in the Rhineland by floods, could attend. However, it seems to have been nothing less than a Rosicrucian ritual. All the leading Rosicrucians were there, including Andreae, Fulke Greville, and Francis Bacon, who himself officiated at the ceremony during which the bride and groom reaffirmed their marriage vows. There were four bridesmaids, whose gowns were decorated with the mystical symbols of earth, air, fire, and water, and Elizabeth wore the rose, the symbol for the fifth element. No record survives of the precise proceedings, but the Rosicrucians themselves certainly regarded it as a mystical ceremony, as they referred to it as the "Alchemical Wedding."

Alchemy is popularly known as the magical procedure of transmuting lead and other base metals into gold. However, it also concerned the search for the philosopher's stone. This was a symbolic reference to the Monad, the supposed fifth element. The philosopher's stone was not meant to be a physical rock or gem, but rather a spiritual idea or a secret knowledge or formula that could transmute anything to a higher state of being. It was indeed supposed to be able to turn lead into gold, but it could also make an ordinary person a genius, cure all ills, and bring about spiritual awareness.

The Alchemical Wedding was an occult term for the mystical rite in which this process could be achieved. The wedding of Elizabeth and Fredrick on St. Valentine's Day had been a political union; the second event, on Mayday, was a spiritual ceremony to bring about the new age of enlightenment that the Rosecrucians expected. Three years later, in 1616, a Rosicrucian work was published in Germany that claimed as much. Entitled *The Alchemical Wedding of Christian Rosencreutz,* it was an anonymous work generally attributed to Andreae. Like Andreae's earlier works, it was highly cryptic and virtually unintelligible to those who were unfamiliar with the coded symbolism in which it was written. It concerned the mythical figure of Christian Rosencreutz and his transcendence to spiritual perfection using the secret knowledge of the Monad.[13]

The work was even more confusing than John Dee's *Monas Hieroglyphica,* and was meant to be: It was apparently written so that only the initiated would understand what the Monad really was. However, it strongly implied that the ceremony on Mayday 1613 had been a physical enactment of the mystical Alchemical Wedding. John Dee's *Monas Hieroglyphica* symbol appears at the beginning of the document, and next to it is a reference to Elizabeth and Frederick's marriage, together with a cryptic verse that was said to reveal the truth about the long-sought-after Monad—the fifth element:

> *This day, this day, this, this [sic],*
> *The Royal Wedding is.*
> *Art thou thereto by birth inclined,*
> *And unto joy of God designed?*
> *Then may'st thou to the mountain's tend,*
> *Whereupon three stately Temples stand,*
> *And there see all from end to end.*
>
> *Keep watch and ward thyself regard;*
> *Unless with diligence thou bathe,*
> *The Wedding can't thee harmless save,*
> *He'll damage have that here delays;*
> *Let him beware, too, light that weighs.*

Below this were written the Latin words *Sponsus* and *Sponsa*—bridegroom and bride.[14] What this enigmatic verse actually means is anyone's guess. Students of the occult have been trying to interpret it ever since it was first penned.

The marriage of Elizabeth and Frederick was, as stated, clearly a Rosicrucian ceremony and those who were invited were key players in the Rosicrucian movement. William Shakespeare, it seems, was one of these. Not only was he one of the guests, but he wrote his play *The Tempest* especially for the wedding and it was performed as part of the celebration. While *The Birth of Merlin* may or may not have been written by Shakespeare, *The Tempest* certainly was. Here, at last, was something to tie William Shakespeare directly to the Rosicrucians.

But there is more. The ceremony involved a sword decorated with two serpents. King James did not attend the event, but he evidently had no objection to it. The Archbishop of Canterbury, on the other hand, did object. Although he was not there in person, he wrote to the king a few weeks later complaining that he had learned that the ceremony involved Francis Bacon performing what the archbishop feared was a pagan rite. Bacon had evidently used a ceremonial sword to draw magic symbols in a bowl of sand—a sword decorated with what the archbishop described as a caduceus symbol. Apparently, the archbishop was concerned that Bacon was performing an ancient Roman rite sacred to the god Mercury. The archbishop's letter was not specific concerning where precisely on the sword the twin-serpent image was, but it might, like Excalibur, have been on the hilt.[15]

If Shakespeare did have a hand in writing *The Birth of Merlin*, then he wrote an allegory concerning the early Rosicrucians. He was almost certainly involved with the Rosicrucians himself, and had played a leading role at their most important ceremony—one involving a sword that sounded as if it might have been a replica of Excalibur. Surely this had some connection with what Glynn Davis had in mind when he said Shakespeare had been privy to some secret concerning the twin serpents on Excalibur's hilt.

Nevertheless, I still failed to see how the historical Merlin might be tied in with it all: Even if the Rosicrucian leaders saw themselves as some kind of latter-day Merlins, even if they did use a sword to represent Excalibur.

What could any of it have to do with the historical Ambrosius, who had died one thousand years before? Frustratingly, very little has survived, or perhaps was ever written, about exactly what went on at this Alchemical Wedding. However, one important part of it does survive—Shakespeare's *Tempest*. Could this explain how the historical Merlin was involved, or why Glynn Davis believed that Shakespeare had been murdered—or for that matter why someone had broken into my apartment and stolen my replica of Excalibur?

9

INTRIGUE

Regardless of whatever someone knew or thought he knew about Excalibur, why would he want *my* sword? It was a replica, and one based on a description from the widely available translations of *The Red Book of Hergest* and published archaeological research. The chances were that it would not have looked exactly like the original in any case. The shape, size, and weight may have matched a sword possessed by a Romano-British leader of the mid-fifth century, but the precise detail of the hilt design was guesswork based on ornamental serpents from contemporary Roman finds, none of them on swords. Beside which, even if someone did regard the replica as a true re-creation, there were pictures of it in my books and on my Web site. It was not only the thief who presumably regarded the sword as important but also Glynn Davis; he had been keen to examine it the day we met in Carmarthen. Why? There had to be something I was overlooking. Only Glynn could answer that question, but he was still in hospital. Perhaps *The Tempest* would help explain the mystery. I had never seen the play, so I read it with anticipation. Was there anything in it to link Shakespeare with Merlin and the Excalibur legend?

The plot was certainly appropriate for the Rosicrucians, as it concerns the occult and its main character is a magician. Having survived a storm at sea, a group of sailors find themselves shipwrecked on an enchanted island where the only inhabitants are a native named Caliban, an Italian magician called Prospero, and Prospero's daughter, Miranda. Prospero was once duke of Milan, but twelve years earlier had been tricked out of his inheritance and was forced to flee to the secluded island with his child. Since then he has been free to practice his magic, in which he is aided by a spirit called Ariel, who appears in the form of a water nymph.

At first, Prospero uses his powers to make the shipwrecked mariners his slaves, but by the end of the play he decides to free the crew, give up his magic, and return home. An elaborate stage set for the original performance was designed by the architect and known Rosicrucian Inigo Jones; it depicted a pool, center stage, with a hut or cell next to it in which Prospero meditated. From the pool, Ariel spectacularly enters and exits the stage and into it Prospero eventually casts his magic book, the source of all his knowledge. The play was appropriate for Elizabeth and Frederick's wedding celebration, as the central theme concerned a love affair between Miranda and one of the mariners, Ferdinand—the high point of the performance being a matrimonial masque involving music, song, and dance, in which Prospero invokes the ancient gods of Rome to celebrate the rites of marriage and bless the couple's union.[1]

The play certainly did appear to link with the Arthurian Merlin: The character Prospero seemed to have been based on him. To begin with, Prospero lives on a mysterious island and, in the Arthurian romances, Merlin frequently travels to the mystical isle of Avalon, where he eventually retires. There is also the character of Ariel, who appears as a water nymph. In the romances, Merlin is aided by a water nymph, the Lady of the Lake. Moreover, Shakespeare depicts his Prospero character as the duke of Milan. The family of Ambrosius, the historical Merlin, had been associated with that very city and Ambrosius's ancestor St. Ambrose had actually been duke of it. Unless this was a remarkable coincidence, Shakespeare not only knew that Ambrosius was the historical Merlin, but he was also aware of his ancestry. Although a magical sword did not feature in the play, Excalibur might also have been alluded to. The source of Prospero's power is his *grimoire*, or book of magic, which, as we have said, he ultimately casts into Ariel's pool, just as Excalibur is thrown to the Lady of the Lake in the Arthurian story.

None of this, however, made me any the wiser. What was so important about Merlin and Excalibur that could have gotten Shakespeare killed, or for that matter impelled someone today to steal Glynn Davis's research notes and my sword?

A week later I finally received a phone call from Glynn, and I was relieved to hear that he was out of hospital and doing well. He called to ask if I had read his research notes. When I told him about the theft, he was deeply concerned. The moment I mentioned the break-in, I regretted it. The last thing a man who just suffered a severe heart attack needs is excitement. Nevertheless, he insisted that I visit him at his home as soon as possible.

When I arrived at Glynn's home in the Welsh capital of Cardiff a few days later, I was impressed. Although it was a fairly modern building, it was filled with antiques. In addition, Glynn had the largest private collection of books on the Arthurian mystery that I had ever seen. Glynn's wife was clearly unhappy about him receiving visitors so soon after leaving hospital but she nonetheless left us alone to talk. First of all, Glynn wanted to know what I had learned since we last spoke, and I quickly summarized.

"You were right about Merlin being a historical figure," I concluded. "I'm also fairly convinced that Shakespeare and the Rosicrucians regarded him as important—exactly why, though, I've no idea."

"Haven't you?" Glynn said with a smile. "What started the Rosicrucian movement?"

"The School of Night?" I suggested.

"The order was an amalgamation of such groups, but what was the event that led to establishment of the wider Rosicrucian fraternity?"

"The new star that appeared in 1604."

"And?"

"The supposed discovery of the tomb of Christian Rosencreutz."

"Precisely!" Glynn left the word hanging in the air, as if it should mean something.

"Sorry, I don't follow," I said. "How does that tie in with Merlin?"

"Christian Rosencreutz *was* Merlin." Glynn obviously expected everything to fall into place with that poignant statement, but it served only to leave me more confused than ever.

"From what I can gather, Christian Rosencreutz was a myth, at least a metaphorical figure," I said. "Even if he did exist, he is said to have been born in 1378 and lived for one hundred and six years until 1484—a millennium after Merlin's time."

"I agree, the account of the tomb's discovery as described in the *Fama Fraternitatis* is symbolic, as is the period of Rosencreutz's life, but think about those dates." Glynn remained silent for a while. "Merlin established the united bloodline of the British kings," he hinted when I failed to grasp the relevance.

"The Romances portray him as initiating the reign of Arthur, whose descendants were said to be the true kings of Britain?" I asked.

"When the Anglo-Saxons finally overran England in the centuries after Merlin's time, the native Britons were forced into Wales and became the Welsh," said Glynn. "After that, the royal bloodline established by Arthur passed down through the kings of Wales. The last of these was Owain Lawgoch, who died in 1378. For the next one hundred and six years, Wales was ruled directly by the English Plantagenet kings and their eldest sons bore the title Prince of Wales. The last of these Plantagenet princes died in 1484 and the following year a Welshman, Henry Tudor, a direct descendant of the original Welsh kings, seized the English throne. He was the first of the Tudors and, during Shakespeare's time, they and their Scottish relatives the Stuarts continued to rule. The period Christian Rosencreutz is said to have lived was symbolic of the period in which Britain was without a monarch from the bloodline said to have been established by Merlin—an important clue to the fact that the two figures were one and the same."

I was far from persuaded. "The dating is interesting, but it might relate to anything. It hardly suggests that Christian Rosencreutz was some kind of allegory of Merlin," I said.

"Not on its own," said Glynn, turning around and taking a couple of books from the shelf behind him. "Are you aware that the Alchemical Wedding in 1613 was not the first Rosicrucian pageant performed for Princess Elizabeth?"

"There was another?"

"Yes, three years earlier, in January 1610, when she came of age. Today most counties regard marriageable age as around eighteen; in early-seventeenth-century England it was the fourteenth year after birth. Although Elizabeth was still only thirteen, 1610 was her fourteenth year and a pageant was held in London before the king, queen, and princess at the start of the year to celebrate the occasion. At the time, King James had been persuaded of the benefits of a Protestant alliance with a united Germany, and the spectacle was designed to proclaim that his daughter would be married to whatever prince the Germans chose to lead them. That was the official story—but it was also a Rosicrucian rite."

"And the king knew?" I asked, wondering if a Rosicrucian ceremony could have been performed so openly.

"Whether or not James I was a Rosicrucian himself has been the subject of much debate. He certainly sympathized with their cause and had no objection to the event at Coombe Abbey on Mayday 1613. Anyway, just as Shakespeare's *Tempest* was performed for Elizabeth's wedding, a masque was performed at her coming-of-age pageant. It was written by Shakespeare's friend and fellow Rosicrucian the playwright Ben Jonson: an elaborate performance involving dance and music with spectacular scenery designed by another Rosicrucian, the architect Inigo Jones."

"The same man who made the scenery for *The Tempest?*" I asked.

"Precisely, and Jones's stage set for the 1610 pageant incorporated a cryptic Rosicrucian message. The masque concerns the opening of a sacred tomb, and the scenery included a re-creation of the tomb of Christian Rosencreutz as described in the *Fama Fraternitatis*."

The books Glynn had taken from the shelf were the script for the masque, complete with Jonson's original notes and Jones's scenery instructions, and a copy of the *Fama Fraternitatis*.[2] Comparing them, I had to agree. The words concerning the discovery of the tomb in the *Fama* were:

> *In the morning we opened the door, and there*
> *appeared to our sight a vault of seven sides and corners,*
> *every side five foot broad, and the height of eight foot.*[3]

Jones's set instructions say specifically that the tomb should be a seven-sided cell, made from panels five feet by eight with a door that opened into it. The masque certainly appeared to concern the same event described in the *Fama*.

"It was obviously a Rosicrucian event, as you say. But what has any of it to do with Merlin?" I asked. I noticed that Glynn had been deliberately keeping his hand over the title and opening verses of the play. Now he made a dramatic gesture of removing it, allowing me to see the name of the character who spoke first. It was the Lady of the Lake and her opening lines identified the tomb's occupant:

> *What nymph I am; behold the ample Lake*
> *Of which I am styl'd; and near it Merlin's Tomb*[4]

"The masque was called *The Lady of the Lake, First Discovered* and her discovery is the discovery of Merlin's tomb," said Glynn. "The *Fama Fraternitatis*, which first appeared in the same year, revealed the finding of the tomb of Christian Rosencreutz, an obvious pseudonym—Christian Rose Cross. The Rosicrucians cloaked everything in riddles and symbolism. Only someone who had read the *Fama* and seen the masque would know who the mysterious Rosencreutz really was—the legendary Merlin."

As I glanced through the script, I could see that this was clearly what Ben Jonson and Inigo Jones were implying. In the *Fama*, it is the appearance of the new star that heralds the finding of Rosencreutz's tomb; in the masque, it is the same star that makes it possible for the Lady of the Lake to find *Merlin's* tomb. She enters holding the star in her hands and places it in a pond, center stage, and in a puff of smoke King Arthur appears. The Arthur character then addresses the audience and explains his presence:

> *And thither hath thy voice pierc'd. Stand not maz'd,*
> *And not been frighted. I thy Arthur am*
> *Translated to a star; and of that frame.*

"You see, Arthur is associated with the star as he is in *The Birth of Merlin* play," said Glynn enthusiastically. "Note how there is a pool beside Merlin's tomb, just as Prospero's cell is next to a pool in Shakespeare's *Tempest*; both are associated with a water nymph, the Lady of the Lake."

Intrigued, I read on. After the monologue by Arthur and a spectacle of singing and dancing, Merlin rises from the dead, leaves his tomb, and gives a speech concerning a new Arthurian era—the age of enlightenment and the grand Protestant alliance with Princess Elizabeth at its heart.

"The Rosicrucian message wasn't conveyed in just one idiom," said Glynn when I finished reading. "It was communicated in pamphlets such as the *Fama* and *The Alchemical Wedding,* the works of playwrights such as Jonson and Shakespeare, and in the set designs of Inigo Jones. Only when they are seen together do the real meanings become apparent: the significance of the new star; Elizabeth as the personification of a new age of religious freedom, scientific discovery, and occult understanding; and at the heart of it all, the discovery of the tomb—Merlin's tomb."

Glynn certainly seemed to be on to something but I could not see why the discovery of a tomb believed to be Merlin's would have been considered so important. "What was supposed to be in the tomb?" I said.

"Exactly what the *Fama Fraternitatis* said it was—the Monad, the philosopher's stone, the fifth element, call it what you will. I have no idea how Merlin might have discovered it, but there are traditions within certain branches of Freemasonry that imply he possessed such knowledge."

"The Freemasons?" I asked in surprise.

I knew very little about the Freemasons. From what I did know, they could be traced back to the guilds or unions of stonemasons formed in the Middle Ages. Over the years, Masonic legends arose that dated their fraternity back to biblical times, when their founders were said to have worked on King Solomon's temple in Jerusalem. The Freemasons had always been a secretive society, as they guarded closely the building techniques upon which their livelihood depended.

However, by the sixteenth century, their membership extended beyond the building profession and had become, in effect, the world's first trade union. By the early 1600s, their interests expanded and turned from actual trade toward moral philosophy, and a number of esoteric elements were introduced to their meetings. Many of these, Glynn explained, were taken from the Rosicrucians. I listened intently as he told me how it all began with the collapse of the Rosicrucian dream.

In the summer of 1613, after his marriage, Frederick returned with his new bride, Elizabeth, to Heidelberg, where he was accepted as the head of the German Protestant Union. Although not a united Germany as such, it was the next best thing: a military alliance with Frederick as its commander in chief. A few years later, however, the alliance was put to the test and failed miserably. In 1619, the state of Bohemia (in what is now the Czech Republic), to the east of the Palatinate, offered to make Frederick its king. Bohemia had been a part of the Catholic Hapsburg Empire but Protestantism had taken a root there. When the Hapsburg emperor Matthias died in August of that year, the Bohemians declared independence and, because he was descended from the pre-Hapsburg dynasty, Frederick was offered the throne. Frederick accepted, and he and Elizabeth were crowned king and queen in the Bohemian capital of Prague in November. The Bohemians adored Elizabeth: She was sprightly, amorous, fun-loving, and, by all accounts, extremely beautiful. So popular was she that she earned the nickname "the Queen of Hearts." However, she has gone down in history with the epithet "the Winter Queen," as a winter was as long as her reign lasted.

War broke out the following spring. Frederick's acceptance of the Bohemian crown had been a dangerous leap of faith. The Hapsburg Empire would almost certainly want it back. Frederick had banked everything on support from the German Union and help from Elizabeth's father, King James of England. However, when the new Hapsburg emperor sent an army into Bohemia, the grand alliance evaporated. Not only did the English offer no assistance, but the German states abandoned their figurehead as well. By the end of 1620, Frederick's gallant but hopeless attempts at resistance were quashed and the last of his forces were routed. Frederick and Elizabeth managed to escape to Holland, where they could only watch helplessly as Bohemia fell back under Hapsburg control and the Palatinate was overrun by the Hapsburg Catholic allies, the Spanish. Not only had the Rosicrucian's political dream evaporated, virtually overnight; the Bohemian affair ignited a protracted conflict that lasted for thirty years, with Protestants and Catholics fighting for control of Central Europe.[5]

"With their political hopes dashed, the Rosicrucians broke apart," concluded Glynn. "Various groups or hermetic orders were founded by some of the fraternity, but many of its leading members joined the Freemasons. In England, for instance, Francis Bacon joined the Masons and introduced a new, mystical aspect to the organization, as did Andreae and others in Germany."

"So the Freemasons knew the Rosicrucians believed that Merlin had discovered the secret of the Monad," I said. "But how do you know what the Masons believe?" Before I finished the question, I knew the answer by the look on Glynn's face. "*You're a Mason.*"

"So you understand why there are certain things I can't reveal. However, I am revealing no secrets by telling you that the Masons inherited certain knowledge about Merlin having discovered the secret of the Monad."

"And the Masons know what that secret is?"

Glynn shook his head. "Only an inner circle of the Rosicrucians seemed to have known that—an elite group referred to as 'the Nine.' Who they were and what happened to them after the wider fraternity broke apart is a mystery. The various Rosicrucian writings suggest, however, that the secret remained where it was found, in the mysterious tomb."

"So the Monad, the fifth element, the ultimate secret, whatever it was, was still to be found in Merlin's tomb," I said, looking up at a picture hanging on the wall above the fireplace: It depicted a knight throwing King Arthur's sword to the Lady of the Lake. "So how does Excalibur tie in with it all?"

"It's only speculation, but I think it revealed the tomb's secret location."

Glynn explained his theory that only a select few Rosicrucians knew where the tomb actually was. One of these was a German count named Michael Maier, who acted as chief spokesman for the fraternity. He wrote a number of books outlining the organization's agenda and in these he gave what Glynn believed were three cryptic clues to reveal the tomb's whereabouts. "The first is in his *Themis Aurea*, the Golden Rule," said Glynn, reaching over and taking two other books from the shelf.[6] Opening one, he pointed out a highlighted verse, which he told me was the first cryptic message: "Pegasus opened a spring of overflowing water wherein Diana washed herself, to whom Venus was handmaid and Saturn gentleman usher."

"I have no idea what this means," said Glynn, "but Maier suggests that only when the tomb is found will the verse make sense. Diana was the Roman huntress goddess and another of Maier's works was dedicated to her." He opened the second book. "This is a copy of his *Atalanta Fugiens*, the Fleeing Huntress, and it contains what I believe to be the other clues to the tomb's location: two illustrations."

He showed me the first illustration, which depicted a brick wall upon which were drawn the naked figures of a man and a woman. Around them was a series of geometric shapes and beside the wall there stood an alchemist with two tapered sticks pointing at two positions on the wall design.[7]

"Look at the plaster on the wall," said Glynn. "It's a map." I examined the drawing carefully as he drew my attention to how the plaster was broken away, leaving the bare bricks exposed in patches. "If you imagine the brick sections as being the sea and the plaster as dry land, then we have a map depicting the mainland with an island above it." Although it was not immediately noticeable, once Glynn pointed it out, the map design became obvious. "Coupling the *Fama* with Elizabeth's coming-of-age masque, we know that the tomb of Christian Rosencreutz was really the tomb of Merlin, and coupling that with Shakespeare's *Tempest*, written for Elizabeth's marriage, we know that the same tomb, represented by Prospero's cell, was on an island. I believe the map depicts that island and that one of the alchemist's sticks points to the site of the tomb."

"Do you know were the island is?" I asked.

Glynn shook his head, almost in despair. "I formulated this theory some time ago, but have not yet found an island that matches the illustration. The chances are I never will until I know more. As you see, only the lower half of the island is visible. It may be merely a small section of its coastline."

"Or perhaps the headland of a larger landmass?"

"No, I'm convinced it's an island," said Glynn. "Early Arthurian legends specifically portray Merlin as ending his life on the *isle* of Avalon."

"That has to narrow it down considerably," I said. "If you are right about all this, then all you have to do is compare the map—if it is a map—with the coastline of the British islands claiming to be the historical Avalon."

Glynn stared at me. "Have you any idea how many that could be?"

My own research had suggested only a few. "Three or four," I said.

"You're kidding! The early Romances and Welsh tales simply say that Avalon lay across the 'western sea.' This could be any one of more than a thousand islands off the coast of Britain or Ireland. Then there are the legends from continental Europe suggesting islands off the coast of France, Spain, even Portugal. I've lost count of how many that is." Glynn held up his hands in a gesture of surrender. "But even if you knew which island Maier's illustration refers to, the chances are that erosion and higher sea levels would make it look very different today, four centuries later."

"I see what you mean. But you said something about Excalibur revealing the tomb's location."

"Yes, which brings me to the second illustration." Glynn flipped the pages of Maier's book. "The first picture is entitled *The Monad,* which in part led me to believe that it contains a vital clue to its whereabouts: in other words, to Merlin's tomb. The second is entitled *The Philosopher's Egg,* another name for the philosopher's stone or the Monad. As you can see, the egg is depicted, as is the sword that is about to crack it open." The illustration shows a large white egg, approximately the size of a football, resting on a table. Beside it is the figure of a man in a Greek or Roman costume, holding up a sword with which he appears to be about to strike the egg.

Glynn continued: "A commentary in Latin, concerning the picture, roughly translated reads: 'Legend tells of a great bird that appears at certain times of the year in a small island in the ocean.' This, I am convinced, is a specific reference to Merlin. His name means the Eagle, a great bird, and the egg is the Monad, the secret buried with him on his mysterious island. It is the sword that can crack it open, or reveal its secret. If I'm right about the heart of the Rosicrucian mystery concerning the tomb of Merlin, then the sword must be a sword specifically associated with him—Excalibur."

"You mentioned Excalibur's hilt, in particular."

"Yes. As you no doubt know, the twin serpents are also found on the caduceus wand." Glynn turned the pages of the book, showing me other illustrations depicting similar strange scenes—some showing dragons and serpents, and one showing the god Mercury holding the double-serpent caduceus wand. "In mythology, the caduceus wand is the magical talisman that enables Mercury to travel back and forth from the realm of the gods. In Celtic legend, Merlin was closely associated with the god Lugh, a god also associated with the twin serpents, and he traveled back and forth from the islands of the Otherworld, one of which was Avalon. I am certain that Maier was implying that something about Excalibur's twin serpents would help reveal the island's location."

"Let me see if I have this right," I said. "The sword reveals the location of the island, the wall map reveals the whereabouts of the tomb on the island, and the Diana verse reveals something about the tomb once the site is found."

"Simply put, but yes."

At that moment, Mrs. Davis put her head around the door to remind Glynn that he was expecting the doctor. "I'd better go," I said, taking my cue to leave.

"No, no." Glynn held up a hand. "We have another half hour."

Before she left, Mrs. Davis cast me a troubled glance. She was obviously concerned that I was keeping her husband occupied. Feeling somewhat embarrassed, I settled back down. "I hope you don't mind me saying that I'm confused," I said. "Not about the cryptic messages," I added quickly when Glynn began turning the pages of the book as if preparing to explain it all again. "About why you are telling me all this. It's obviously your passion to find this tomb. Aren't you concerned that I might jump in on the act? You were—" I picked my words carefully, "a bit reticent the first time we met."

Glynn leaned back in his chair, linked his hands behind his head, and stared up at the Lady of the Lake picture on the wall. "You're right. I would never have told anyone any of this a few weeks ago. The truth is that I am no longer in any fit state to go searching for anything. This is my second heart attack, and I might not survive a third. Besides, I've sworn I'd give it all up." He glanced toward the door as if to indicate to whom the promise had been made.

"I understand," I said.

"I don't think you do," said Glynn, staring me right in my eyes. "I want you to find the tomb . . . before they do."

"They?"

"The people who broke into your place."

"You know who they are?"

"Unfortunately, no. If I did, I'd see them charged with unlawful entry, illegal surveillance, and computer hacking, and I'd sue them for aggravating my state of health. I'd better explain."

Glynn told me how he had made no secret about his interest in Merlin's tomb; he even gave talks about it, although in his talks he did not reveal the important clues he believed he was on to. Then, shortly before we first met, a bugging device had been found in his study. A plumber had been called in to fix the radiators and, quite by chance, had discovered a small, rectangular piece of electronic equipment attached behind some pipes. At first Glynn was mystified as to what this was, until a friend told him that it looked like some kind of miniature transmitter. Glynn took the device to the police, who confirmed the suspicion, but unfortunately there was nothing they could do to trace who put it there.

"Fingerprinting revealed nothing, and the device is sold on the Internet all over the world. Thousands are bought every week, apparently. Makes you wonder just how many people are into bugging: jealous lovers, unethical salesmen, journalists, voyeurs, the list is endless. These days it's not only military intelligence that can have you monitored around the clock; it's anyone who can afford to spend a few hundred pounds."

"Surely there had to be a receiver somewhere nearby. Couldn't the police find that?"

Glynn shook his head. "Evidently it was a quartz-controlled UHF device, which meant nothing to me. Apparently it had a transmitting range of over a mile, which meant that locating the receiver would be nigh on impossible."

"Aren't you worried they may still be bugging you?" I asked as I looked around the room.

"The police checked the entire place and put me in touch with a security company that offers effective countermeasures equipment to industry—bug detectors, to you and me. The company installed its own devices so that if any unusual radio signals are detected, it knows at once."

"So what made you think that whoever was responsible for the bugging had an interest in your Merlin research? It could have been something else."

Glynn smiled. "Sad to say, I do nothing of any conceivable interest to anyone, apart from my research into the Arthurian legend and, in particular, the search for Merlin's tomb. However, the proof came when the security company checked my computer and found it was infected by a Trojan—you know, a backdoor into your computer, an illegal program that gives someone access to all your files."

I knew what he meant. These programs can be downloaded from

Web sites automatically. If you don't have the proper anti-Trojan software, you never know that your files have been stolen. "Computers are being infected by these things all the time," I said, "by people who want to get your credit card details, send spam e-mails, and do whatever else they do. What makes you sure it had anything to do with your Merlin research?"

"The security company was able to determine which particular files had been accessed and discovered that it was only those that had relevance to my search for Merlin's tomb."

It all sounded a bit extreme to me. I couldn't quite see a group of Arthurian enthusiasts going to so much trouble and expense, let alone breaking the law. Then again, my own place had been burgled. "You say you've had all these sophisticated countermeasures installed for the last few weeks. All the same, someone must have known you sent your research notes to me."

"I know. Thinking my computer was safe, I sent you an e-mail confirming that I'd posted you the notes."

"I know, I got it."

"And so did someone else. When you told me of the break-in the other day, I asked the security company to recheck my computer. Apparently, someone had managed to remotely download something called a keylogger, a more sophisticated program that somehow managed to get around its best security measures. Evidently, whoever these people are, they know their stuff."

"What did you send me, anyway?"

"Luckily, nothing of any importance. Just a few notes that told you little more than you tell me you've discovered yourself. When I sent them, I had no intention of filling you in on everything I've told you today."

"So why *are* you telling me? You say you want me to find the tomb before they do?"

"Yes, it makes me mad to think that someone has had the impudence to invade my privacy and . . ." Glynn took a moment to calm down. "I would love for someone else to find it before those bastards do!"

"I see." It was a shock to hear such a refined old gentleman swear. "So why me? For all you know, I might be the one who's been bugging you."

"I thought you were," he said after a few seconds of silence. "You were one of the few people I knew who, having researched the relevant material, would be a prime culprit. That's why I originally wanted to meet you. I'm a pretty good judge of character and I wanted to sound you out. After meeting you, it seemed fairly obvious that you were not the guilty party, but to be on the safe side . . ." Glynn stopped and reached out for something on the table, then flopped back in his chair. "Can't get used to not smoking."

"To be on the safe side?" I prompted him.

"I hired a private detective and had you followed." Glynn was visibly embarrassed by the admission.

"A small, thin, shifty-looking guy with wiry gray hair," I said.

Glynn looked shocked. "You know?"

I told him about the man I had seen in Nevern churchyard and at the well in Brittany, but assured him I had no problem with it. I didn't really mind, it all sounded quite exciting. "So you trust me now," I said.

"Yes, and I'm sorry. In fact you are one of the only people I know for certain I *can* trust. It has taken me a long time to discover the clues to the tomb's location. I can't carry on myself and you seem to be good at solving these kinds of mysteries." Glynn fell silent for a moment. "*Will* you try to find it?"

I needed no persuading. "I'll do my best. I'm hooked on the Merlin mystery now anyway. I would love to find proof of his historical existence and . . ."

"No, you don't understand," interrupted Glynn. "This is not just academic. I really believe that the tomb does hold something far too important to fall into the wrong hands."

I was prepared to accept that the Rosicrucians discovered what they thought was Merlin's tomb, but I was still skeptical regarding the Monad. "What do you think the Monad actually is?" I asked.

"The Logos," he said quietly. "What the ancients regarded as the true name of God."

I decided not to question Glynn further about his belief as the doctor would be arriving soon: He told me that everything I needed to know was in his complete research notes, which he promised to give me before I left. Nevertheless, I had a nagging question for which I could find no logical answer. "I understand why Excalibur or something about the legend may be important to solving Maier's clues, but I don't see how my replica is important."

"It isn't," said Glynn, looking down. "I'm ashamed to admit it, but I told you that in order to mislead you. In case you were the . . . well, the enemy, so to speak."

"What about what you told me concerning Shakespeare being murdered because of what he knew about Excalibur?"

"That was true. Shakespeare's fellow playwright and Rosicrucian, Ben Jonson, was drinking with Shakespeare on his last night. Jonson later became a Freemason and some of his private writings are preserved by the lodge with which I am associated. Unfortunately, I am bound not to disclose exactly that they say other than to tell you that they reveal that Shakespeare discovered something—Jonson does not say what—about the serpents on Excalibur's hilt that led Shakespeare to discover the whereabouts of the tomb."

"Wouldn't he have known anyway, if he was a Rosicrucian?"

"He clearly wasn't one of the Nine. Neither was Jonson."

"So the Nine killed him to keep him quiet?"

"No. Jonson says Raleigh killed Shakespeare, just as you suspected."

I tried to get Glynn to tell me more. If his Masons really did have writings in Johnson's own hand accusing Sir Walter Raleigh of Shakespeare's murder, it would be not only eyewitness testimony to support my own theory; it would be a literary bombshell. However, Glynn would reveal nothing else apart from that Raleigh had personal reasons for wanting the whereabouts of the tomb kept quiet.

"But if Raleigh wasn't one of the Nine, how did he know where the tomb was?" I asked. "Why didn't he want it found?"

"Unfortunately, Jonson doesn't say."

I had a thousand questions to ask, but Glynn politely refused to tell me any more. Apparently to do so would have been to betray certain Masonic secrets, although he assured me they gave no further insight into where the tomb was, what it contained, or what Shakespeare had actually worked out. We changed the subject to who the enemy could be.

"They could be a part of any number of so-called esoteric groups, or maybe an individual acting alone with no ties to any organization," said Glynn. "I've thought about it a lot, as you can imagine, but I have no clues at all." Glynn left the room for a while and returned with a black leather briefcase. "These are all my notes. You can learn everything that is relevant from them. Please keep them safe and make sure that you don't commit anything to writing, certainly not on a computer, until . . . if you find the tomb. I advise you to also have your home checked by the security people I use. I'll give you their number."

"Do you think it could be Freemasons who've been bugging you?" I asked.

Glynn smiled. "Most unlikely. The culprits stole your sword, which presumably means they believed the lie I told you. No one with any real knowledge of Freemasonry, coupled with the kind of research into the Rosicrucians these people must have been doing, would have fallen for that."

I wanted to know what such Masonic knowledge was, but realized I would get no answer. However, another question occurred to me, one I had to have an answer to. "When we first met, you said there were people today who would kill to find out what Shakespeare knew. I assume now that you were referring to whoever's been bugging you. These people might be prepared to illegally eavesdrop, burgle, and hack into computers but—murder?!"

Glynn remained silent for a moment. "Just a figure of speech," he said eventually. "I didn't mean that they would actually murder anyone. Not that I know of," he added with a laugh, which hardly disguised the fact that he was suddenly concerned. Clearly something else had happened that he was reluctant to tell me about, and I remembered he had mentioned wanting to sue the mysterious parties in question for damaging his health. It seemed that they had done more than just put him under surveillance. I didn't push the matter but had a pretty good idea why he didn't want to tell me. If I thought the enemy, as he called them, were physically dangerous, I might decide to drop the entire thing.

Soon after, the doctor arrived and I prepared to leave. It was only when I stood up that another disturbing thought occurred to me. "Did you talk to anyone about misleading me regarding the Excalibur replica?" I asked. Glynn shook his head. "Or type anything about it on your computer?" I pressed on.

"No."

"Then you must have been bugged the day we first met."

"Impossible! The security company gave me a personal detector. Look!" Glynn showed me an object that looked like a cell phone. "I keep it on me all the time; it beeps if you're bugged."

"In that case someone must have followed you to the pub and been there in the beer garden, close enough to overhear everything you said."

I had no idea how dangerous these people were, but they were certainly serious—seriously obsessed.

10

WHERE WAS AVALON?

Reading through Glynn Davis's research, I found that he had originally been investigating only the historical Merlin, and had reached much the same conclusions that I had now drawn regarding Ambrosius. However, this work was sidelined once he concluded that Merlin's tomb had been discovered in 1604. Convinced that the discovery was genuine, all Glynn's efforts were then directed to deciphering the Rosicrucians' cryptic writings and symbolism, much of it taking him down blind alleys, until he finally homed in on Michael Maier's clues.

At this point, he seemed to have become stuck and, unable to solve Maier's message, concentrated his research on the Rosicrucian movement itself and what might have become of its descendants. Glynn believed that the inner Rosicrucian elite, the Nine, had continued on as an underground society, preserving the secret of Merlin's tomb and passing it down from one generation to the next. There were pages and pages of notes concerning various esoteric groups that emerged between the breakup of the wider Rosicrucian fraternity in the early 1600s and the present day. Evidently, though, Glynn had found no evidence that any of them were associated with the Nine. Unfortunately, in my opinion, Glynn's fixation with the Rosicrucians had diverted him from any further research into Merlin himself.

I agreed with Glynn's theory that through Ben Jonson's coming-of-age masque for Princess Elizabeth, together with the *Fama Fraternitatis* and Shakespeare's *Tempest* performed at the Alchemical Wedding, the Rosicrucians were implying that Merlin's tomb was discovered in 1604. However, there were two problems with that as far as research into the Merlin mystery was concerned. First, the allusion to Merlin's tomb may have been as allegorical as the mythical Christian Rosencreutz; and second, even if the Rosicrucians really found a tomb, who was to say it was actually the tomb of the historical Merlin? They may simply have *thought* it was.

Then there was the problem with what was supposed to have been inside the tomb: the Monad, whatever that might be. Was there any historical evidence to suggest that Merlin, or at least the historical Ambrosius, acquired mystical wisdom the Rosicrucians would later regard as significant? I had discovered that Ambrosius was regarded as a bard, and my research in Brittany suggested that he could have inherited the knowledge of the ancient Druids. Could the Monad have had something to do with Druidism?

One thing occurred to me that might have linked the Rosicrucians with the Druids: the fact that Shakespeare is often referred to as "the Bard." However, I soon discovered that this title originated with the eighteenth-century English actor David Garrick, who in 1769 wrote a tribute to Shakespeare in which he said: "For the bard of all bards was the Warwickshire bard." Garrick, like most people, thought that a bard was simply the ancient name for a poet and the nickname stuck.

But what about the Druids themselves: Was there any evidence that their beliefs incorporated anything concerning the supposed fifth element? The trouble was that, although Julius Caesar and other Roman writers referred to Druid beliefs, they said very little about their actual practices. They supposedly had the gift of prophecy, had an affinity with nature, and employed various healing practices. Most significant, they were said to have developed amazing memory techniques. How they trained in these skills goes unmentioned, and none of it, in any obvious way, seems to have anything to do with the Monad. Alternatively, Ambrosius might have known something about the Monad from Greek or Roman sources, or perhaps from early Christianity or Jewish tradition. However, I had so far discovered nothing about Ambrosius from which to draw any conclusions, while Glynn's research into Ambrosius took things only to the point I had now reached myself. As fascinating as they were, Glynn's research notes were not really going to help. If I was going to find Merlin's tomb, I would have to go about it some other way.

I had told Glynn I was hooked on the mystery of Merlin, and it was true. I wanted to find out more about Ambrosius, and finding his tomb would make a fantastic discovery. I decided there was no point, at least for the time being, in trying to solve Michael Maier's clues. If Glynn couldn't manage it with all his background knowledge on the Rosicrucians, what chance would I have? Besides, I didn't even understand how Glynn had decided which particular verse or illustrations in Maier's works were important. Evidently, that had something to do with his knowledge of Freemasonry, but there was nothing specifically concerning it in the notes.

I knew next to nothing about the Freemasons, and seriously doubted that any member of the organization would willingly enlighten me. If I was going to try to locate Merlin's tomb, I would have to concentrate on the Arthurian Romances, which implied that he was buried on the isle of Avalon. However, as Glynn had observed, locating Avalon was easier said than done.

Many of the Arthurian romances refer to Avalon, but none of them says specifically where it is. If it really did exist, its location had seemingly been forgotten by the Middle Ages. A number of British islands have been proposed as a possible Avalon, and two of them I had already investigated.

The first was the most famous: the small town of Glastonbury, in the county of Somerset, in western England. Nestling amid a small cluster of hills, with much of the surrounding countryside once submerged, Glastonbury was an island during Roman times and the Dark Ages. It is certainly an imposing location, for its highest hill, Glastonbury Tor, with its solitary stone tower at the summit, can be seen for miles from the fertile Somerset plain. Personally, though, I doubted that Glastonbury was a viable candidate for the mysterious island.

Glastonbury's link with Avalon arose as a result of a discovery said to have been made there in the late 1100s, within the grounds of the town's abbey. The impressive ruins of Glastonbury Abbey that survive today date from the late twelfth century, replacing much older buildings destroyed by fire in 1184. In 1190, during reconstruction following the fire, the abbey monks claimed to have discovered a grave containing the bones of a tall man. Along with the remains, a lead cross was said to have been found bearing the Latin inscription: "Here lies the renowned King Arthur in the isle of Avalon." Neither the bones nor the cross exists today, so nothing can be proved with certainty one way or the other. However, the incident is at best suspicious. The discovery of the grave was, to say the least, lucky.

The abbey desperately needed funds for rebuilding, and the only sure way to raise money was to attract large numbers of pilgrims. Stories of King Arthur were so popular at the time that nothing else could hope to bring in so many visitors. The inscription on the cross was also rather convenient, telling the world not only that was Arthur buried there, but also that Glastonbury was the secret island of Avalon. In fact, linguists have pointed out that the style of Latin is medieval and not that employed in the sixth century when Arthur is said to have died. Today the affair of Arthur's bones is considered so suspect that few historians take it seriously.

There is certainly no evidence that anyone prior to 1190 ever associated Glastonbury with Avalon. On the contrary, early historians seem completely unaware of any such notion. The English historian William of Malmesbury, for example, writing in the early twelfth century, compiled an exhaustive history of Glastonbury but not once does he link it with King Arthur, nor does he refer to the town in connection with Avalon.[1]

The other candidate for Avalon that I had already investigated was the isle of Anglesey, off the coast of North Wales. In Britain there was an ancient tradition that Jesus's mother, the Virgin Mary, had come to this country with some of the first Christians to escape persecution by the Romans, and the story recounted that she was buried on the isle of Avalon. In 597 A.D. Britain's first archbishop, Saint Augustine, located what he believed to be Mary's tomb on Anglesey and so the implication was that Avalon and Anglesey were one and the same. However, although Anglesey may well have been considered the site of Avalon at the time

Augustine lived, it cannot have been the same island that the romancers—or at least the authors of their original sources—had in mind for the island where Merlin ended his life. Merlin is said to have made a significant sea voyage to reach Avalon, but Anglesey is separated from the mainland by a strait that is only a few hundred feet wide. A regular ferry service crossed it in Roman and post-Roman times, which could hardly be described as a sea voyage. It seems that the Avalon where Merlin ended his days was somewhere farther away.[2]

Nevertheless, this still left hundreds of possible locations off the coast of Britain alone, and various authors have made equally convincing cases for a number of them as candidates for Avalon. If I hoped to discover where Merlin was buried, I would have to examine the life of Ambrosius. The problem was that none of the historical sources reveals where he was buried either. It would help, I decided, if I could determine the whereabouts of Ambrosius's power base.

Around the year 459, Ambrosius returned to Britain and, presumably with the help of the last of the Roman legions from Gaul, he defeated Vortigern's successor, Vitalinus, in South Wales. Unfortunately, although the various historical sources, such as Gildas, Bede, and Nennius, refer to Ambrosius as leading the Britons for the next few decades, none of them actually says where he ruled from. It seemed unlikely that he would have made his power base at Vortigern's fort in South Wales or at Dinas Emrys in North Wales. Both were too far to the west to have been significant, strategic locations from which to have directed successful warfare against the Anglo-Saxons.

A more convincing location was the site that later became King Arthur's capital, and this was somewhere that I previously had been able to identify. In 1992, when Martin Keatman and I were working on our book *King Arthur: The True Story,* we investigated the historical period in which the Arthurian legends were set. Although we had not investigated Ambrosius, we did identify a historical figure upon whom King Arthur may have been based.

In the Arthurian Romances, Arthur is portrayed as Britain's one true king. According to Nennius, however, he is the leader of an alliance of British kings. Either way, if he existed, Arthur must have ruled from the country's mightiest stronghold. Historically, around 500 A.D. Britain had fragmented into a number of kingdoms, and the largest and strongest was the kingdom of Powys. Now merely a Welsh county, in the late fifth and early sixth centuries Powys covered much of what is now the center of England and Wales. The likelihood is, therefore, that the historical Arthur came from, or at least ruled from, Powys, the heart of which is in what is now the English country of Shropshire. Indeed, one of the oldest surviving references to King Arthur, "The Song of Llywarch the Old," a war poem written around 650, actually refers to the kings of Powys at that time as Arthur's descendants.[3] So who had ruled the kingdom of Powys around 500 A.D.?

A tenth-century manuscript detailing the family trees of important Dark Age chieftains, cataloged as Harlein MS 3859 in the British Library, provides the answer. He was one Owain Ddantgwyn—Owain White Tooth. Nothing else was recorded concerning the reign of Owain Ddantgwyn. All the same, this discovery was at first disappointing. It appeared that the man who was presumably the most powerful British leader when Arthur is said to have lived was not called Arthur after all. However, closer examination revealed that the name Arthur may not have been a personal name but rather, like the name Merlin, a title. Many Dark Age kings were given honorary battle names—often the name of a real or imaginary beast that was thought to typify their qualities—and Owain Ddantgwyn was no exception. Gildas, writing a generation later, actually refers to him by the title "the Bear" and in the British language of the time, and preserved in modern Welsh, the word for "bear" was *arth*. This title Arth, the Bear, could well have been where the later name Arthur originated. Martin and I were convinced we had located the historical figure behind the Arthur legend, and we next set out to determine his capital.[4]

In the medieval tales, Arthur ruled from the magnificent city of Camelot. Unfortunately, the writers disagree on its location, and its whereabouts have long remained a mystery. However, wherever it was, the city would not have been called Camelot during the historical Arthur's time. The name Camelot was an invention of the twelfth-century French poet Chrétien de Troyes, and as the name of Arthur's city had been forgotten by Chrétien's time, the name Camelot was adopted in the popular imagination. No records survived of what Arthur's capital was really called, so where exactly was this mysterious city? If the historical Arthur ruled from the kingdom of Powys, it could well have been its capital: an old Roman city called Viriconium.

During the last years of Roman rule, Viriconium was one of the four largest and most important cities in Britain. The others were London, Lincoln, and York. Well before 500 A.D., these other three cities were overrun by the invaders, effectively making Viriconium Britain's capital. Unlike London, Lincoln, and York, which are thriving cities today, all that remains of Viriconium are its ruined walls in the quiet countryside outside the Shropshire village of Wroxeter. (Situated some five miles southeast of Shrewsbury, the site is now open to the public. A small museum displaying artifacts found during the excavations is open all year round.)

Over the last thirty five years, many archaeological excavations have taken place at Viriconium. They show that, unlike most other Roman towns that had been abandoned for more easily defended hilltop fortifications, the city was still a thriving, walled town in the late fifth century. The latest archaeological excavation at Viriconium took place in the 1990s and revealed that there had been a major rebuilding of the city during the mid- to late 400s. The nerve center of this new Viriconium was a massive winged building that must have been the palace of an extremely important warlord. As the work seems to have begun at the very time the Britons were defeating the Anglo-Saxons, it may well have been the seat of power for the British chieftain who led the Britons at the time—in other words, the historical Arthur. Arthur, however, does not appear to have become British ruler until around the year 500, which means the city was already refortified before his reign. In fact, it seems to have been refortified at exactly the time Ambrosius was leading the Britons.[5]

That this led me to consider the possibility that Ambrosius was buried in the same site where Owain Ddantgwyn had been laid to rest. "The Song of Llywarch the Old," the seventh-century war poem that mentions King Arthur, refers to the burial place of the kings of Powys.[6] This was a fortified hillock some twelve miles northwest of Viriconium called the Berth. In the Arthurian romances, Arthur is said to have been buried on the isle of Avalon, and the Berth was indeed an island during the Dark Ages.

The ruins of Glastonbury Abbey in Somerset, England. It was here that medieval monks first wrote the accounts of Merlin and his burial on the isle of Avalon.

This ancient bust found at Amesbury Abbey may be the oldest surviving statue of Ambrosius Aurelius.

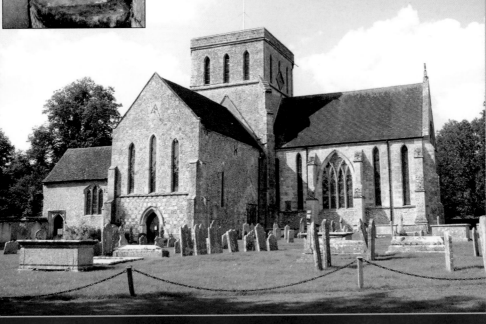

Amesbury Abbey in Wiltshire, England. Its ancient archives contained documentary evidence

The ruins of the Roman city of Viriconium, the fifth-century capital of Britain. Was this the historical Camelot?

Graham Phillips looking toward Silbury Hill in Wiltshire. Traditionally believed to be the burial place of Ambrosius Aurelius, this artificial mound was actually built more than 1,500 years before his time.

Graham Phillips examines a grave, said to be that of Guinevere, at White Ladies Priory in Shropshire. Was this legendary queen really the daughter of the historical Merlin?

Graham Phillips with the Excalibur replica made by Wilkinson Sword.

Detail of the Excalibur hilt, ...ociated with M

The ruins of Whittington Castle in Shropshire. According to the medieval romances, this was the Grail Castle to which Merlin retired after leaving Arthur's court.

The White Cliff at Hawkstone Park in Shropshire. It was in a labyrinth of caves at the summit

that Merlin was buried.

The sun sets over the lake in the forest of Broceliande, which in French folklore was the home of the Lady of the Lake.

The picturesque stream near the town of Paimpont in Brittany. According to the thirteenth-century *Estoire de Merlin*, it was here that Excalibur was forged.

Harvington Hall in Warwickshire, central England, the last known headquarters of the British Rosicrucians in the early seventeenth century.

Guy's Cliff Chapel near the town of Warwick, the meeting place for the School of Night in the 1590s.

The Philosopher's Egg from Michael Maier's *Atalanta Fugiens,* published in 1617. Does this illustration hold a clue to an ancient and secret bloodline?

The Monad from Michael Maier's *Atalanta Fugiens.* Is this enigmatic illustration a cryptic code revealing the whereabouts of Merlin's tomb?

The Chestertown Windmill in Warwickshire, built in 1632 by the architect and Freemason Inigo Jones. What was its link to the mysterious tower in Newport, Rhode Island?

Laurel Hall in Cuttingsville, Vermont. Built by the wealthy Freemason John Bowman in the 1880s, its purpose has remained a mystery for more than a hundred years.

Graham Russell and his wife Jodi examine the Venus fountain on the grounds of Laurel Hall.

Cuttingsville cemetery, landscaped by John Bowman in the 1880s with strange statues and gravestones. Was it all an elaborate code to reveal the secret of Merlin's grave? (Photograph by Jodi Russell)

The Bowman family mausoleum in Cuttingsville cemetery, boarded up after being vandalized. (Photograph by Jodi Russell)

Megalithic monuments at Avebury in Wiltshire, England. Although these standing stones were erected more than 3,000 years ago, the Celtic Druids used them for ritual purposes in the fifth century A.D.

The enigmatic standing stones on Manana Island off the coast of Maine. Do these monuments, remarkably similar to British megaliths, mark the grave of the historical Merlin?

Graham Phillips stands on one of the dozens of unexplained stone structures in woodland near Rochester, Vermont.

One of the Cuttingsville gravestones inscribed with the Rosicrucian symbol for the new star that appeared in 1604.

Hodnet Hall in the village of Hodnet near Shrewsbury. This was the ancestral home of the Vernon family, direct descendants of the historical Merlin.

Coughton Court near Stratford-upon-Avon. It was here that Sir Walter Raleigh was staying when Shakespeare mysteriously died.

Princess Elizabeth as a child.
(Contemporary portrait by
an unknown artist, now at
Coombe Abbey)

Coombe Abbey in Warwickshire, the setting for Princess Elizabeth's Alchemical Wedding in 1613.

Although the surrounding land has now been drained, the Berth at the time stood in the middle of a lake.

However, although it may well have been the burial site of Owain Ddantgwyn, the historical King Arthur, it did not fit with the supposed location of Merlin's final resting place. Crossing the lake to reach the island on which the Berth was situated could hardly be described as a sea voyage. In fact, in ancient times a stone causeway crossed the lake and a boat journey of a mere one hundred yards would not have been necessary.[7] The Berth might have given rise to the legends of Arthur being buried on Avalon, but it could not have been the Avalon that the romancers had in mind for Merlin's final resting place. Besides which, unlike Owain Ddantgwyn, Ambrosius was not one of the Powys kings and so is unlikely to have been buried in their family cemetery.

I had to return to the medieval Arthurian Romances. Although many of the stories end with Merlin sailing away to the isle of Avalon, no details are given as to where that actually is. The next best thing I could do, therefore, was to ascertain where Merlin was thought to have ended his life in Britain before he sailed away. Perhaps there would be clues to be found there. Once again, however, this is a mystery, as it is said to be at the Grail Castle—the secret location where the Holy Grail was believed to have been kept.

The Arthurian romances portray the Holy Grail as the cup used by Jesus at the Last Supper, which was later used to collect a few drops of Christ's sacred blood during the Crucifixion. Said to possess miraculous healing properties, it had been brought to Britain by Christ's disciple Joseph of Arimathea and left under the guardianship of a family who lived in a secret castle. Four and a half centuries later, the Grail is needed to cure King Arthur, and Merlin sends the Knights of the Round Table on a quest to discover its mysterious hiding place. It is eventually found by the knight Sir Perceval, and when Arthur is restored to health, Merlin returns the Grail to its secret castle and retires there with Perceval, who becomes the guardian of the holy relic. This mysterious Grail Castle is where Merlin ends his life in Britain before sailing off to Avalon. Although the story is clearly a fictional account, I hoped that it might reflect some earlier, historical account of where Ambrosius spent his later days in Britain. So where was the Grail Castle thought to be?

The Arthurian stories that refer to the Grail Castle are collectively called the Grail romances, and most of them refer to Merlin retiring to the Grail Castle after he leaves King Arthur's court for the last time. Although none of these says specifically where the Grail Castle is, five of them give important clues. In order of composition, they are as follows:

1. The first of the Grail Romances was a poem called *Le Conte del Graal* (The Tale of the Grail), written by the French poet Chrétien de Troyes around the year 1190. Introducing the work, Chrétien says he obtained the story from a book given to him by his patron Count Philip of Flanders.[8]

2. Chrétien's work was followed in approximately 1195 by another French poem, this time by an anonymous author. Known as the *First Continuation*, it is so named because it was the author's attempt to continue the story where Chrétien left off. Unlike Chrétien, however, the author provides no information regarding his source.[9]

3. Circa the year 1200, a Grail Romance in prose was written by another anonymous author. This is now known as the *Didot Perceval*, after a Parisian manuscript collector named Firmin Didot, who discovered the copy of the story in the eighteenth century. Although the author fails to reveal his immediate source, he claimed that it came from a copy of an original story by a monk named Blayse who lived in the sixth century.[10]

4. In or about 1220, another Grail Romance appeared called *Perlesvaus* (Perceval Disinherited). Although written in French, it was penned by an anonymous English author who claimed to have translated the story from an earlier Latin work, which he failed to identify.[11]

5. In addition to the medieval Grail romances written in French, there is a Welsh Grail story, which may have been composed before the others. Called *Peredur* (the Welsh version of the name Perceval), it now survives in *The Red Book of Hergest*. It was certainly written by the mid-thirteenth century, as parts of it are found in fragments in manuscripts dating from this time, but linguistic analysis suggests that it dates from as early as 1150.[12]

All of these are versions of the same story concerning Sir Perceval searching for the Holy Grail and finding it at the mysterious Grail Castle. The whereabouts of this enigmatic place has long been a mystery to literary historians, as the Romances do not employ modern names for the location. However, they agree on what it appears to have been called at the time of writing, which was approximately the year 1200. Chrétien refers to the Grail Castle simply as the White Castle, but offers no clues to its whereabouts. However, the *Didot Perceval* refers to it as the "the White Castle in the White Town." *Perlesvaus* also locates the castle in the White Town. The *First Continuation* goes one stage further, saying the White Town is in a region it calls "the White Land," as does *Peredur*, which adds a further detail by saying that the White Land is an area situated in the "Old Marches."

Did this White Town really exist or was it just a literary invention? It so happens that less than twenty miles to the northwest of the ruins of Viriconium, the likely location for Ambrosius's capital, there was a village called the White Town. In fact, it is now called Whittington, from the early English meaning literally "white town." This small community of just a few hundred people, with a couple of stores, a pub, and a church, also has a castle—a castle known locally as the White Castle because it was built from light-colored stone.

Moreover, during the Dark Ages, Whittington had been part of the kingdom of Gwynedd, which in Brythonic meant "white land." Not only is Whittington Castle a white castle, in a white town, in a white land, but it is also in an area once known as the Old Marches (the marshy northern border between England and Wales in medieval times), precisely the term used in the *Peredur* account as the location of the White Town. The question of the historical or mythological content of the Grail romances aside, there can be no doubt that Whittington Castle was the location that the medieval authors had in mind for the setting of the Grail Castle, to which Merlin retires after leaving Arthur's court.

Remarkably, there was also a separate Grail legend attached to Whittington Castle. During the late twelfth century, around the time that the Grail Romances were being composed, the owner of Whittington Castle was an English baron named Fulke Fitz Warine. Like King Arthur of many years before, Fulke became something of a hero when he rebelled against the unpopular king John, and many romantic stories were written about him.

One of these, a romance called *Fulke le Fitz Waryn*, composed circa 1260, associated him with the Holy Grail, which was said to have been kept in his castle chapel.[13] Although the most popular stories of the Grail depicted the relic as the cup of the Last Supper, some portrayed it as the cup of Mary Magdalene. The legend went that Jesus's follower Mary Magdalene used an ointment jar to collect a few drops of Jesus's blood after the Crucifixion and that it was this that became the Grail sought by Arthur and his knights. Known as the Marian Chalice, or Chalice of Magdalene, it was this relic that supposedly was kept at Whittington Castle.

In fact, Fulke's descendants possessed a cup that they claimed was the Chalice of Magdalene until the nineteenth century, when one of them, Thomas Wright, a Shropshire historian, decided to hide it when he had no heir to pass it on to. Fascinatingly, Wright left a series of elaborate clues to reveal the whereabouts of the cup, including a stained-glass window he designed and installed in the parish church of Hodnet, a Shropshire village close to his home. The window scene, which still survives, depicts a figure that appears to be Mary Magdalene holding a chalice with the image of an eagle above her head. In the 1920s, the cup was discovered, hidden in an eagle statue in a cave at nearby Hawkstone Park. The cup, which is about two inches high, shaped like an eggcup, and made of onyx, has been identified as a first-century Roman ointment jar, just as the Marian Chalice is said to have been. Although this was no proof that the artifact actually belonged to Mary Magdalene, the existence of the relic showed that Whittington Castle was firmly associated with the legend of the Holy Grail.[14]

I had already investigated the story of the Marian Chalice for my book *The Chalice of Magdalene*, first published in 1995, and knew of Whittington Castle's connection with the Grail legend. However, rereading the *Fulke le Fitz Waryn* romance, I discovered that it too associated the castle with Merlin. The author, quoting an earlier unidentified source, related that Merlin had spent time at Whittington, where he made a prediction concerning a hero who would one day oppose tyranny from his stronghold at Whittington Castle. The author of the romance saw this as a prediction relating to Fulke Fitz Warine. Whether or not Merlin's prophecy related to Fulke, the fact remains that there was a separate tradition to the Arthurian Grail Romances, one that specifically associated Merlin with the area.

To my mind, there was no doubt that Whittington was where Merlin retired after leaving Arthur's court. Although the present castle dates only from the twelfth century, it was built on the earthen ramparts of an earlier fortification that has been dated to the immediate post-Roman period. This earlier fort was here during Ambrosius's time, so the stories associating Merlin with the castle could have been based on much earlier accounts relating to this original defensive structure.

The problem was that this was no help in locating where Avalon was thought to be. The nearest sea was some distance away: Whittington was thirty miles from the north coast and almost fifty miles from the west coast of Wales. However, the *Fulke le Fitz Waryn* romance indirectly gave me the vital clue I was looking for. Although the story was based on the historical life of Fulke Fitz Warine, it also romanticized his exploits and embellished them with clearly mythological events.

In fact, the author portrayed his hero Fulke as a medieval successor to King Arthur and incorporated Arthurian themes into Fulke's life story. One such theme concerned a voyage that Fulke had supposedly made to mysterious islands far across the western sea. The story was obviously fictional as it included sea monsters, mermaids, and all sorts of fantastic adventures. Nevertheless, the author made reference to Fulke following in Merlin's footsteps. In fact, the hero was depicted trying to rediscover the fabled isle of Avalon. Although the story was of no direct help in locating where Avalon was thought to be, it made reference to Merlin under a variation of his name that I had not come across before. This was Maelduin, the Irish version of his name.

When I next visited the National Library of Wales in Aberystwyth, I made a search for Merlin under the name Maelduin and was astonished by what I found. An old Irish saga written in the eighth century was called the *Immram Curaig Maelduin Inso*—"The Voyage of Merlin's Boat." In the Arthurian Romances and early Welsh poetry, there were only passing references to Merlin's final voyage, but this Irish tale gave the whole story in remarkable detail. I had not considered researching Irish legends for evidence concerning Merlin, but here was an Irish saga that revealed exactly where Merlin was believed to have gone. It was the last place on earth I thought it would turn out to be.

11

THE VOYAGE OF MAELDUIN

In Irish literature, Merlin is portrayed as visiting Ireland in the footsteps of St. Patrick, the patron saint of the country. Patrick was a historical figure whose father had been an important British citizen during the last days of Roman rule—the equivalent to mayor of a town somewhere on the western coast of what is now northern England. When he was just sixteen, Patrick was kidnapped by Irish raiders and taken to Ireland, where he lived as a slave for six years. He managed to escape, eventually, and returned to Britain to find that Roman rule had ended.

Soon after, he met Germanus, the bishop of Auxerre, who had been sent to Britain as an envoy of the pope. Under his influence, Patrick became a priest. In 433 Patrick decided to return to Ireland, where he spent the next sixty years successfully converting the Irish to Christianity. For this reason, by the year 500 there were close ties between Britain and Ireland, and the Arthurian romances depict both Arthur and Merlin traveling to Ireland on a number of occasions. According to *The Voyage of Maelduin's Boat,* it was from Ireland that Merlin ultimately set off on his final voyage.

As in the Arthurian Romances, the Irish stories seem to have confused history and mythology regarding Merlin. Like Geoffrey of Monmouth's

Merlin, the Irish Maelduin was depicted as the son of a princess who became a nun; he is raised in secret and his father's true identity is kept secret. Also, like the Merlin of the Arthurian romances, Maelduin is the son of a supernatural being, although his father is identified as being a legendary Irish figure. This was a mythical king named Ailill, a demigod who traveled freely between the world of the living and the mystical Otherworld—the island realms of the gods and the home of the divine race, the Tuatha De Dannan. In *The Voyage of Maelduin's Boat*, Maelduin decides to set sail for the Otherworld himself, in search of his father's spirit.

A number of versions of the story still survive; the oldest exists in an eleventh-century manuscript known as the *Lebor na h Uidre* (Book of the Dun Cow) in the library of Trinity College, Dublin, although linguistic analysis has dated its original time of composition to the early to mid-eighth century.[1] As would be expected with an Irish tale concerning Merlin, the story is embellished with elements from Celtic mythology—in particular, mythical traditions concerning the god-hero Lugh (the same figure with whom the Arthurian Merlin and the historical Ambrosius were associated). Although the anonymous author asserts that the voyage was a historical event, on my first reading of the account it seemed purely fictional; the events appeared to be too fantastic to have anything to do with history.

In *The Voyage of Maelduin's Boat*, Maelduin and a number of companions set sail in a single vessel on a long and perilous voyage to the islands of the Otherworld. The first lands they reach are a group of islands, one of which is inhabited by giant sheep. Another is so full of birds that they cannot land. Deciding that these are not the islands of the Otherworld, Maelduin's party sail on into what is described as an endless ocean. Here they encounter many strange lands, the first of which is inhabited by a race of giant blacksmiths.

> Now when they had been voyaging for a long time, they saw an island far off. As they approached it they heard a great noise, as if it were the sound of a gigantic forge with a giant smith hammering iron upon an anvil . . . Then the smith came out of the forge, holding in his tongs a huge load of red-hot iron which he hurled toward the boat;

and the sea boiled and they fled from the island and out far into the great ocean.[2]

After many months on the open sea, they again sight land, but this time it is a cold and desolate place where nothing grows: "And they saw no living thing or beasts among that craggy land, only stony gravel and green sand."[3] For weeks they find nothing that is habitable; the only place they come across is a curious floating island.

Thereafter they voyaged until they saw a great column that was bright like silver. It had four sides, the width of each being two full oar-strokes of their boat . . . Completely barren and with no earth upon it, there was endless ocean and nothing living thereabouts. It towered above them and its base was far below; how far, they could not see.[4]

Subsequent to several more months of encounters with other strange marvels, they reach a forested island having miles upon miles of beaches of pure white sand. Here they replenish their food and fresh water before sailing on until finally discovering the islands of the Otherworld. On one of these islands they find a hermit who tells the travelers that he too had come there from Ireland many years before. His companions are now dead and he lives alone, guarding a stone upon which is inscribed a sacred text. The voyage has taken the mariners well over a year and, homesick, they decide to return to Ireland.

In some versions of the tale, Maelduin goes with them; in others, he remains on the hermit's island, never to be seen again. *The Voyage of Maelduin's Boat* does not reveal which of the Otherworld islands this was thought to have been, but another Irish tale of about the same age identifies it. This is the *Imram Brain*—"The Voyage of Bran"—in which a hero called Bran departs Ireland on a similar journey.[5]

Written around 750, *The Voyage of Bran* is considered by most literary historians to be a reworking of the Maelduin tale. Bran was a mythical hero, probably taken from an original Celtic god, whom the Arthurian Romances depict as the Grail guardian: Perceval takes over the Grail guardianship at the White Castle from Bran.

The Voyage of Bran is similar to *The Voyage of Maelduin's Boat*, except that it is Bran who leads the expedition, rather than Maelduin. Another difference is that the island where Bran and his mariners end up is actually identified—it is the home of the Celtic sea god Manannan. As discussed in chapter 6, this is the Manannan Island (named after the deity), where the god-hero Lugh, according to the Irish Invasion Cycle, lived as a youth before traveling on to Avallach.

The word *avlach*, whence the name Avallach was derived, means "of apples": Among other things, Avallach was the god of orchards and apple trees. As established earlier in this book, as well as historically, Avalon—the place—is associated with apple orchards.

Given that *The Voyage of Bran* also refers to Manannan Island as Emain Ablach (which sounds like Avallach), it was very possibly the case that the Gaelic Avallach became corrupted into the place-name Avalon. This was obviously the mistake that had been made by the authors of the early Welsh Arthurian tales, as they refer to Avalon as Ynys Afal, Apple Island. Geoffrey of Monmouth also appears to have made the same error, for in his *Life of Merlin* he actually calls Avalon *Insula Pomorum*, Latin for "Isle of Apples."

In contemporary Gaelic the word *emain* refers to a fort or stronghold and the word *ablach* means a carcass or corpse. *Emain Ablach*, therefore, appears to have meant something like the Place of the Dead.

In any event, and notwithstanding this confusion over Avallach versus Avalon, the island where Merlin ended up was thought not to be Avalon itself. This supposition is actually revealed by a verse in *The Voyage of Maelduin's Boat*. Early on in the voyage Maelduin falls asleep and dreams of Avalon, with a city built from crystal, silver, marble, and bronze. In the dream, Maelduin and his companions arrive at the island to be greeted by its queen, a beautiful giant woman:

> She wore a white mantle, with a circlet of gold in her hair . . . Two sandals she wore on her feet and a silken smock she wore next to her white skin, tied with a brooch . . .[6]

This was certainly not the island where Maelduin ultimately decides to remain: Apart from the hermit, it said to be quiet and uninhabited; there is no crystal city and no giant queen.

None of this, however, appeared to be of much help in determining where the historical Merlin's tomb was. *The Voyage of Maelduin's Boat* seemed to be a mythological account. Floating islands of silver, giant smiths hurling molten metal, islands with green and white sands: It all sounded make-believe. That is, until I was diverted to another avenue of research, after rereading the verse concerning the hermit's island. In it, the hermit identifies himself:

> I am the fifteenth man who accompanied Brenainn of Birr. We voy-
> aged into the ocean and came to this island. All others have died and
> I am left alone.[7]

Brenainn is the Irish name for a Dark Age Christian missionary known as Saint Brendan, a man who is also said to have made a voyage to some far away islands. Unlike Merlin, whom most historians regard as a mythical character, Brendan was a known historical figure. He was an Irish bishop born around A.D. 484. After founding a monastery at Birr in County Offaly, southern Ireland, Brendan spent his life sailing around northwest Europe spreading the Christian faith until his death in 577.

Sometime around 510, while still a young man in his mid-twenties, Brendan is said to have gone on his longest voyage, during which he founded a small colony on a mysterious island somewhere in the west. In the Middle Ages this was thought to have been a real island and medieval maps often showed Saint Brendan's Isle at various locations to the west of Ireland, far out in the Atlantic Ocean. The hermit's words in *The Voyage of Maelduin's Boat* clearly imply that Manannan Island and Saint Brendan's Isle are one and the same.

If I could identify Saint Brendan's Isle, I would presumably have found the island where Merlin was thought to have been buried. The problem, however, was that the precise location of Saint Brendan's Isle had been long forgotten by the Middle Ages. Additionally, although the story of Maelduin's boat was believed to have been a historical event, Brendan's expedition seemed just as fanciful as Maelduin's voyage, which threw its veracity into question. Coupled with this, and upon closer reading, both accounts appeared be one and the same event.

By the Middle Ages, the story of Brendan's voyage had been made famous throughout Europe by an anonymous Latin account entitled the *Navigatio Sancti Brendani*—"The Voyage of Saint Brendan." The oldest surviving copy dates from the tenth century, but linguists date the original to around the mid-eighth century.[8] I needed only to start reading a copy of *The Voyage of Saint Brendan* to realize that it bore a remarkable similarity to *The Voyage of Maelduin's Boat*.

After setting sail, the first group of islands Brendan's crew encounters are referred to as "the islands of sheep," as they were full of sheep "the size of an ox." One of the islands is called "the paradise of birds." In the *Maelduin* story, the first island Maelduin visits is inhabited by giant sheep and another of the same group of islands is covered by a vast number of birds. Sometime later, Brendan and his crew come to an island that sounds very like the land of the smiths described in the *Maelduin* tale, the only difference being that the smiths are described as demons.

> They saw far away in the north a dark country full of stench and of smoke; and as the ship drew near it they heard great blowing and blasting of bellows, and a noise of blows and a noise like thunder . . . And with that there came demons thick about them on every side, with tongs and with fiery hammers, and followed after them till it seemed all the sea to be one fire . . . And then the demons began to roar and cry, and threw their tongs at them and their hammers . . . Then the south wind drove them farther again into the north, and they saw a mount all on fire and like as if walled in with fire, and clouds upon it, and if there was much smoke in that other place.[9]

After this, Brendan's crew encounters a number of strange, floating islands described as "crystal pillars," which again sounds remarkably similar to the floating island of silver in the *Maelduin* tale. Sailing on past barren lands "with rivers of ice," Brendan eventually discovers what the author of the account refers to as the "Isles of the Blessed," evidently the same islands as the islands of the Otherworld in the *Maelduin* tale. Some of the crew decide to stay behind on one of these islands while Brendan and others return to Ireland; one of those who remains, it seems, was the hermit in the *Maelduin* story.

Both stories appear to be different versions of the same account, although literary scholars did not seem to have fully recognized this. Although the voyages are portrayed as separate ones—one of Brendan's crew is already on Manannan Island when Maelduin lands there—the descriptive similarity of the two accounts, with marvels being described in almost identical terms, suggested to me that both came from one original source.

Literary scholars had concluded that *The Voyage of Bran* was derived from the same source as *The Voyage of Maelduin's Boat;* surely this also applied to *The Voyage of Saint Brendan.* The surviving versions of all three tales date from approximately the same period, the mid-700s, and they each refer to an event that supposedly took place two centuries earlier, around 510 A.D. This is when the twenty-six-year-old Brendan is said to have made the voyage; Arthur's reign began (allegedly around 500 A.D.); and the Arthurian romances depict the Grail guardian Bran as bequeathing his guardianship to Sir Perceval (approximately one decade later). This is also said to be when the aging Merlin finally sails off to his mysterious island.

Either three almost identical stories were composed simultaneously, about an event that was believed to have occurred at almost *exactly the same time*—which seems highly unlikely—or three separate accounts were written, *over time*, concerning the same voyage. The latter scenario is far more probable: The stories all concern the same event, with their respective authors concentrating on separate members of the expedition and describing the events from a different perspective.

The *Brendan* account tells the story from a Christian perception: for example, referring to the fiery land as the "borders of Hell" and its fire-hurtling inhabitants as demons, while in the *Maelduin* and *Bran* accounts, the story is told from a traditional Celtic viewpoint. In *Maelduin* and *Bran*, the same island is the home of the smith-god Goibniu, who makes weapons for the Tuatha De Dannan, the demigods of the Otherworld.

In any event, on the face of it, all three stories appeared to be purely fanciful tales, bearing no relationship to reality—or did they?

Unlike Merlin and Bran, whom most historians regarded as mythical characters, Brendan was a known historical figure and, for many years, some scholars speculated that *The Voyage of Saint Brendan* was an embellished, but nonetheless real, account of a historical voyage. One of these scholars was the British exploration historian Tim Severin. In the 1970s, Severin theorized that the seemingly fanciful accounts of the marvels said to have been witnessed during Brendan's voyage were early interpretations of natural phenomena previously unknown to the sailors. In fact, he suggested that such descriptions in *The Voyage of Saint Brendan* could have been made only by someone who had sailed far into the North Atlantic.

Tim Severin became convinced that Brendan's voyage was a real event when he realized that the description of the first group of islands in the account was remarkably similar to what are, in fact, the Faroe Isles. The Faroes consist of eighteen islands lying approximately 175 miles northwest of Scotland and some four hundred miles due north of Ireland. Now belonging to Denmark, the islands were known to the Dark Age Vikings of Scandinavia, who called them the Føroyar, from which the name Faroe comes. Føroyar means literally "islands of sheep" and, according to *The Voyage of Saint Brendan*, the first islands its mariners encountered were full of sheep. The account actually calls them "the islands of sheep."

There are still sheep on the Faroes today, descendants of an ancient variety that existed there, in isolation, for hundreds of years. Surviving skeletons of this ancient variety reveal that they were much larger than the common sheep of today. This might explain the description in the Brendan account of *giant* sheep. Furthermore, the *Brendan* account calls one of the islands "the paradise of birds," and one of the Faroe Isles, the isle of Mykines, still supports one of the densest colonies of seabirds in the North Atlantic.

If Brendan visited the Faroes, Severin reasoned, he was heading north; and if he continued on a northerly course, he would need to sail only another 250 miles to the northeast before reaching the coast of Iceland. Another description in *The Voyage of Brendan*, indeed, seems to tally with Iceland. A few weeks after leaving the islands of sheep, Brendan is said to have reached "a dark country full of stench and smoke." Iceland is an island with many active volcanoes and one of them, Severin suggested, might have been erupting when Brendan arrived. The sound of "a great blowing and blasting of bellows"; "a noise of blows and a noise like thunder"; "a mount all on fire"—what else could this be but an erupting volcano? There are no volcanoes in Ireland, or in any other part of northwest Europe that Brendan is known historically to have visited. Being unfamiliar with volcanic eruptions, it is understandable that the mariners would equate a volcano ejecting molten rocks with demons hurling fire into the sea.

And yet some scholars believe that Brendan's voyage went even farther than the Faroe Islands. The huge floating crystals described in *The Voyage of Brendan* might refer to icebergs of the North Atlantic, and the land of rivers of ice might be a description of Greenland and its immense glaciers. Greenland is less than three hundred miles across the Denmark Strait from Iceland, so such a voyage was possible.

However, Tim Severin speculated that Brendan traveled even farther than this. During their visit to the Isles of the Blessed, Brendan and his crew are said to have discovered a place called the Land of Promise. Unlike the fiery land that may or may not have been Iceland, and the ice-covered wasteland that may or may not have been Greenland, the Land of Promise is depicted as a lush and welcoming place:

> The trees were full of fruit on every bough, and the apples were as ripe as at harvest time. And they were going about that country through forty days and could see no end to it . . . and the air neither hot nor cold but always in the one way, and the delight that they found there could never be told. Then they came to a river that they could not cross but they could see beyond it the country that had no bounds to its beauty.[10]

This huge fertile land, Severin suggested, might have been none other than the mainland of North America!

For years it was thought that Christopher Columbus, in the late fifteenth century, was the first European to discover America. Then Viking remains, dating from approximately 1000 A.D., were found in Canada. When Severin aired his theory that an Irish bishop visited North America almost five hundred years before even the Vikings, he was met with intense skepticism. It was impossible, historians protested: The kind of boats the Irish had in the sixth century were mere fishing vessels used for coastal voyages, capable of sailing only to Britain or mainland Europe at best. There is no way that they could have made it all the way across the Atlantic. However, after examining both written and archaeological evidence from sixth-century Ireland, Severin concluded that such vessels *could* have made the journey. Yet rather than argue his case academically, Severin decided to prove it—by undertaking a similar journey himself.

Drawing upon textual and archaeological evidence from sixth-century Ireland, Severin reconstructed an original Irish *carrach:* the type of vessel *The Voyage of Brendan* describes. It was thirty-six feet long and eight feet wide, made from ox hides and oak bark stretched across a wooden frame. This twin-masted boat could either be rowed or sailed. In May 1976, with a crew of four, Severin set sail from the west coast of Ireland; by June, they had reached the Faroes and by July were in Iceland. Not knowing how long their attempt to sail around Greenland and on to Canada would actually take, Severin and his crew decided to postpone the all-important, last leg of the crossing until the following spring.

They finally set off in May 1977 and, against all of their expectations, arrived in Newfoundland, Canada, almost two thousand miles away, in less than two months! Severin could easily have made the entire Atlantic crossing, from Ireland to Canada, in less than four months. It took courage and a lot of hard work, but Severin proved that crossing the Atlantic in a sixth-century Irish boat, by island-hopping through the Arctic in summertime, was far easier and quicker than anyone had ever imagined it could be.[11] Tim Severin may not have known it, but he had proved not only that Brendan's voyage was possible, but that Merlin's voyage was possible too.

The Voyage of Saint Brendan and *The Voyage of Maelduin's Boat* were so similar that they had to be different accounts of the same voyage. Although in the *Maelduin* story the hermit, one of Brendan's crew, is already on Manannan Island, this was due probably to some confusion that arose between the time the event apparently occurred in the early sixth century and the writing of the accounts two hundred years later. It was speculation, but it seemed more likely that Brendan and Merlin, contemporaries, had gone on the same voyage. It was not only the descriptions of the Faroes, Iceland, and icebergs that were virtually identical in the two texts, but *The Voyage of Maelduin's Boat* also gives a description of what had to have been the coast of Greenland.

I had always wondered how this vast island got its name: It is a cold,

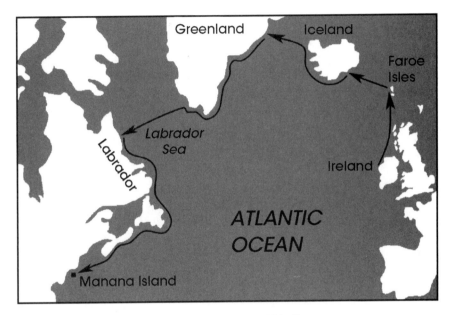

Map 4. The voyage of Merlin

barren place, and anything but green. It had, in fact, been named after the exotic green sands that stretch along its eastern coast, which is dominated by the Kronprins Fredrik Bjerge mountain range. (The vivid green is caused by a rare variety of sandstone that consists of glauconite, potash, and phosphate of lime.) After visiting the island of the smiths, *The Voyage of Maelduin's Boat* describes it as a craggy land, with beaches of stony gravel and *green sand*.[12]

One criticism of Tim Severin's theory was that although Brendan may have made it to Greenland, and it was *possible* to have made it to Canada, there is nothing in *The Voyage of Saint Brendan* that specifically described anything that could uniquely be identified as on the North American mainland. In *The Voyage of Maelduin's Boat*, however, there is. The account relates that, after passing the land with green sand and after the encounter with what seem to be icebergs, Maelduin's crew eventually reached a forested country with beaches consisting of mile upon mile of pure white sand.[13] As unlikely as such a place might sound, there is a stretch of the North American coastline that matches this description exactly. A magnificent white sandy beach known as the Porcupine Strand stretches for

155

more than twenty miles along the coast of Labrador on mainland Canada, directly across the Labrador Sea from Greenland. (The unusual color of the sand is derived from quartz deposits left by retreating glaciers at the end of the last ice age.) This unique coastline, set against a backdrop of the forested Mealy Mountains, has to have been the place described in the tale.

As incredible as it sounds, a group of intrepid explorers had made a transatlantic voyage from Ireland to North America by island-hopping through the Arctic in the early sixth century. And if *The Voyage of Maelduin's Boat* is to be believed, Merlin was one of them. Some of these early explorers returned to tell the tale and others died, but Merlin is said to have remained behind on one of the islands that had been discovered in this new land. The crew had been searching for the mystic islands of the Otherworld, but instead, it seems, they had discovered the islands of northeastern America.

Where, then, was the island on which Merlin was supposedly buried? Where exactly was Saint Brendan's Isle, the island where Brendan is said to have founded a small colony, also thought to have been Manannan Island, the island home of the Celtic sea god?

The Voyage of Maelduin's Boat depicts the expedition sailing south from the land of the white sands before discovering the islands of the Otherworld, while *The Voyage of Saint Brendan* depicts the Isles of the Blessed as having a much warmer climate than that of Labrador. If these accounts are accurate, it seems that the mariners had to have crossed the Gulf of St. Lawrence to New Brunswick or Nova Scotia. In fact, reference to apples being found in the Land of Promise in the *Brendan* account suggests that the voyagers may have traveled as far south as the coast of Virginia in what is now the United States. (The most difficult part of their journey would have been getting to Canada; after that, there is no telling how far down the American coast they might have gone.)

The only indigenous American variety of apple large enough to have been those described in the Brendan account is *Malus angustifolia*. Commonly known as the southern crab apple, it grows no farther north than Virginia.

Since Tim Severin demonstrated that the journey to North America could have been made in the sixth century, various researchers have found what they believe to be early Irish inscriptions in the northeastern United States. Markings inscribed on rocks found in Virginia and New England were identified as Ogham script, the form of writing developed in Ireland by the fifth century[14] (as discussed in chapter 5). However, although initially considered to have been made by members of the Brendan expedition, or by other Irish explorers who followed them, the date of these inscriptions has not been reliably determined. Without attendant human remains that could be carbon-dated, or datable historical artifacts, there is no way of knowing exactly *when* the inscriptions were made. They might have been made by Dark Age Irish explorers or, by the same token, they might have been made by Irish settlers in the seventeenth century. They could even be modern fakes.

In any event, a number of such inscriptions written in the old Celtic script have been found at the sites of early Irish colonies in Maryland and Massachusetts. Ironically, archaeological proof that pre-Viking transatlantic voyages had been made was to come not from America, but rather from Europe. Remarkably, Native Americans had actually crossed the Atlantic, traveling from North America to mainland Europe, well before the Celts had.

The indigenous population of New England were the Beothuk, who inhabited the area for thousands of years before the Europeans arrived. Originating in Maine, they were a fishing culture who produced a surprisingly seaworthy catamaran capable of carrying up to fifty people. With these boats, the Beothuk not only hunted whales, but they also migrated up the Atlantic coast, settling in Newfoundland, Labrador, and Baffin Island. By 1500 B.C., they had crossed the Davis Strait into Greenland. From here the Beothuk sailed around the southern tip of Greenland and crossed the Denmark Strait into Iceland.

Archaeological excavations at Akranes and Ingolfshofoi in Iceland have unearthed ancient Beothuk burial sites dating from as early as 1000 B.C. and as late as the seventh century A.D. After this time, the climate suddenly became much colder, putting an end to such distant voyages. If all this is not surprising enough, there is evidence that the Beothuk actually made it to Norway! The British who first encountered these Indians in America in the sixteenth century describe how they used red ocher, an earthen dye, to adorn their bodies for burial and before going into battle. A number of archaeological sites in Norway, dating from the first to third centuries A.D., have uncovered quantities of red ocher, which scientific analysis has determined could have come only from New England. Although no identifiable Beothuk bones have yet been found, the inference is that these Native Americans were in mainland Europe centuries before any European set foot in America.[15]

So transatlantic crossings were possible in the early sixth century; and the detail in the *Brendan*, *Bran*, and *Maelduin* accounts—probably accounts of the same voyage—could not have been told unless at least one Irish expedition had made such a voyage around the year 510. *The Voyage of Maelduin's Boat* indicates that Merlin departed on such a voyage, and remained on an island *The Voyage of Bran* identified as one believed to have been the home of the sea god Manannan. This appeared to be one and the same island that the medieval writers referred to as Saint Brendan's Isle. I never in my wildest dreams imagined that the search for the historical Merlin would lead me to seriously consider the possibility that he was buried somewhere in America. However, if he really was buried on an island off the coast of North America, this actually made matters worse regarding my search for his tomb. There were hundreds of possible islands off the coast of Britain, but there were thousands off the coast of northeastern America! Judging by the descriptions in the old Irish accounts, the island in question could have been any island along a stretch of coastline more than two thousand miles long.

Spending time at the National Library of Wales, searching through all these ancient sources, I had almost forgotten why I was looking for Merlin's tomb. If Glynn's theory was right, then the Rosicrucians claimed to have found it in 1604. Just before I left the library, I made a search of its database to see if there was record of a European presence in northeastern America at that time. I was astonished by the result. In 1604, an English ship had been sailing the coast of New England. Not only was it charting newly discovered islands, but the leader of the expedition was a high-profile member of the Rosicrucians as well!

12

MEONIA

One place associated with navigation more than any other in the world is Greenwich in southeast London. Here, a brass line set into the courtyard of the Royal Observatory building marks the Greenwich meridian—longitude zero degrees. Unlike latitude zero—the equator—the Greenwich meridian is an imaginary line that could have been drawn anywhere on the globe; it is *here* because this is where the problem of determining longitude was solved.

If you know your latitude and longitude, you know your exact whereabouts on the face of the earth. Calculating latitude by using the sun and the stars is relatively simple; establishing longitude is far more difficult. In the early centuries of transatlantic voyages, ship after ship was lost at sea for lack of a way to determine longitude. Accordingly, in 1675 the English king Charles II established the Royal Observatory at Greenwich as an institute to study the means of fixing longitude, and fifty years later it was finally achieved. Longitude is possible to calculate by the heavenly bodies if one compares the time on two clocks, one adjusted to keep showing local time and another remaining unaltered.

The problem facing early sailors was that clocks were far from accurate, especially those that needed to keep running while aboard ships that were constantly jostled on the high seas. Motivated by a financial reward offered by the Royal Observatory, an Englishman named John Harrison finally managed to devise such a timepiece in 1735. From then on, the ships of the British navy always kept one clock according to the time at Greenwich (which became known as Greenwich Mean Time, or GMT), and the longitude of Greenwich became longitude zero. The rest of the world followed suit in 1874 when, at a conference held in Washington, D.C., the international community agreed to standardize the Greenwich meridian as zero longitude for all maps of the world.

Because of its importance in the history of seafaring, in 1934 the Royal Observatory and a number of nearby buildings became Britain's National Maritime Museum. The observatory building itself is now a museum of astronomy, and the museum's historical collections are housed in the adjacent Queen's House, a seventeenth-century mansion that had been built for the English queen Anne, wife of James I. The Queen's House and its two flanking wings currently hold one of the world's most important collections concerning the history of cartography, shipbuilding, and nautical science. The Queen's House also has exhaustive records of British and European seafaring dating back to the fifteenth century, as well as the largest maritime historical reference library in the world. Here I found everything I needed to know regarding the early charting and exploration of the coastline of North America. In the National Library of Wales I had found only a brief reference to the voyage of 1604, but the archives of the National Maritime Museum provided much more detail regarding the expedition that had been instigated by Sir Walter Raleigh.

One of Sir Walter Raleigh's most prolific young protégés was fellow Englishman Martin Pring. Like Raleigh, he loved the sea and shared a passion for colonizing the New World. On April 10, 1603, while still only in his mid-twenties, Pring left on the last voyage Raleigh organized during Queen Elizabeth's reign. (She had died just a couple of weeks earlier, on March 24.) The intention of the two-ship expedition of the *Speedwell* and *Discoverer* was to chart the coast and explore the rivers and islands of New England.

The expedition reached the coast of Maine in the late spring and sailed south as far as Virginia before returning for home in August. When Pring arrived back in England, he reported to James I that, although the expedition had encountered some hostility from the Native Americans, they had generally been friendly and he was convinced that the land was well suited for a large-scale English colony. However, the new king did not initially share his predecessor's enthusiasm for American colonization, and the initiative was taken up by another of Raleigh's friends, a Frenchman named Pierre Dugua.[1]

The forty-five-year-old Dugua was a close friend of Raleigh and shared his enthusiasm for exploration; he was also a libertarian and a member of the School of Night. Like Raleigh, Dugua dreamed of a world free from religious bigotry, and shared Raleigh's vision of founding a tolerant society in America. Dugua had intended to join Pring's expedition, but illness forced him to remain behind; the following year he was well again and determined to lead his own voyage. However, he could expect no help from King James, and Raleigh was of no use to Dugua either, as he had been locked up in the Tower of London after being implicated in the Bye Plot the previous year. Dugua therefore sought sponsorship in his native France, and received backing from the French king Henry IV.

In March 1604, with five ships carrying 120 men, Dugua set sail from France to establish an advance settlement in the New World with the view to later colonization. After exploring various possible locations, Dugua decided on an island in the estuary of the St. Croix River, now the international boundary separating Canada and the United States between New Brunswick and Maine. By September, buildings had been completed and supplies were laid in for winter. Sadly, the Europeans' lack of knowledge concerning the local climate was to cost them dearly. They were on the same latitude as temperate France and expected a similarly mild winter, and thus were unprepared for the Arctic airflow that brings bitter winters to that part of America.

Their river estuary became a death trap of broken ice sheets, making the island a winter prison. Provisions were quickly exhausted and, to make matters worse, the settlers ran out of firewood and began to freeze. By the time spring arrived, nearly half the original company had perished and the remainder managed to survive only with the help of the indigenous Passamaquoddy tribe. Luckily, Dugua had taken along a Native American who had returned to Europe with Pring's expedition. This Indian spoke the local Passamaquoddy and Beothuk dialects fluently, and with the settlers too weak to hunt or forage for themselves, he was able to barter for provisions. When summer came, the colonists moved to a more favorable location on the shores of the present-day Annapolis basin, in Nova Scotia, and in August Dugua returned to France.[2]

If I interpreted *The Voyage of Maelduin's Boat* correctly, Merlin ended his life on an island somewhere along the coast of northeastern America. The Rosicrucians claimed to have found Merlin's tomb on some mysterious island in 1604, and that same year, an expedition had traveled to northeastern America, led by one of Raleigh's colleagues. Furthermore, Pierre Dugua not only was a member of Raleigh's School of Night, but he, as previously noted, appears to have been a leading member of the Rosicrucian fraternity as well.

For more than a decade, Pierre Dugua had been one of the most outspoken libertarians in Europe. When he was in his twenties, France was an unsafe place for anyone with such ideas; it was a strict Catholic country with harsh edicts against those who advocated religious tolerance and encouraged freedom of scientific or philosophical thought. Consequently, in the 1580s, Dugua spent much time in England, where he befriended Raleigh and joined his School of Night. Following the assassination of the French king Henry III in 1588, a bloody civil war ensued between two rivals for the throne: Henry, king of Navarre (a sovereign state to the south of France), and Charles, the duke of Mayenne (in the north of the country). The duke was a harsh Catholic traditionalist, while Henry, although a Protestant, promised a country of free religious choice if he became king. A keen supporter of Henry's ideology, Dugua returned to France and enlisted in his army.

Henry was a remarkable man. When he ultimately triumphed and was crowned Henry IV of France in 1594, he decided to convert to Catholicism to unite the country and show the Catholics they had nothing to fear. His pledge to make the country a nation of religious choice was kept and France became one of the most liberal states in Europe. As in the Netherlands, Britain, and Germany, scientific research was encouraged and ancient philosophy and even occult ideas were tolerated. Although the Rosicrucian movement was centered in England and Germany, it initially gained a far wider following in France; when the *Fama Fraternitatis* publicly announced the existence of the Rosicrucian fraternity in 1610, the document was circulated in Paris, and one of the first to publicly respond to it was Dugua.[3]

Contrary to the king's hopes, there were still extremist elements in France, both Catholic and Protestant, who wanted to see an end to religious tolerance. The views expressed in the *Fama Fraternitatis* were not only regarded as dangerously liberal, but they were also attacked for their cabalistic content. (Cabalism is a school of occult thought based on Jewish mysticism, and was regarded as contrary to Christian doctrine.) The *Fama* and its message were widely condemned by both Catholics and Protestants, and Dugua openly denounced its critics, even risking his position at court by becoming embroiled in the debate. A few years after his expedition to America, Dugua had been made a captain of Henry's royal guard, a position similar to that which Walter Raleigh had held under Queen Elizabeth in England. As a member of the royal household, Dugua was expected to remain above the world of politics, religious or otherwise. However, although he never admitted to being a Rosicrucian, historians have long speculated that Dugua was one of the organization's leading figures. To begin with, apart from his connection with Raleigh and the School of Night and his defense of Rosicrucianism, there were other Rosicrucian links throughout Dugua's life.[4]

On May 14, 1610, Henry IV was assassinated in Paris by a fanatical Roman Catholic named François Ravaillac. Sadly, when Henry died, so did liberalism in France. Because his son and heir Prince Louis was only nine years old at the time, the boy's mother, Marie de Medici, assumed the powers of regent. The Queen Mother was not only a devout Catholic, but she was also half Hapsburg, and so immediately began to undo everything her husband had accomplished. For a few years France was to witness some of the worst persecutions of Protestants and Nonconformists anywhere in Europe and Dugua found himself dismissed from office. He returned to his home in Brittany for a few years, whence he wrote a number of antigovernment pamphlets, which he had smuggled out of the country to be printed in Germany. There were a great number of printing companies in Germany and the fact that Dugua's publisher was the same company in the principality of Hesse-Cassel that published all the Rosicrucian documents, such as the *Naometria* and the *Fama Fraternitatis*, was one link that suggested that Dugua had connections with the fraternity. Another was his ongoing association with members of the organization.[5]

In 1615 the Queen Mother discovered Dugua's authorship of the pamphlets and ordered his arrest. With a price on his head, Dugua fled to the Netherlands, where he stayed with an old friend: an Englishman named William Brewster, who was closely associated with the Rosicrucian movement. Brewster had been a student of Greek and Latin at Cambridge University in the mid-1580s, at the same time as William Shakespeare's colleague Christopher Marlowe. Through Marlowe, Brewster had met Walter Raleigh and began to attend the meetings of the School of Night, and accordingly struck up a close friendship with Dugua. After leaving Cambridge, Brewster became personal assistant to the secretary of state in London, but in the 1590s he returned to his family home of Scrooby Manor in the county of Nottinghamshire in central England.

After witnessing the unscrupulous methods of the English Protestant regime firsthand, Brewster had become disillusioned by the Church of England and set up a printing press to publish papers questioning established religion. He was smart enough to make sure he never crossed the line by specifically leveling his criticisms at the Anglican Church by name. Nonetheless, like-minded individuals got the message and dozens wrote to him in support. One of these was a fellow Cambridge University man, John Robinson, an ordained Anglican minister who had been dismissed from the Church of England for his militant views. In the late 1590s, he joined Brewster in Nottinghamshire and proposed a radical and dangerous idea: He decided to found his own congregation outside the Church of England.[6]

Like Brewster, Robinson was appalled by the corruption of the Anglican Church and horrified by its unchristian treatment of dissenters. Nevertheless, Robinson had no sympathy with Roman Catholicism. In fact, he had been thrown out of the Church of England for preaching sermons against elements of Catholic ritual that the Anglicans still retained, such as ecclesiastical courts, clerical vestments, altars, and the practice of kneeling for prayer. Sometime around the year 1600, the informal meetings that were being held by Brewster and Robinson at Scrooby Manor became a formalized church with Robinson as its pastor and Brewster as chief of nine elected elders. Within a few years, the congregation, who became known as Separatists, had grown to hundreds from around the county of Nottingham, and Brewster's pamphlets inspired others to found

Separatist churches elsewhere. Although the Separatists were a thorn in the Church of England's side, no official action was taken against them while Elizabeth was queen. However, shortly after James I came to the throne, the Separatist Church was declared an illegal organization. In 1608, Robinson and Brewster obtained properties in the town of Leiden in the Netherlands and the Scrooby congregation emigrated there to begin a new life.[7]

Until 1581, the Netherlands comprised a group of small states known as the Low Countries. (Holland, the name by which the Netherlands is also known in the English-speaking world, was actually just one of these.) The Netherlands had been ruled at various times by the French, the Hapsburgs, and the Spanish, but in 1581 it became a single, independent Dutch republic. (The constitutional Dutch monarchy was not established until the nineteenth century.) Protestantism took firm root here, and because of its democratic form of government, the Netherlands made dissenters welcome. The Separatists were allowed to settle in the country and a sizable community of English expatriates grew up in the town of Leiden. It was here that Brewster set up a new printing company in order to publish leaflets promoting the Separatist aims. He also published pamphlets supporting the Rosicrucian cause, and it was to Brewster's home in Leiden that Dugua fled in 1615.[8]

Further evidence for Dugua's association with the Rosicrucian movement comes with the last known Rosicrucian document, which was published by Brewster in Leiden in 1615. Published in Latin, it was called the *Confessio Fraternitatis,* or Confession of the Fraternity, and was written under a pseudonym, Philip à Gabella (Philip the Cabalist). Some scholars have reasoned that its true author was Pierre Dugua. Not only is its style similar to Dugua's own writings, but its tone precisely matches his sentiments at the time as well. Although the *Confessio* repeated some of the earlier Rosicrucian message, it was far less compromising in its voice. Indeed, it was aggressively anti-Catholic. It called for the destruction of the Catholic Church, and specifically attacked Marie de Medici, calling her a murderess. (After Dugua escaped to the Netherlands, members of his family were arrested on the Queen Mother's orders and some were executed for heresy. This, of course, was circumstantial evidence for Dugua's direct involvement with the Rosicrucians.) However, the fact that the *Confessio* had been published from precisely where Dugua was living seems more than coincidental. (Although the original Latin manuscript was, like the other Rosicrucian documents, published in Hesse-Cassel, an English translation had been printed shortly after by Brewster in Leiden.[9])

It seemed to me that Pierre Dugua was right at the heart of the entire Rosicrucian mystery. He was a member of the School of Night, the Rosicrucian precursors, and he had other close links with the Rosicrucian movement itself. Indeed, if he was the author of the *Confessio*, he must have held a senior position in the organization. If Glynn Davis's theory *was* correct, and my own research supported its veracity, it would appear that Dugua's visit to North America in 1604 was connected to the Rosicrucians' claim of having found Merlin's tomb there that same year. And when I realized that Dugua would almost certainly have been fully acquainted with the Merlin legend, I was left with little doubt that Dugua was indeed the man responsible for finding Merlin's tomb.

Dugua was born in Royan, a town in the old province of Saintonge on the west coast of France, but when he returned home from England in the 1590s, he bought a château in Paimpont, in Brittany, where he spent a considerable amount of time.[10] This was in the center of the Broceliande forest where Merlin folklore was rife. As a seafaring man, chances were that Dugua was familiar with *The Voyage of Saint Brendan*—the supposed location of Saint Brendan's Isle was shown on many contemporary maps of the North Atlantic.

In fact, Dugua *must* have known the story. In the *Brendan* account, the land that the saint discovered near the Isles of the Blessed was called the Land of Promise. This was taken from Greek mythology, in which the Land of Promise was another name for a place called Arcadia, the mythical garden country of the gods. Arcadia was the name Dugua christened the area of mainland America that the British called New England. If he was familiar with the Merlin legend and *The Voyage of Saint Brendan,* the chances are that Dugua was also familiar with *The Voyage of Maelduin's Boat.* If so, he was well placed to identify the island on which Merlin was said to have been buried.

It seemed to me that the scenario was something like this. On his expedition, Dugua wittingly or by chance discovered what appeared to be Merlin's tomb. At the same time in Europe, the School of Night regarded the sudden appearance of the new star in the constellation of Ophiuchus, the twin serpents, as heralding a new age of enlightenment. Merlin was associated with two serpents, and when the School of Night learned of Dugua's discovery, they saw the simultaneous discoveries as being mystically linked. Whatever it was that had been found in the tomb, it was regarded as having spiritual significance for the new age, and the two monumental events initiated the wider Rosicrucian movement. The Rosicrucian mystery now fit into a historical perspective, but the big question still remained: Where was Merlin's tomb?

If it was on an island off the coast of northeastern America, Dugua must have been the man who found it. But on which of the many islands he might have visited could it have been? It may have been the island on which Dugua first located his settlement: the island at the mouth of the St. Croix River, now called St. Croix Island. It could equally have been one of a number of other islands along the coast of New England. In the summer of 1604, after leaving the colonists on St. Croix Island, Dugua sailed south as far as what is now New York so that his cartographer, Samuel de Champlain, could chart the coastline. Unfortunately, though, Dugua's log of the voyage no longer survives. Champlain's maps do; but they included dozens of islands along the coast of what are now the states of Maine, New Hampshire, Massachusetts, Rhode Island, Connecticut, and New York. Although Champlain's maps narrowed things down somewhat, I needed more to go on.

Dugua's own writings might have solved the entire enigma, but the relevant works no longer exist. Most of Dugua's surviving works are tomes on exploration and navigation, or texts discussing religious issues, but one gave an account of his travels. His autobiography described his journeys throughout the world, but infuriatingly, the surviving work consists of a mere two volumes of what had been a much longer composition; and his voyage to America in 1604 is not included in the extant text.[11]

Nevertheless, it indirectly provided a new lead. One chapter concerns the events that appear to be the curtain call in the history of the Rosicrucian movement. In the early weeks of 1620, Dugua records that he spent time in the Netherlands, visiting his old friend William Brewster. Annoyingly, Dugua describes his visit to the city only from a tourist's perspective, mentioning its galleries, culture, and architecture. He leaves out anything concerning why he was there or who he met during his stay.[12] However, it so happens that, at the same time, just about every other known Rosicrucian of any consequence was also in the city of Leiden.

In 1617, with the support of certain nobles, the sixteen-year-old Louis took over the reigns of power in France and sent his mother into exile. Dugua was able to return home, but even under the new regime, France was not the country it had been in King Henry's day. Although the religious persecutions had ceased, the new king's advisers had decided to implement a form of absolute monarchy, which would remain in France until the Revolution in the late 1700s. Dugua seems to have decided that he would never see the anticipated new age of enlightenment during his lifetime. It was not only in France that things went badly for the Rosicrucian dream.

After Elizabeth and Frederick's rash attempt to rule Bohemia in 1619, the Hapsburgs, as previously noted, reoccupied the country and their Spanish allies invaded Frederick's home state of the Palatinate. This led to the so-called Thirty Years War, in which the Catholic Hapsburg empire and its Spanish allies fought the Protestant states of Germany for control of Central Europe. In 1620, when Elizabeth and Frederick were driven out of Bohemia, none of the German states would accept them, and Elizabeth's own father, King James, refused to let them return to England. He had been embarrassed by the entire affair and distanced himself from what he saw as a fiasco. In fact, by this time James had become an Anglican extremist; draconian measures were taken against anyone who refused to subscribe to Church of England ideology. This included not only Roman Catholics, but also other Protestants, such as the Calvinists, Nonconformists, and Puritans. Just about the only place in Europe where liberalism was still tolerated was the Netherlands, but it seemed that even this would soon end as the country was under threat from the Hapsburgs and the Spanish, who were, at the time, winning the war in neighboring Germany.[13] The Rosicrucian dream of a free and tolerant Europe had evaporated and it appears that, in the early months of 1620, the Rosicrucians gathered in the Netherlands for one last meeting.

After Elizabeth and Frederick fled Bohemia in 1620, the reason they sought refuge in the Netherlands was not only because of the liberal principles adopted by the republic, but also because of the hospitality offered by Maurice, the prince of Orange (a tiny independent principality in the south of France from where his family originally came). Maurice had been educated at Heidelberg University in the Palatinate, where he had met Simon Studion and other founding members of the Rosicrucian movement. He came to sympathize with their philosophy, and also became a close friend of Frederick's family, the rulers of the Palatinate. During the first two decades of the seventeenth century, and until his death in 1625, Maurice was the Stadtholder (the chief government official) of the Netherlands provinces of Holland and Zeeland: the southern coastal states, which included the towns of Amsterdam, Leiden, and The Hague. It was Maurice, in fact, who had offered the English Separatists a safe haven in Leiden in 1608. After their flight from Bohemia, Maurice granted Elizabeth and Frederick asylum in Holland. He let them use his home in The Hague and gave them another residence in Leiden.[14]

Even before I visited the National Maritime Museum I had begun to suspect there had been some kind of Rosicrucian gathering in the city of Leiden. It was not just that Elizabeth and Frederick had fled there; it was also that the other Rosicrucians, for supposedly different reasons, all congregated in that area at precisely the same time, in February 1620.

Johann Valentin Andreae, the author of the *Fama Fraternitatis,* was already there, having left Germany when war broke out. Fulke Greville, whose London house was used for the early meetings of the School of Night and who had been present at Elizabeth's Alchemical Wedding, was there, supposedly to visit Leiden University to see an exhibition of paintings. Francis Bacon was visiting the prince of Orange in his official position as English lord chancellor to discuss the legality of a trade treaty with the Netherlands. The playwright Ben Jonson was present in Leiden, performing a play at a new theater. And the architect Inigo Jones, although not staying in Leiden itself, was in nearby Amsterdam working on plans for a church he had been commissioned to build in the city. In fact, just about the only known major Rosicrucian players who were not in or near Leiden in February 1620 were William Shakespeare, Walter Raleigh, Simon Studion, and John Dee, and they had good reason for not being there—they were all dead.

Despite the seemingly unrelated reasons for all these people being in virtually the same place at the same time, surely there had to be some other agenda: The laws of probability just couldn't stretch that far. Although it cannot be proved, it seems reasonable to assume that the Rosicrucians had gathered in the city after the overthrow of Elizabeth and Frederick in Bohemia in order to decide what to do given that the anticipated new-age dream was over and the libertarian flame was rapidly dying in Europe. I had already read up on the lives of those involved, but so far had found nothing to confirm my suspicions with any degree of certainty, nor had I found any new information regarding the likely whereabouts of the mysterious island.

However, while reading an English translation of Dugua's autobiography, I found mention of a new voyage to America that might somehow be linked with the Rosicrucian's final plans.[15] Having been conceived by Dugua's friend William Brewster in February 1620, it was in fact one of the most famous voyages in history—the voyage of the *Mayflower*.

At the very time that the Rosicrucians were gathered in Leiden, the English Separatists in the city decided the only hope for religious freedom lay in North America. Together with the congregation's pastor, John Robinson, Brewster suggested they hire a ship, sail to New England, and establish a colony. A few weeks later, Brewster returned to England and by May had arranged to hire two ships: Martin Pring's old ship the *Speedwell* and the *Mayflower*. In July, a large part of the Separatist congregation sailed to England in the *Speedwell* for a rendezvous with the *Mayflower* at Southampton, and on August 5, with ninety of them on board the *Mayflower* and thirty more on the *Speedwell*, they set out for the New World. However, the *Speedwell* was in no condition to make a transatlantic passage, and that boat was forced to turn back. Ultimately, the voyage involved only the *Mayflower*, which finally set sail from Plymouth in southwest England on September 6, with 102 passengers. John Robinson actually remained behind in Leiden, but Brewster was on the voyage, as were all the Pilgrim Fathers (the name later given to the original nine elders of the church.) [16]

Could the voyage of the *Mayflower* actually have had some link with the Rosicrucians' final plans, before their movement disbanded? The most important Rosicrucians were in Leiden and the most important Rosicrucian secret was evidently whatever it was that the tomb of Merlin contained, a tomb that may have been discovered in northeastern America—precisely where the Separatists were going. Moreover, Pierre Dugua, the man who seems to have originally found the tomb, was staying in Brewster's home at that very time that Brewster came up with the idea of sending the *Mayflower* expedition to North America! Given all of these seeming coincidences, might it be the case that the Nine—the mysterious Rosicrucian elite who were supposed to know the whereabouts of the sacred tomb—were actually the nine Separatist elders, the Pilgrim Fathers?

There was no evidence I could discover that any of the Separatists other than Brewster was involved with the Rosicrucians. In fact, although they shared a belief in freedom of religious choice, the Separatists were Puritans with no interest whatsoever in the kind of mystical views held by the Rosicrucian fraternity. Nonetheless, there was no known objection to Brewster's association with the organization or his printing of the *Confessio* in 1615. He made no secret of his Rosicrucian leanings and, as he was chief elder and cofounder of the Separatist movement, this bent of his was obviously tolerated.

Perhaps a shared abhorrence of the orthodox Christian establishment brought together the Rosicrucians and the Separatists, or perhaps it was something more practical. There is some mystery about where the Separatists got the financial backing for their expedition. Perhaps the Rosicrucians funded the *Mayflower* voyage. But if so, what was their motivation?

Dugua gave no hint one way or the other in his book; he simply said that when he returned to France in late February, Brewster had already decided that the only hope for Separatism lay in the New World and that he was planning what would eventually be the *Mayflower* voyage. Had Dugua and Brewster inspired the Separatists with the secret that had supposedly been found at the mysterious tomb? According to the *Confessio*—possibly Dugua's own words—the secret was "the word of the Lord." So great was it that "if all other knowledge were lost it would be possible to rebuild from it alone." It could conquer hunger, poverty, and all manner of wickedness, and it was "as if to read in one book all that is in all books."[17]

The *Fama Fraternitatis* suggested that it was what Glynn Davis referred to as the Logos, the true name of God, a divine word passed down from the time of Moses that held awesome power. As fundamentalist Christians, this might have been something that appealed to the Separatists. This mysterious divine word is referred to in the opening lines of St. John's Gospel of the New Testament:

> In the beginning there was the Word, and the Word was with God, and the Word was God ... And the Word was made flesh, and dwelt amongst us. (John 1:1, 14)

This was a reference to Jesus Christ, so whatever this word was, it would have been of immense significance to the early-seventeenth-century Puritans.

If—and it was a big if—the Pilgrim Fathers were somehow involved with the mystery of Merlin's tomb, perhaps the Rosicrucians decided these purist Christians were worthy of its secret. I had no doubt that Merlin's tomb and the Rosicrucians' secret lay on an island off the coast of New England. Perhaps the Separatists went there on the *Mayflower* before establishing their colony on the mainland. There were a lot of *ifs*, but with nothing else to narrow down the location of the island, it was an idea worth considering. The next question, therefore, was where did the *Mayflower* go?

On November 11, 1620, the *Mayflower* first anchored off Cape Cod in what is now Provincetown Harbor in the state of Massachusetts, and after a few exploratory expeditions by the crew, it sailed across Cape Cod Bay. There the settlers went ashore on Plymouth Rock, near where the first colony was established. Unfortunately, the log of the *Mayflower's* captain, John Smith, no longer survives, and it is unknown whether the *Mayflower* previously landed elsewhere. I had taken my research in England just about as far as I could; I would obviously have to go to New England to continue with it, and the Cape Cod area seemed as good a place as any to start.

It was as I was leaving the National Maritime Museum that I found myself staring into the face of one of the men at the center of the Rosicrucian mystery. In the entrance hall of the museum there was a bust of Inigo Jones. A plaque beneath the bust explained that Jones was the architect who designed the Queen's House (now the main building of the museum). By 1616, Jones had risen to fame as a designer of court entertainments and in that year the English queen commissioned his first major architectural enterprise. This was her house at Greenwich, which apparently was to be a place of private retreat. It was obviously a coincidence that the building I was in had been designed by one of the Rosicrucians, as it had nothing to do with navigation until well after Jones's day. Nevertheless, it started me thinking.

One thing I had been puzzling over was the death of William Shakespeare. According to Glynn Davis, Shakespeare was murdered in 1616 by Walter Raleigh because of something he knew. Whether or not Raleigh acted alone, Glynn had not said. Evidently, to reveal more would necessitate Glynn giving away certain Masonic secrets: the information Glynn gave me apparently had come from the writings of Ben Jonson, which had been preserved by Glynn's Masonic lodge. Shakespeare obviously knew the tomb of Christian Rosencreutz was really the tomb of Merlin and knew it was on an island, as demonstrated by *The Tempest* and its performance at the wedding of Princess Elizabeth. According to Glynn, Shakespeare had been able to work out where this island actually was.

For a while I had considered the possibility that Shakespeare left clues in his works to reveal the secret location of the tomb. If he did, however, the clues were lost on me. I then turned to the works of Ben Jonson. As he wrote the masque for Elizabeth's coming-of-age pageant, he too must have known as much as Shakespeare concerning the tomb. Also, given that Shakespeare was Jonson's close friend, Shakespeare may have confided his discovery to Jonson. Glynn had said Jonson's writings revealed that he knew that something to do with the serpents on Excalibur's hilt had led his fellow playwright to work out the tomb's location; if true, this implied that Jonson knew the secret too.

Had Jonson, I wondered, secretly shared Shakespeare's sentiments and left cryptic messages in his own works to reveal the tomb's whereabouts? With this in mind, I read through all of Jonson's works, as well as his obituary in the First Folio edition of Shakespeare's plays, but I found nothing I could interpret as being relevant. I had, therefore, given up that line of research. However, on seeing the bust of Inigo Jones, an idea occurred to me. It was a long shot, but did Inigo Jones leave any clues?

Jones had not only worked closely with the two playwrights, designing their sets, but he also worked on both Elizabeth's coming-of-age pageant and her wedding. As a close friend of both Shakespeare and Jonson, could he too have known where the tomb was and covertly wanted to reveal its whereabouts? The Rosicrucians' cryptic clues to reveal that the tomb of Christian Rosencreutz was really the tomb of Merlin were in Jones's set designs for Elizabeth's "entertainments"; could he have left unauthorized clues to the whereabouts of the tomb in his architecture? The Queen's House was designed for Elizabeth's mother the year Shakespeare died. While I was there, there was nothing to lose by looking around.

For some time I wandered around the outside of the Romanesque mansion, built of pure white stone, examining its decorative Greek columns and ornate balustrades, but saw nothing that struck a familiar chord. Inside it was the same. In what had once been the bedchambers and staterooms of a succession of English queens, with flamboyant plasterwork, elaborate fireplaces, and priceless works of art, there was nothing that presented any obvious connection with the Rosicrucians, the tomb of Christian Rosencreutz, or the legend of Merlin.

There was, however, an exhibition in one of the upstairs galleries concerning the life and works of Inigo Jones, and it was here that I found something of interest. The exhibition included paintings, photographs, and plans of the architect's works, but none of it seemed to have any relevance to my search. However, one of the pictures soon captured my attention. It was a photograph of the strangest-looking windmill I had ever seen. The structure was a round tower with white sails, raised high above the ground by brick supports that formed a series of open arches. According to the pamphlet that accompanied the exhibition, it was Jones's last work, built around 1632. It was not originally a windmill, it seems, as the sails and mill-working were added later in the 1700s.

Its original purpose was a mystery. Some thought the wealthy owner of the land on which it stood commissioned Jones to erect a folly on the highest hill on his estate. (A folly is an ornamental structure with no practical purpose: in other words, just for show.) Others thought the structure was designed as an observatory to house a telescope. One clue to its original purpose, however, was the name that Jones called it—the Esplumoir. *Esplumoir* is an old French word meaning "molting cage": a building where birds of prey were kept. It seems the place was built as a birdhouse. However, this rare word immediately jumped out at me—because it was associated with the legend of Merlin. One of the medieval Grail Romances actually says that Merlin ended his days in an esplumoir.

The *Didot Perceval Romance,* composed around 1200 (see chapter 10), does not actually reveal where (in the world) Merlin's life ended; the story closes with Perceval becoming the Grail guardian and Merlin deciding not to return to Arthur's court. However, it does say in passing that Merlin ended his life living in an esplumoir. The consensus among literary scholars regarding this strange statement is that it was a symbolic reference somehow related to Merlin's name that meant the Eagle.

Given all of this, there had to be some connection between the name of Jones's last structure and the fact that Merlin allegedly died in a similar structure. Before going to America, I decided I must visit Jones's bizarre-looking tower.

13

ISLAND OF THE DEAD

Now known as the Chesterton Windmill, the strange building that Inigo Jones built stands on top of the aptly named Windmill Hill, a few miles to the southeast of the county town of Warwick. The solitary structure can be seen for miles around; it stands alone on the treeless hill overlooking the Warwickshire countryside. A narrow road winds its way upward to a parking verge beside a farm gate, from where a muddy track crosses a field to the windmill some two hundred yards away.

In summertime, visitors no doubt visit this site by the carload to admire the scenery, but it was now winter, and the day I arrived a bitter wind tore across the empty hillside. There was no one out walking and only one car was parked on the verge: a black hatchback with the driver and one passenger inside. Perhaps they had decided it was just too chilly to brave the walk. You didn't actually need to leave your vehicle to take in the spectacular view. Beyond the M40 motorway running along the base of the hill, most of the English Midlands could be seen, as far away as the mountains of Wales more than sixty miles to the west. Despite the cold, the sun shone brightly, silhouetting Jones's eccentric creation, which stood out in stark contrast against the skyline.

I made my way across the fields and stood looking up at the building. An arrangement of six rectangular brick pillars and round arches that acted as stilts—some of which were fifteen feet tall—supported a cylindrical stone tower set with a few oddly placed windows and capped with a domed metal roof. The entire thing was about thirty five feet high and its painted white sails remained fixed like huge angel wings spread out toward the west.

As I walked around its base, twenty or so feet in diameter, I could see that it was a most impractical design for a windmill. A mill's sails are meant to rotate to face into the wind. Old windmills were made from wood, with the upper section free to turn on bearings, but this solid structure was built from sandstone bricks and blocks of limestone and could face in only one direction.

It had clearly never been designed as a windmill. Yet, although Jones had called it the Esplumoir—a shelter for birds of prey—it could not have served as a birdhouse, either. Like a dovecote, an esplumoir would have been ringed by holes for birds to fly in and out; this had no such openings. Despite the brilliant sunshine, the setting was an eerie one. The lonely, exposed tower of yellowish gray stone, covered here and there with patches of moss, moaned and wailed against the biting wind. The sails, which no longer turned, shrieked in the storm-force gusts while the open stone arches groaned in chorus. It sounded almost as if the building were occupied by a condemned community of men, women, and children all crying out in pain.

Stepping through one of the arches to get in out of the wind, I was surprised to find that I was not alone. A bearded man of thirty-something, wrapped up in a colorful scarf and a green anorak, was huddled on a narrow stone bench behind one of the pillars supporting the upper tower. He was scribbling on a pad resting on his lap, desperately trying to prevent it from being blown away. He was a local artist, and he was there making preparatory sketches for a landscape he was intending to paint. Fortunately, he knew all about the windmill, and when we got to talking, he told me more of its history.

It had been built in 1632 for the lord of the local manor: Sir Edward Peyto, a mathematician and keen astronomer. He originally commissioned one of Jones's students, John Stone, to build an observatory to house one of the telescopes that had recently been invented. However, before work started, Jones himself intervened to design the structure, with Stone to oversee its construction. Sir Edward was thrilled to have England's most celebrated architect come up with any design he saw fit; when it was finished, he was proud to have one of the country's oddest-looking follies dominating the landscape for miles around. It served its purpose as an observatory, but it was also the talk of the county.

After we had been chatting for a while, I asked the artist if he knew why the building was called the Esplumoir. "Interesting question," he replied. "It was certainly never used for birds. Evidently, it has to do with Merlin."

"Merlin!" I said the name with such surprise that the man took a step back.

"In the King Arthur story, Merlin built an observatory to study the stars and make predictions," he said. "It was called the Esplumoir."

It took me awhile to realize what he was talking about, but as we chatted I put it together. In Geoffrey of Monmouth's *Life of Merlin*, Merlin marries a mysterious woman named Gwendolena.[1] Nothing is revealed about her background except that she came from Wales. Other romances portray her as the mother of Guinevere, who married King Arthur. When Merlin is old, he decides to finish out his days as a hermit and, consequently, urges his wife to take another husband. She agrees, but before leaving Merlin, she has a tower built for him whence he can observe the stars.

In this particular account (as discussed in chapter 1), Geoffrey has confused the legends of Ambrosius and Lailoken. Yet also in this account, Geoffrey depicts Merlin as a forest-dwelling recluse in the north of England. Nevertheless, Merlin's tower became part of Arthurian folklore. In the story, the tower was built to observe the stars and planets—in other words, it was an observatory. Such buildings were constructed in medieval times, well before the invention of the telescope. Used for astrological purposes, they were set with tiny windows: frames of reference from which to plot the positions of the heavenly bodies as seen from a central viewing point. I had not appreciated it before, but from the outside, these buildings looked very much like dovecotes and birdhouses, something that might well account for why the *Didot Perceval* romance describes Merlin ending his life in an esplumoir.

An observatory and/or esplumoir is where Merlin ends his days in some of the Arthurian tales. Inigo Jones went out of his way to design such a building, his last one. By naming it after Merlin's final habitation, might he have been alluding to clues here as to the location of Merlin's final resting place? With this in mind, I wandered around the tower several times, yet could see nothing that seemed to be a coded message that might lead to Merlin's tomb, or to a mysterious island off the coast of North America. Perhaps there was something inside. The upper section comprised two rooms—the way up was through a trapdoor—but without a ladder, there was no way of reaching them.

"Any idea why it's raised up on columns?" I asked.

"Some people reckon it's a copy of another building. I've seen pictures and it does look very similar. It's in America."

"America!" Once again my enthusiastic response startled the man.

"Yes, it's a circular stone tower about the same size, built on top of arched columns, just like this. It has no roof anymore, but in all other respects it's virtually identical."

"And it was there when this tower was built?" I asked, surprised. In 1632, few stone buildings had been erected in the American colonies.

"That's where the controversy lies. Some people say Jones had seen drawings of the one in America and built this as a copy. Others say the American tower was a copy of this one. No one really knows which came first. The owner of the land in the States where the tower stood came from around here. I believe he was the English governor of Rhode Island."

"Rhode Island!"

"Yes, that's where the tower is."

This had to mean something! Merlin's tomb was apparently on an island off New England—Rhode Island is on the coast of New England. The artist knew no more about the Rhode Island tower, so I was keen to get away and look it up.

"I should get myself a job as the official guide here," said the artist as I turned to leave. "It's the second time in half an hour I've been asked about its history."

"Perhaps you should," I said nonchalantly.

"They also raced off the moment I mentioned the tower on Rhode Island," he said.

The hairs on the back of my neck stood up. "Who were they?"

"A young couple—Germans, I think. When I arrived they were trying to scale the side of the building to get inside. They asked if I knew anything that linked this building with an island in the United States. I think they were on some kind of treasure hunt; they got really excited and took off the moment I told them about Rhode Island." The artist could see I was concerned. "You must have bumped into them on your way up. They left only a few minutes before you arrived."

The couple in the black hatchback! I looked along the path to see if their vehicle was still there, but the brow of the hill obscured the view. I thanked the man and quickly made my way to the parking lot, but the mysterious couple's car was gone. As I gazed across the landscape for the vehicle, my mind raced. I had almost forgotten that others were apparently searching for Merlin's tomb and following the same clues as I. Were these the people responsible for bugging Glynn Davis and for breaking into my apartment? The answer seemed clear enough when I got to my car. The passenger window was broken and my attaché case was missing from the front seat! I had taken Glynn's advice and put nothing new on my computer. Since leaving his home a few weeks earlier, I made only handwritten notes—and they were all in that attaché case.

The theft could not possibly be a coincidence. This mysterious couple had to be the enemy (as Glynn Davis called them). If only I'd taken a better look at them, or taken notice of their license plate. But why should I have? I had only seen them briefly in profile; as for the car, I had no idea what make it was. I knew nothing about these people, but they obviously knew everything about me. In fact, as they now had all my notes, they also knew everything I knew—and they would be heading for Rhode Island. I took out my cell phone and dialed the airport.

The next afternoon, I was high over the Atlantic on a flight bound for Providence, Rhode Island. I had a few good hours to think, and I tried to find an alternative explanation for the events at the Chesterton Windmill. By chance, an innocent tourist couple had been visiting the place, and had been excited by the discovery that it bore a resemblance to one in the States. By chance, my car had been robbed by a passing thief who noticed my vehicle on the deserted road. Yet try as I might to convince myself that this could have been the case, it didn't seem likely.

But if the couple were the enemy, why were they at the windmill at the same time as I? Whoever these people were, they knew their stuff. They must have outwitted Glynn's security company and were still been bugging his place. They must have been following me for weeks. But why did they think my attaché case worth stealing? They must have been at the National Maritime Museum. I had the case with me then and was making notes while searching through the library and its database. To have known about the windmill, these people had to have been in the Inigo Jones exhibition gallery. Observing me, it would have been obvious, as I examined the photograph and read up on the windmill, that I considered the windmill significant.

I tried to think back. Who had been in the library? Quite a lot of people had been milling around, but to me they were all faceless tourists. No one seemed to stick out. I had no idea how surveillance worked, but Glynn's private detective had managed to follow me into Wales and halfway across France. But he had been easy to spot. These people, however, were more covert. Who were they?

Whatever their identity, they obviously shared Glynn's belief that whatever was at Merlin's tomb was worth a great deal of trouble to discover. The artist thought they were German. The Rosicrucian movement had been centered in Germany. Was there a connection? All sorts of crazy notions went through my mind about who they might be: descendants of the Rosicrucians searching for the secret of their ancestors; renegade Freemasons who held a grudge against Glynn Davis; even the grandchildren of Nazi war criminals hunting for treasure! The truth was, I had no idea who they were! All I knew is that they were smart, obsessed, and prepared to go to extraordinary lengths to find the mysterious tomb. Whether or not they would resort to physical violence, I shuddered to think.

I considered dropping the entire thing: Was the potential discovery of a fifteen-hundred-year-old tomb really worth the risk? Yes it was, I decided. I was hooked, so much so that I was ready to throw caution to the wind. What had begun as an academic exercise was now an impelling mystery. What *was* it that had excited poets, explorers, and academics from all over Europe to found a secret society in the seventeenth century? What was so important that a young couple—and possibly others as well—were spending a great deal of time, effort, and money trying to rediscover it?

These people clearly knew their business when it came to covert activities—but were they really that smart? They seemed to have needed Glynn, and now me, to solve the mystery for them. We were nearing the end of the road, I was certain of that, and I intended to beat them to the answer we were all seeking. But how? They would presumably follow my every move. Nervously, I looked around at the other passengers. They could be on this very flight!

It was around eight in the evening when I finally arrived at the Newport Tower (as it is known). Located in a small park close to the sea in the city of Newport, it is something of a tourist attraction, and was illuminated by floodlights. The official name of the state is actually the State of Rhode Island and Providence Plantations. In addition to the state being called Rhode Island, Newport is situated on an island that is *also* known as Rhode Island, and is currently called Aquidneck Island. It was first settled in the 1630s by the English; by the 1660s, it had become part of a thriving British colony.

As I approached the tower, I noted that it was indeed very similar to Jones's windmill, and virtually the same size. It consisted of a cylindrical stone tower supported by a series of pillars and semicircular arches. It even had a similar arrangement of windows. The only differences were that this was more of a ruin, having no roof or glass in the windows, and there were no sails. It also appeared to be much older than Jones's structure. Rather than being made of neatly cut sandstone bricks and limestone blocks, like the Chesterton Windmill, the Newport Tower had been built from roughly hewn stones and shale. It was, nevertheless, a solid stone building, cemented together in a manner unlike anything known to have been used by the Native Americans.

Some North American Indian tribes, such as the Anasazi in New Mexico, Colorado, and Utah, built sizable stone structures, but none of these Indians had employed the use of cement, and no known indigenous peoples of North, Central, or South America are known to have developed the arch. In the Old World, even the ancient Egyptians and Greeks never developed the arch—it was invented by the Romans.

I had read up on the Newport Tower on the flight over and discovered that America's smallest state holds one of the biggest mysteries regarding the history of European colonization. Who built the tower, when, and why are pieces of a historical puzzle that has yet to be solved. The artist had told me the governor of Rhode Island in the 1630s had come from Warwickshire. However, he seemed to have gotten that a bit mixed up. The first historical reference to the tower was made by the English governor Benedict Arnold in 1677, who simply mentioned it in passing in his will. Benedict Arnold (not to be confused with the man of the same name who was active during the War of Independence) had, it seemed, come from Warwickshire, but this was more than thirty years after the Chesterton Windmill had been erected. English settlers were in Rhode Island about the time that Jones's building was erected in England, but whether or not the Newport Tower was standing then is an open question.

The Newport Tower was seemingly not built by the Native Americans. Was it built by English settlers after the 1630s? Apart from Jones's windmill, there is nothing anywhere else in the world that looks anything like it. However, the fact that its builders employed the Romanesque arch suggests they were Europeans.

Some have suggested that the tower was built much earlier than the 1630s by the Vikings. They are known to have settled in Nova Scotia and probably explored the coast of New England. Those who subscribe to the theory that St. Brendan visited America have suggested it could have been built by Irish settlers in the sixth century. Both of these peoples had the technical expertise to erect such a structure—but did they?

In the 1940s, the first archaeological survey of the tower was made by a team from Harvard University. After excavating the foundation of the building, they found nothing to solve the enigma one way or the other. Colonial artifacts were discovered in the vicinity, but there was nothing under the actual foundation from which to date it. Even today, no one knows for sure who built it. The similarity with Jones's windmill suggests that it existed in the 1630s, but whether Jones copied it or the Newport Tower builders copied Jones is anyone's guess. If Inigo Jones knew the whereabouts of the Rosicrucians' secret island, and the Chesterton Windmill was in some way a clue to its location, did it mean the island in question with regard to Merlin was, in fact, the island that Newport is located on?[2]

Now linked to the mainland by bridges, Aquidneck Island is located among a group of other islands in Narragansett Bay, approximately fifty miles down the coast from Plymouth Rock, where the Pilgrim Fathers landed. If the Separatists were somehow involved with the Rosicrucian mystery, they could indeed have come here. The Narragansett Bay islands were certainly charted by Pierre Dugua's expedition in 1604; they appear on his cartographer Champlain's charts.

Was this island that Newport is located on really the island where the Rosicrucians, presumably Dugua's expedition, discovered the enigmatic tomb? Was it Saint Brendan's Isle, the island thought to be Manannan Island discovered in *The Voyage of Maelduin's Boat*? If it was, was this mysterious tower the site of Merlin's grave? No one had proposed a satisfactory explanation for its purpose. Was it a tomb marker? Was the Newport Tower itself Merlin's tomb? If it was, what would be its associated discovery, a discovery of such profound significance that it inspired the founding of the Rosicrucian fraternity? If Glynn Davis was right, whatever was found at the tomb remained there. If it remained there, and Newport Tower was that tomb, whatever had been discovered obviously was no longer there.

Walking around and around the old building, examining the brickwork inside and out, there was nothing about the mysterious construction that seemed significant. As far as I could tell, nothing had been found there, either by archaeologists or by anyone else, that could conceivably be linked with the Monad that the tomb was supposed to have contained.

The problem was that I didn't really know what form this Monad took. If it was a word that, for whatever reason, was thought to be the true name of God, I could only assume it was an inscription of some sort. That seemed the most likely answer. After all, *The Voyage of Maelduin's Boat* said that when the sailors arrived at the island they found a hermit there who was guarding a stone upon which a sacred text was inscribed (see chapter 11).

No inscriptions, though, had been found on the Newport Tower. If this was not Merlin's tomb, perhaps Inigo Jones was implying that it was somewhere nearby. I needed to go to the Newport public library and see if I could discover more about Rhode Island. Perhaps there was another structure resembling a tomb that had been found in the area.

The next day, my search through the library's exhaustive collection of books on the local history was initially disappointing. There was nothing that seemed relevant. If a fifteen-hundred-year-old European tomb ever existed in the Newport area, it had probably been dug up as the modern city evolved. Perhaps neither I nor the mysterious enemy would ever know the Rosicrucian secret. However, as I was looking through a book concerning the controversial Ogham texts that had been found in New England, I saw a reference that leaped off the page at me.

It concerned what appeared to be an Ogham inscription found on a rock on one of the New England islands. It wasn't in Rhode Island, however, but rather on an island off the coast of Maine, Manana Island.

The island on which Merlin was said to have ended his days was thought to be Mannanan Island, named after the Celtic sea god. Manana Island—Mannanan Island—was there a connection? From the reference material, I learned that Manana was the original Native American name for the island, derived from a Beothuk word meaning "island in the sea."[3] If the Irish landed there in the early sixth century and discovered the similar name, they may well have thought they discovered the island of Manannan. But it was not only the name of the place that captivated me; it was also the fact that an Ogham inscription had been found there.

On the western side of the island, on a headland overlooking the sea, was a boulder inscribed with what looked like Ogham characters, although no one, as far as I could discover, had been able to date or even decipher them. Just below the boulder was a spring that bubbled out of the rocks to form a pool, and next to it there were two standing stones, about four feet tall. They had definitely been shaped and erected by man, but again, no one knew how long ago. If Inigo Jones's set designs for Princess Elizabeth's coming-of-age pageant and her Alchemical Wedding were anything to go by, Merlin's tomb stood next to a pool. Did these man-made standing stones actually mark Merlin's grave? Was the mysterious inscription the long forgotten secret of the Rosicrucians?

I had to curb my excitement! For all I knew, the enemy was watching me right now. How would I know whether a microscopic tracking device had been attached to my clothes? To prevent this possibility, that morning I had changed into a new set of clothes that I purchased in a shop in the hotel.

By taking a long detour through downtown Newport, I had tried to ensure that I had not been followed to the library. Once there, I looked up at its surveillance cameras: Perhaps the enemy could tap into these. To confuse anyone who might be watching, I wandered from section to section, browsing through books, making enthusiastic expressions over nothing of interest, finally leaving the library with a defeated look on my face.

The truth is that I was now sure that Manana Island was the island in question. I had no idea how it related to the Newport Tower, or whether Inigo Jones built his windmill as a clue to it, but Manana Island fit. It was definitely known about in Dugua's day. I had not noticed a specific reference to Manana Island from my research from the National Maritime Museum, but a book in the Newport library described how, in 1603, Martin Pring first discovered the island and went ashore.[4] There was a Beothuk fishing community there, and one of the island's inhabitants returned with the expedition to England. (This was the same man who acted as interpreter on Pierre Dugua's expedition the following year.)

Dugua had visited the island also, and on two occasions: once on the voyage out and again on the way home when he returned the Native American (who sadly is not named) to his people. Unfortunately, though, neither account describes what actually happened on the island. All the same, I was sure this was the island I was looking for. Given the names similarities, the fact that both Pring and Dugua had gone there, the mysterious inscription and standing stones next to a pool—it was all too much to be coincidence.

Manana Island lies around two hundred miles northeast of Rhode Island, situated some ten miles off the coast of Maine. It is a windswept, treeless island of just a few dozen acres, lying a couple of hundred yards across a strait that separates it from its larger companion, Monhegan Island. Although Monhegan Island has a small population of approximately one hundred people, Manana is unpopulated; its only building is an automated fog-warning station.

Even in summertime hardly anyone goes there, and I wanted to get there in the middle of winter! Regular ferries serviced Monhegan Island during the vacation season, but in winter there were only three crossings a week, and they departed only when the weather held.

Driving my rental car north along Interstate 95 later that day, the signs weren't good. The skies had darkened and fresh snow began to fall. I had called the ferry service that departs from Port Clyde, at the tip of Maine's Saint George peninsula (the closest mainland point to the island), and had been told there would be a service departing at 9:30 the following morning—provided the weather didn't get any worse. Even if I did make it to Monhegan Island, I had no idea how I would get to Manana. My only hope was to find someone to row me across.

By the time I got to Port Clyde, the snow had stopped falling. I checked in at the ferry house, where I was told that the boat was still scheduled to depart the following morning. Port Clyde is only a small fishing village: a cluster of wooden buildings set around a tiny harbor. There were a number of small hotels in the area that catered to summer tourists, but they were all closed. However, the man who ran the ferry house gave me the name of a couple who lived a few miles out of town who ran a bed-and-breakfast.

When I booked in for the night, the couple, Sam and Kerri, were intrigued by why I wanted to get to Monhegan Island in the dead of winter. Although I didn't tell them anything about Merlin or the Rosicrucians, I did tell them that I hoped to see the mysterious inscription that had been found on the island.

"I can save you the trip," said Sam. "It's hardly visible anymore; it's been vandalized. But I have a picture of what it used to look like."

He had a collection of old books on the history of Maine and one of them was a rare book written in 1930 by an American artist who had investigated the Manana inscription. The author, Ida Sedgwick Proper, had started the debate about whether the inscription was Ogham script, and in her *Monhegan: The Cradle of New England*, she included a picture of the inscription from the nineteenth century.[5]

Looking through the book, I learned that the first record of the inscription was made in 1808. Sometime later, local fishermen thought the inscription might be a form of Viking writing composed of runes. However, Proper decided that it bore no resemblance to runic writings and that it far more resembled Ogham script. Examining the drawing made in 1855, when the inscription was still clear, I had to agree with her. A series of short straight lines were grouped in clusters in a horizontal arrangement. Runes were more intricate and were usually written vertically.

The problem was that although Proper thought the inscription might be an Ogham script, she was unable to translate it. In fact, I discovered from Sam and Kerri that no one has been able to prove it is an Ogham inscription at all.

"The local Indians probably carved it for some reason," said Sam.

"Has any archaeological work been done?" I asked.

"Not that I know of, but some people have speculated that the pool beside the boulder might have been sacred to the Beothuk."

"What about the standing stones?" I asked.

"There's no way of knowing how long they've been there. Ida Proper doesn't mention them in her book. I guess they could have been put there recently. Groups of hippies used to stay there in the sixties. They scratched things all over the rocks, virtually obliterating the original markings on the boulder."

The next morning, when I heard the ferry had been canceled due to technical problems, and that the next boat would not be departing until after the weekend, I began to wonder if it was worth going to the island at all. Nothing had been found there and any historical evidence would have been contaminated by the hippies. I had everything I needed in Ida Proper's book. If the inscription did relate to the Monad, the Logos, or whatever it was the Rosicrucians considered important, I could make a photocopy of the inscription and have Sally Evans take a look at it when I got back to England. Beside which, the island would be covered in snow, I probably wouldn't be able to find the site in any case. However, when I asked Sam and Kerri where on the island on the inscription was located, my decision was made for me.

"The best way to get up to it is from the west, up a gully between two rocky outcrops. You can't miss them; they look like giant fish heads. The Indians used to call them the two serpents," said Sam.

Two serpents! Merlin was associated with two serpents. Intrigued, I queried Sam further about what he knew.

"Sadly, very little is known about the Beothuk, as they became extinct in the nineteenth century: wiped out by European diseases from which they had no immunity," he explained. "The last of them died from tuber-culosis in 1829, before anyone bothered to make a written study of their culture. From what is known, however, giant serpents featured prominently in their mythology. The fact that they regarded these rocks as serpents suggests to me that the site, which includes the spring and the inscribed rock, was sacred to them."

This meant far more to me than Sam and Kerri could have realized! If these rocks were called the two serpents when the Irish arrived in the sixth century, the place might indeed have been considered Manannan Island. Not only did its name bear an uncanny similarity to the mythical island of the Celtic sea god, but also serpents were associated with the god-hero Lugh, who was said to have been raised on the island. This might explain why the historical Merlin would have stayed there. He was old: Why not end his days on the island where Lugh, whom the Britons thought he personified, was raised?

Even more interesting was a possible link with William Shakespeare. Glynn Davis had said that Shakespeare discovered the location of the island because of something having to do with the two serpents on Excalibur's hilt. The original charts of the area, made by Dugua's cartographer Samuel de Champlain, no longer survive, but if they had included the names of these rocks, Shakespeare may have realized where the tomb was.

There was now no doubt, in my mind at least, that I had found what the Rosicrucians thought was Merlin's tomb. Manana Island had to be the island described in *The Voyage of Maelduin's Boat*, and, as such, it might well have been the burial site of the historical Merlin. After all my searching, I had to go there in person, if only to beat the enemy. There had been no sign of them since arriving in the States, but this didn't mean they weren't close on my heels. It would be only a matter of time before they made the connection to Manana Island. In fact, they could arrive in Port Clyde at any time. I did not want to wait another few days.

When I told Sam and Kerri that I needed to get back to England but didn't want to have wasted the journey to the States, they made a phone call to a friend, a local fisherman. The fisherman, Mat Walker, owned a boat and often dropped lobster pots around Manana Island. He had not planned to go out on the water that day, as the weather forecast wasn't very good, but my offer of two hundred dollars changed his mind.

189

At 11 A.M., on board the cramped boat with Mat and his crew of three, I set off from Port Clyde on a choppy crossing that was expected to take approximately an hour and a half. There was a strong north wind blowing and I had never known such cold. The crew found it amusing that, despite being wrapped up in rain gear that Sam had kindly lent me, underneath which I had on God knows how many layers of clothing, I was frozen stiff. I was also sick within ten minutes of casting off. They found that hilarious, too. I was almost considering paying Mat another two hundred dollars just to turn back, but I started to feel better once the last vestiges of my breakfast had been heaved overboard. Around an hour later, I wished we had, indeed, gone back.

The weather deteriorated; the wind was rising and snow began to fall. Mat spoke to the weather station on the radio and all indications were that the weather was only going to get worse. Unexpected storm-force winds were driving south from the Arctic. Mat would have returned to Port Clyde, but he was now much closer to Monhegan Island and could shelter there. The winds were slowing our progress and it was well after 1 P.M. when we finally sighted land. Although it was the middle of the day, Monhegan's lighthouse was flashing every few seconds from the highest point of the island. The harbor was situated on the west of the island, and we were just rounding the southern headland when the waves grew stronger and the current began to force us toward a cluster of jagged rocks called Lobster Point.

Inside the cabin, Mat spun the wheel to force us against the current, throwing the tiny fishing vessel high into the air each time we crashed through a wave. Every few seconds the forward view would be obscured completely by a blast of icy spray. The crew somehow managed to keep standing, but even though I was holding on to a safety rail, I kept losing my footing, with the result that I dangled helplessly from the handhold before being thrown repeatedly against the wall.

"Hang on!" screamed Mat. Too late! I lost my hold and was hurtled against the opposite side of the cabin, where I found myself sliding around on the floor.

"If we can make it around the point, we'll have a chance of making land," Mat shouted.

I looked ahead of him at the cliffs of the snow-covered headland that appeared occasionally between the relentless sheets of the driving blizzard. But just as I thought there was hope we would make it around Lobster Point, my stomach leaped as the boat dropped suddenly deeper into the violent sea. For a few seconds there was an icy calm. The howl of the wind became a dull moan and the freezing torrent no longer pounded the windows. Then the terror hit me. The vessel had sunk into the trough of an enormous wave. Its dark crest towering before us momentarily shielded the boat from the relentless storm and shrouded us in a cold shadow of impending doom. We were directly in the wave's path and it was heading right for the rocks! As the dreadful wall of water drew closer and the vessel began to rise, the skipper spun the wheel furiously in an attempt to turn the bow into the oncoming wave.

So it was that six months after beginning my search for the origins of the Merlin legend in the town of Carmarthen, it seemed that my life was about to end in the bitter waters ten miles off the coast of North America.

14

THE FIFTH ELEMENT

We hit the wave head on. The bow rose high into the air, lifting the boat close to vertical. Even the experienced crew members were jolted from the safety rails. Two of them went tumbling with me to crash into the back of the cabin, while the third was left dangling helplessly from his handhold. Incredibly, the skipper managed to remain at the wheel. For a few seconds the vessel remained almost still as the engine roared and diesel smoke filled the air. But just as it seemed the boat was about to flip over onto its back, it came crashing down upright. We were propelled across the deck, but Mat fought for control and steered on unyieldingly into the violent waves.

Then, suddenly and unexpectedly, the sea calmed. It was actually as rough as it had been when we left the harbor, but compared to what we had just been through, we could have been floating on a millpond. The crew scrambled to their feet and one of them helped me up.

"You hurt?" he asked. I was disorientated, but managed to shake my head. "We're okay now," he said, pointing through the window to a new headland that had appeared on our port side. Manana Island now stood mercifully between us and the mighty waves that rolled in from the North Atlantic: We were in the channel between the two islands. The current was still strong and the wind continued to howl, but the boat chugged forward to dock a few minutes later in Monhegan's tiny harbor.

After about an hour, the snow stopped and the winds abated. Mat had to fix a few things on the boat, and told me that one of his crew, a guy named Del, would take me across to Manana Island in a dinghy. I was terrified to take to the sea again—the skies were still dark and the air was bitter cold—but we sped across to the island in the little motor-boat without incident.

Monhegan Island rises to over 160 feet, and on the hillside above the harbor a cluster of wooden buildings nestles in a small forest of hardy pines. In contrast, Manana Island was a snow-covered, barren hump, rising out of the sea like the back of an enormous whale, with patches of exposed rock here and there. Sam had told me that the best way to reach the inscribed boulder was through the gully on the west of the island, but the rough seas made that impossible. Instead, we landed on the sheltered, eastern side and pulled the dinghy onto the rocks.

Leading the way up the snowy hillside, Del told me what everyone else had been telling me: this was a waste of time. There would be nothing to see; everything would be covered with snow. I was hoping he was wrong; it wasn't that deep where we were. However, the moment we climbed to the top of the island, I could see what he meant. It was a terrace of driven snow, with nothing to be seen but the fog station sticking out in the middle. The deep resonance of the station's foghorn sounded every so often, as if in response to the beam of the Monhegan lighthouse, sweeping the darkened landscape every fifteen seconds.

After putting on the pair of snowshoes that Sam had lent me, I followed Del as we trudged our way across a few hundred yards of gray-white wasteland to finally reach a depression in the snow. It was thirty feet across and surrounded by a ring of partly exposed rocks. "Well, here you are," Del said. "Told you there'd be nothing to see."

Apparently, the inscribed boulder was deep under the snow; even the four-foot standing stones, which were evidently on higher ground, were complete covered. In the past, when I imagined the setting for Merlin's tomb, I envisioned a tranquil land of sunlit meadows, singing birds circling overhead, the air filled with the scent of summer flowers. Instead, I was on a dark and frozen headland, the sound of angry waves breaking on the rocks below us, the air bitter with the smell of salt. The only signs of life of any kind were the eerie foghorn and the clanging of a buoy bell somewhere out at sea.

Del sat down on one of the rocks and lit a cigarette. He chuckled as he watched me try to clear away the snow. "Packed solid," he said. He was right. A combination of wind, sea air, and intense cold had turned the snow virtually to ice. There was no way I was going to see anything here until spring. Still, I had made it, and seemingly before the enemy—at least no one in Port Clyde had heard about anyone else, other than the locals, coming anywhere near Manana Island for weeks.

In my own mind I was convinced Manana Island was the place where Merlin ended his days, and I was sure I was standing on the very spot that Pierre Dugua and others had thought was the site of Merlin's grave. However, the only way to know if anyone was buried here was to organize an archaeological dig. Unfortunately, a proper excavation seemed extremely remote. Not only was the island government land and miles from anywhere, but it would also take more than stories of Merlin to motivate qualified archaeologists.

But what about the great secret the Rosicrucians supposedly discovered? Was it the inscription, which, in any event, was no longer visible? My thoughts were interrupted by Del, who informed me that it was time to leave. The weather was forecast to hold for only a few hours and we had to be heading back.

It was certainly an anticlimax. I was sure I had found what I was looking for, but there was nothing to see. I had also expected to meet up with the enemy, but presumably I had managed to lose them—which was, quite ironically, very disappointing.

When I returned to England, Sally Evans examined the drawing of the inscription on the boulder. I was hoping for something revelatory. Unfortunately, she could offer no translation. She said it looked similar to a sixth-century variation of Ogham script that had been found on a few inscribed stones in Ireland; sadly, however, not enough such inscriptions had been found to render them interpretable. If the inscription on Manana Island really was an Ogham text, its message was destined to remain a mystery, at least for the foreseeable future.

At first, Sally's failure to translate the inscription left me deeply disappointed. However, I eventually got to thinking. If Sally Evans, a modern expert on ancient Celtic script, couldn't decipher it, then it seemed unlikely that anyone in 1604 would have been able to read it either. If Dagua or anyone else found something on Manana Island that he believed was the Monad, the Fifth Element, the name of God, or suchlike, then whatever he found was surely something other than the inscription!

Glynn Davis thought whatever they had found was still there, but he might well be wrong. It could have been taken away by Dugua, the Rosicrucians, or their successors. There was certainly nothing there now. I therefore tried one final line of investigation. A mysterious group of Rosicrucian successors known as the Nine had supposedly kept the secret. If they were the Pilgrim Fathers, as I had speculated, was there any written evidence concerning them that might throw new light on the enigma?

Studying the writings of the Plymouth colonists, I found nothing that could be remotely linked to Merlin, the Rosicrucians, or anything esoteric. Nor could I find anything of any conceivable relevance regarding their descendants—that is, until I concentrated on the family of William Brewster. I had purposely left Brewster's descendants for last, as they might prove to be the most interesting. Although there was no proof that the other Pilgrim Fathers were Rosicrucians, their leader, William Brewster, almost certainly was. He was a member of the School of Night and he printed Rosicrucian literature, and Pierre Dugua had been staying with him in Leiden when the final meeting of the fraternity seems to have taken place in February 1620. Even if the Pilgrim Fathers were not the Nine, the chances were that Brewster would have known as much about Dugua's discovery as anyone else. He was Dugua's close friend and right in the thick of it all.

Brewster's descendants initially proved difficult to follow, until I discovered that, in 1931, a Boston scholar named George Bowman had managed to trace the Brewster genealogy.[1] In fact, what had gotten him interested was that the Brewster family tree was linked with his own. George Bowman discovered that in 1814 Brewster's sole surviving descendant, one Mary Brewster, married into the Bowman family of Cuttingsville, in the New England state of Vermont. Two years later she gave birth to a son, John Bowman, who was the only one of her three children to reach adulthood. John married a woman named Jennie in 1849, and they had two daughters. Sadly, their first daughter, Addie, died

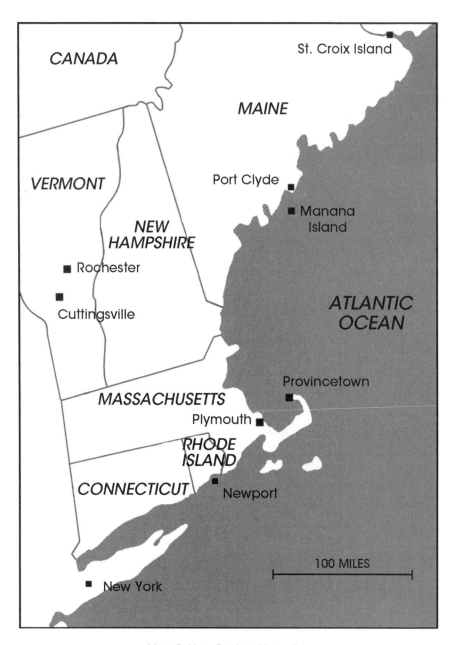

Map 5. New England key sites

in 1854 at the age of four months, and his second daughter, Ella, died in 1879, still in her teens. When his wife died in 1880, John Bowman was left childless, so when *he* died in 1891, so did the last known descendant of William Brewster.

It was when I read up on John Bowman that I discovered something exciting. Toward the end of his life, he had embarked upon a most peculiar project, one that seemed to link directly with the mystery of the Rosicrucians.

John Bowman was a self-made man. Having begun life as a relatively poor farmer's son, he eventually made a fortune selling leather goods to the U.S. government during the Civil War. There was nothing remarkable about Bowman's life until after the death of his wife. Left alone, without a family, he spent vast sums of money creating the most unusual monument to his wife and daughters.

To begin with, he had a large mausoleum built in the Cuttingsville cemetery. The Egyptian-style tomb was the largest memorial in the entire state: More than twenty feet high, it was constructed from 750 tons of granite, fifty tons of marble, and twenty thousand bricks. Outside the entrance, Bowman erected a life-size stone statue of himself. Inside were busts of his family surrounded by pillars and the walls were covered with huge mirrors. In addition, Bowman reconstructed the entire cemetery by repairing damaged graves and adding a perimeter wall.

In the graveyard he erected statues of Greek and Roman figures, together with fountains and stone monuments carved with strange designs and symbols. And if this was not enough, Bowman had a large, three-story, twenty-one-room mansion built directly across the road from the mausoleum. It was appointed with hot and cold running water, luxurious carpets, ornate wallpaper, and lavish woodwork. On the grounds were a barn, an icehouse, and a cottage for a permanent caretaker. Bowman never lived in the house, however. No one did. Incredibly, it had been built purely as a memorial to his dead family. When Bowman died in 1891, he left a fifty-thousand-dollar trust for the maintenance of the estate. A huge sum of money in those days, it paid for the caretaker and a household of servants to keep the mansion clean and tidy. This is how it remained: a piece of nineteenth-century history suspended in time, until the fund finally ran out in 1950.

Most people in Cuttingsville thought the deaths of Bowman's wife and children had sent the poor man mad, but others thought the eccentric creations were an intricate code that led to buried treasure. When he died, apparently a great deal of Bowman's fortune was unaccounted for.

Historians suggested that the strange imagery was associated with Freemasonry. Bowman had been a Mason, and some of the symbolism he employed in the project was undoubtedly Masonic, such as the statue of a man in the cemetery grounds that held up a giant pair of dividers. However, when I read about a number of gravestones Bowman had erected to replace older, broken ones, I was sure that more than Masonic symbolism was involved. Evidently, the gravestones were carved with a hand, fist clenched, with its index finger pointing upward to a star. This is precisely the symbol the Rosicrucians had used for the new star that appeared in 1604—the supernova that occurred in the same year that the grave of Merlin supposedly had been found. As the last descendant of William Brewster, did the childless Bowman build the elaborate memorial as a series of clues, not to lead to buried treasure, but instead to preserve the secret that had been discovered at Merlin's tomb?

I needed to return to the States and find out for myself.

It was still winter when I arrived in Cuttingsville, but spring was near and much of the New England snow had melted. The sun was bright overhead and Bowman's white-painted timber mansion almost shone beside the road that ran down the hill to the center of the small town. A short flight of steps led up to a covered porch that adorned the front of the house. Above the porch were two other levels, topped by a jumble of yellow-slate roofs and a pinnacled tower.

The mansion certainly looked mysterious, like the traditional haunted house from an old horror movie. I was accompanied by Graham and Jodi Russell, a couple from America who had helped me with historical investigations in the past; they were as curious as I to see the strange things John Bowman left as his epitaph.

We were in for a series of bitter disappointments, however. Bowman's house is now called Laurel Hall, and the Vermont guidebook we bought said it was a museum, open to the public year-round. It was, as we immediately discovered, no such thing. The building stood locked and empty.

We were peering in through the windows to see if anyone was around when a woman drove up and asked what we were doing. She seemed agitated and highly suspicious of us. When we showed her the guidebook and told her we thought the house was a museum, she shook her head in exasperation. Whoever had written the guide, she said, had obviously never been there. The house belonged to a private trust. The trust was attempting to renovate the building, which was in an advanced state of disrepair.

This woman was connected with the trust and was keeping a close watch on the place. Apparently, only a week or so prior to our arrival there had been a break-in, and considerable damage was done. Paneling was torn from the walls, floorboards were ripped up, and parts of the ceiling were pulled down. The mausoleum too had been vandalized, as was the cemetery, from which nearly all of Bowman's statues and inscribed stones were removed.

The road that passes the house is a quiet one, and with no occupied buildings within sight of the area, it evidently had been possible for the robbers to pile everything into the back of a truck undetected. Still, it must have taken some effort. Of the statues that John Bowman had erected, only two remained: the life-size effigy of himself outside the mausoleum and a figurine of the Roman goddess Venus, which stood on the lawn in front of the mansion. No wonder the woman was so upset. Annoyingly, the break-in had left the trustees so wary that there was no way we would be allowed inside.

After she left, we walked across the road to the cemetery and found that we could not even get inside the mausoleum. The door to the windowless white marble structure was boarded up with heavy metal sheets; even Bowman's statue was covered over by solid metal panels. In the graveyard we found the remains of the pedestals that had supported the statues, but anything of interest seemed gone. For more than a hundred years, Bowman's mysterious creations had stood quietly in this picturesque cemetery, in the tranquil shadow of the tree-lined mountains of central Vermont. Then, just a few days before we arrived, they had all been stolen. The damage to the mansion may not have been as mindless as the woman seemed to think. The fact that the perpetrators had torn away paneling suggested they were looking for something. Returning to the mausoleum,

I gave the metal sheeting an angry kick. A deep booming resounded inside the tomb. I may have beaten the enemy to Manana Island—but they had obviously gotten here first.

I half hoped that I was wrong about John Bowman knowing anything about the Rosicrucians, and that the robbers too would be following a red herring. All their trouble pulling apart the mansion and hauling away heavy stone statues would have been a waste of time. Then Jodi discovered one of the gravestones carved with the hand and star. It lay broken and flat on the ground, hidden behind a pile of stones in the corner of the cemetery. It was the remains of a gray stone grave marker, normal in all respects apart from its circular, rose-colored inlay, about a foot in diameter, which showed a relief of a hand pointing upward to a five-rayed star. There could be no doubt about it; it was identical in every way to the symbol used by the Rosicrucians for the new star of 1604.

Surely John Bowman had to have known something about his ancestor and the mystery of Merlin's tomb!

Returning to the car, we stopped to look at the sole remaining statue. About four feet tall, it was a metal sculpture of the goddess Venus standing in a carved bowl representing a shell. This, in turn, stood on a rusting iron pedestal, about the same height again, in the center of what had once been a pond. The Venus figure was actually a fountain, and the water would have poured from an urn she held on her shoulder. Presumably, the only reason this had not been taken was that it was made of metal, filled with plumbing, and firmly riveted down.

"Wasn't Venus mentioned in the Rosicrucian writings?" asked Graham Russell as we examined the figurine.

I had brought along copies of the Rosicrucian works that Glynn Davis had given me. One of them, Michael Maier's *Themis Aurea*, contained what Glynn believed to be one of the three clues to the secret discovered at Merlin's grave (see chapter 9). The cryptic verse read:

> *Pegasus opened a spring of overflowing water wherein Diana washed herself, to whom Venus was handmaid and Saturn gentleman usher.*

The fountain was an overflowing spring, and the figure of Venus could indeed be described as the handmaiden who fed the pool. There was no Pegasus, Diana, or Saturn, but perhaps the other statues had represented them. Finding no one around to speak to, we headed for the county library, in the nearby town of Rutland, a few miles to the north. Hopefully there we could find more information about the interior of Bowman's mansion and the mausoleum, and learn more about the missing statues.

Unfortunately, at the library we found no photographs, or even illustrations, but there were a few descriptions of the statues that had been stolen. Beside the figure, which held up the dividers, there was a winged horse, the Grim Reaper, and a woman holding a horn. In classical mythology, Pegasus is a winged horse, Saturn is the god of time and death, and Diana, the huntress, is often depicted with a hunter's horn. Although they were not named, these statues were almost certainly the other mythical figures from the enigmatic passage in Maier's *Themis Aurea*.

Looking through Maier's other book, the *Atalanta Fugiens*, I realized that the statue of the figure holding the dividers may also have been relevant. The picture that Glynn Davis believed was one of the other two clues showed the alchemist beside the wall, holding what I had taken to be two tapered sticks. I could now see that they were, in fact, a pair of huge dividers, the place where they joined being hidden by the alchemist's arm. Taking all this into account, I was now certain that John Bowman knew all about whatever it was that had been found at Merlin's grave.

What confirmed my belief was something else we discovered about the interior of Laurel Hall. Most of the decorations had been removed and sold off after Bowman's trust fund ran out in 1950. There was a copy of the inventory, but nothing seemed relevant apart from a wall mural in one of the first-floor rooms. It showed a scene from a Shakespearean play—*The Tempest*. This was the very play that Shakespeare had written for Elizabeth's Alchemical Wedding!

Like everything else that John Bowman had gone to such lengths to preserve, the picture could no longer be seen; it had been painted over in the 1960s when the building was used briefly as book depository.

Fortunately, though, there was a record of what it had depicted: act 1, scene 2, in which the magician Prospero and his daughter, Miranda, stand alone, talking beside Prospero's cell.

Surely this was more than coincidence! Inigo Jones's original set design was identical to the one he designed for Elizabeth's coming-of-age masque, where the same cell was depicted as Merlin's tomb. John Bowman had left gravestones inscribed with the symbol for the new star of 1604, statues that connected with Michael Maier's cryptic clues, and a painting showing what Jones, Shakespeare, and Jonson used to symbolize Merlin's last resting place. But what did it all mean?

For a while it seemed we had reached a dead end. There was, though, one other thing we discovered about the mansion that could be significant. Opposite the mural depicting the scene from *The Tempest* there was another mural. It was a landscape of a wooded hillside called West Hill, near the town of Rochester, some thirty miles to the north. Evidently, it had been a favorite spot of Bowman's; he and his family had often gone camping there.

Looking up the location, we found that it did, indeed, hold a mystery. Across an area of some forty acres on West Hill, there are approximately eighty huge piles of stones known as cairns. Most of them are between six and ten feet high, around fifteen feet wide and long, and built from thousands of roughly shaped stones. The oldest surviving record of them goes back to 1838, when the owner of the land described them as "Indian burial mounds."

However, no bones have ever been found inside them, and today they are somewhat of a mystery to archaeologists. John Bowman's interest in the area may have been innocent enough, but as the area was so close by, we decided it was worth a visit.

West Hill is now part of the Green Mountain National Forest, and on the day we arrived the whole area was still covered with snow. Nevertheless, the piles of gray and rust-colored stones stood out clearly every fifty feet or so across the length of the wooded escarpment. Covered by patches of green moss and yellow lichen, with dead brown leaves having been swept among the stones, most of the cairns were solid structures, but some had niches at the base, just large enough for someone to crouch inside.

Over the years, spring meltwater had reduced many of the cairns to elongated piles of rubble, but those that were best preserved had a common feature: Considerable trouble had been taken to make them flat on top. Rather than cairns, which are mounds of stones usually built by ancient peoples as grave markers, these appeared to be platforms, erected specifically to provide a series of flat surfaces on the sleep slope.

As we trudged through the snow from pile to pile, I tried to reason what purpose they might have served. Unfortunately, the Algonquian tribes who are known to have occupied this part of Vermont were extinct by the nineteenth century, and little is known about them. It was Graham Russell who proposed the most logical explanation: Some Native Americans tribes incinerated their dead; might these have been used for cremations? I agreed that it would explain why no bones had been found.[2]

"Surely only one cremation platform would be needed," Jodi said, as we discussed the idea. "Why, then, are there so many?"

"Perhaps each one was used for the funeral of a different person, and they then became individual memorials," Graham suggested.

Jodi looked around at the dozen or so stone piles that were visible from where we stood. "So they might be monuments to a whole succession of tribal chiefs, each one representing a different generation?"

Jodi's words seemed to jog something in my memory. For some weeks, I could not help but feel that a common theme ran through the Rosicrucians' cryptic messages. I had no idea what it might be, but when Jodi talked about the cairns representing a series of generations, it seemed to mean something. "It probably has nothing to do with this place specifically," I said, "but there's something about the Roscicrucians' codes. For some reason, the idea of a *family* just sprang into my mind."

"You think that's why John Bowman left the painting of this place—to reinforce the idea of a family graveyard?" Graham asked.

"Maybe! I don't know. I think it's just what you were talking about. It made me think of families." I tried to focus my thoughts, but the tantalizing notion began to recede.

"Is it something to do with the Alchemical Wedding?" Graham suggested.

"Michael Maier's cryptic verse is all about a wedding," said Jodi. Graham and I had no idea what she meant. "A handmaiden and an usher," she said, looking at us as though it was obvious. "What else could it refer to but a wedding?"

I thought for a moment. Whatever the connection was, I was close to grasping it. "The goddess Diana was also mentioned in the verse," I said. "Apart from being the goddess of hunting, Diana was a fertility goddess and deity of childbirth. She was . . ." I cut off mid-sentence. Suddenly it became clear. The Rosicrucian clues all concerned *procreation*!

It was not only Michael Maier's cryptic verse that concerned the theme of male and female union; it was also his two mysterious illustrations. One was of the man with a sword about to break open a giant egg. This could well have symbolized male penetration and fertility—the sword being a phallic symbol and the egg being the female ovum. Glynn Davis had thought the significance of the other illustration, the one depicting an alchemist with a pair of dividers, was that it was a map designed to reveal the location of Merlin's tomb.

I was now sure that it was something else entirely. As well as being a Masonic emblem derived from the fraternity's origins as stonemasons, in the Middle Ages a set of dividers was used symbolically in art to stand for sexual union—it represented a pair of open female legs. Moreover, on the wall in the illustration was a drawing of a naked couple.

My friends agreed that I was on to something, but Jodi was still confused. "What could any of that have to do with Merlin's tomb?" she asked.

The stone platforms: monuments to generation after generation of tribal leaders. It may or may not have been Bowman's intention, but thinking about the platforms helped me to make sense of the Rosicrucian code. "It's all to do with an ancestral bloodline," I said. "The *Fama Fraternitatis* metaphorically portrayed Merlin as Christian Rosencreutz, the mythical figure that supposedly lived for the one hundred and six years between 1378 and 1484—the years when Britain was without a monarch from the royal bloodline, a bloodline established by Merlin. It drew attention not only to Merlin, but also to his descendants."

"You mean it's all connected with Merlin's ancestral bloodline?" asked Graham.

"It *must* be. In Maier's illustration, the man wields a sword, which Glynn Davis believes to be Excalibur. If so, then this figure in Roman costume was either Arthur or, more likely, Merlin, the man for whom the sword was originally made."

"If it was Arthur's bloodline, then it was also Merlin's," said Jodi. "Wasn't Guinevere said to be Merlin's daughter?"

"Yes! That has to be why Bowman depicted Prospero and Miranda in the mural," I said. "If Prospero symbolized Merlin, then his daughter Miranda must have represented Guinevere."

I had no idea whether John Bowman's mural of West Hill was actually one of his clues. Perhaps it had been his intent to draw attention to the theme of ancestry. Perhaps it was just a coincidence. Nonetheless, I was now sure that the heart of the Rosicrucian mystery in some way concerned Merlin's bloodline. After all, Princess Elizabeth was seemingly one of his descendants. She was certainly descended from the man who appears to have been the historical King Arthur—Owain Ddantgwyn (see chapter 10).

Owain's genealogy is preserved in the *Welsh Annals*, which lists his descendants as kings of central Wales until 855, when the last of his direct male line, a king called Cyngen, died without issue.[3] The line then passed on through Cyngen's sister, a woman called Nest, whose husband, Rhodri, inherited the title of king. He became known as Rhodri the Great, as he extended his kingdom throughout much of Wales, and it was his direct male heirs who became the Tudor monarchs of England in 1485. The last of the Tudors was Queen Elizabeth I, who died unmarried and childless in 1603. Her nearest relative was her second cousin James I, the father of Princess Elizabeth.[4] Standing on top of one of the enigmatic stone piles, looking across to the mountains over the valley below, I reasoned that I had discovered just about all I could concerning John Bowman.

A few days later, I returned again to England with a mystery half-solved. All the same, I had found what I was certain was Merlin's tomb, and I knew about as much concerning the Rosicrucians as it seemed I ever would. I had promised Glynn Davis that I would tell him everything I discovered once my adventure was over, and now was the time.

Calling him, I was delighted to hear that he had recovered and that new medication was keeping his heart condition in check. His wife probably wasn't too happy about it, but Glynn offered to meet me in the beer garden of the Carmarthen pub where we had first met.

Glynn listened intently as I told him about Manana Island. He was ecstatic, and agreed that this had to be the location of Merlin's tomb. And when I went on to explain how I believed the mystery somehow concerned Merlin's descendants, he nodded knowingly. Apparently, this was something he had already come to suspect since we had last met.

"I have no idea how the mysterious Monad ties in with it all," I concluded. "You told me you thought the Monad would be found at Merlin's tomb. I've no clues as to what that was. I'm afraid the enemy, as you call them, are probably in a much better position to discover whatever *that* is."

Glynn smiled. "I think they'll find it's been a wild-goose chase," he said. "No doubt they expect to discover something that will give them power. From what you've told me, I now think the Monad was simply another clue to the fact that it was a descendant of Merlin's that was important. True, John Dee and others spent years trying to discover the Fifth Element. However, I think the Rosicrucians employed the notion of the Monad as the Logos, the Word of God, simply as part of their cipher."

"I'm not with you," I said.

"You know how 'the Word' is referred to at the beginning of St. John's Gospel: 'In the beginning was the Word, and the Word was with God, and the Word was God.' Some biblical scholars speculate that this refers to the Hebrew word Peru-Urevu. According to the original Hebrew Bible, this was the first word God spoke to Adam. In the modern English Bible it is translated as 'Be fruitful and multiply.'[5] If this is what the author of the *Fama Fraternitatis* had in mind, it was yet another clue concerning procreation."

"So you don't think there is anything else to be discovered?" I asked.

"My passion was to find the mysterious tomb; I think you've solved that mystery for me. You may not share my beliefs, but I believe that occult power is very real. I believe the Fifth Element is a universal force that, if discovered, would be a dreadful thing in the wrong hands. My fear has always been that the secret of the Fifth Element was to be found at Merlin's grave. I now realize that this does not seem to be the case. It was the Star Child that was important all along."

"The Star Child?" I had no idea what he meant.

"The *Naometria*, the very first Rosicrucian manuscript, written by Simon Studion in 1604, refers to someone called the Star Child who was supposedly born in 1596. In that year, another new star had appeared in the constellation of Cetus, the Sea Dragon. It was not a supernova, however, but rather what astronomers now call a variable star. Its brightness changes over time, and it became visible with the naked eye for a while in 1596. Not only Studion, but other astrologers as well regarded this as heralding the birth of a sacred royal figure, just as the star of Bethlehem accompanied Christ's birth.

"When the much brighter star appeared in 1604, Studion decided it was a second omen regarding this important individual; and as *this* star appeared in the constellation of the serpents, he linked it with Merlin. Coincidence or not, the fact that Merlin's tomb was found in the same year, 1604, merely confirmed his idea that someone who was born in 1596—a direct descendant of Merlin's—would become a monarch and found a royal dynasty that would rule in a brave new age of enlightenment. For that reason, he referred to this person as the Star Child."[6]

"Princess Elizabeth!" I said.

"She was born in 1596, the year the first star appeared. Studion and his fellows in the School of Night were more than familiar with the Arthurian romances, and knew the tradition that the Tudors and Stuarts were of the bloodline of the Welsh kings, a kingship said to have been founded by Merlin, through his own daughter Guinevere. This variable star was called Mira, after a woman from Greek mythology, which, I'm sure, is why Shakespeare called Prospero's daughter Miranda. Although it's now a common name, Shakespeare actually coined it. Many people think it came from the Latin word *mirandum,* meaning wonderful, but I think it was yet another clue to the fact that a monarch from Merlin's bloodline was at the heart of the mystery."

"Elizabeth *did* become a monarch in her own right," I said. "She became queen of Bohemia—but it didn't last long. The Winter Queen, as they called her, must have been a bitter disappointment to the Rosicrucians."

Glynn shook his head slowly. "But Elizabeth wasn't the Star Child," he said. "The true Star Child's descendant has yet to be crowned."

I was confused. "Elizabeth was descended from Merlin—Arthur certainly. She was the person all the fuss was about: the coming-of-age pageant; the Alchemical Wedding. You said she was born in the right year."

"Elizabeth was certainly important for the hopes of a grand Protestant alliance, but I think she was a diversion. Although it's misogynistic, ancient European lines of succession always passed through the male heir: the eldest son. If there was no male heir, it passed through the oldest daughter; and if there was no daughter, then to the king's brother; and if he had no brother, to his eldest sister. Most unfair, I know, but this is how it worked. In the Rosicrucians' time, this was still the way to trace a direct bloodline. Suspecting that the real Rosicrucian mystery concerned Merlin's bloodline, I looked into the genealogy of the ancient Welsh kings and found that the Arthurian romancers had gotten it wrong. Going by their own logic, the Tudors were not the most direct Arthurian descendants."

Glynn reminded me that in 855, the Welsh king Cyngen died childless and that his sister Nest married Rhodri. "Rhodri became a highly successful king, so all the attention remained with him," he said. "However, Nest was actually the younger of Cyngen's two sisters; his older sister, a princess named Cynddia, was the one who really carried on the bloodline. She was married to a less important chieftain named Ynyr, a prince of Gwent in South Wales, and the most direct bloodline continued with their descendants."

I had traced this genealogy myself when I was researching Whittington Castle. Cynddia and Ynyr's last direct male successor was a Welsh baron, Cadfarch, whose daughter married the English earl of Hereford in the late eleventh century. Their sole heir, Lynette, married another English baron, Payne Peveril. Payne Peveril's granddaughter and sole heir, Mellet, married a certain Fulk Fitz Warine, and their son, also called Fulk, was baron of Whittington Castle at the close of the twelfth century. It was he who possessed the Marian Chalice, the cup that was said to be the Chalice of Mary Magdalene and the true Holy Grail.[7]

"I realized that Fulk was descended from the historical King Arthur," I said, "but I didn't realize that this line of succession was more direct than that of the Tudors."

"Here we have another case where confusion over daughters comes into play," said Glynn. "Payne Peveril's youngest daughter was the mother of Fulk's wife. His eldest daughter was Adelise Peveril, and she married Sir Richard Vernon of Shropshire in the year 1100. She and her descendants were the direct line, as far as traditional hereditary is concerned. In 1596 their direct descendant Lady Elizabeth Vernon gave birth to a daughter named Penelope. It is she who I believe was the true Star Child."

"Would the Rosicrucians have known of her?" I said.

"Elizabeth was married to the Earl of Southampton. He was not only Shakespeare's patron for a while in the 1590s, but he was also a close friend of Christopher Marlowe and Walter Raleigh, and a member of the School of Night."

"The Earl of Southampton was Penelope's father?"

Glynn smiled. "That's where the mystery lies. The earl never acknowledged her as his daughter; besides which, he was a self-confessed homosexual. Many historians have speculated that William Shakespeare was the true father. It's known that he was estranged from his wife at this time, and in the mid-1590s he wrote more than one hundred and fifty love sonnets to a mysterious woman, often referred to as the Dark Lady. The only woman who is known to have been close to Shakespeare at this time was his patron's wife, Elizabeth—Penelope's mother."[8]

"So you think that although Elizabeth was important politically, it was Penelope who the Rosicrucians really thought would establish this new, mystical dynasty?"

Glynn nodded. "And it may have been the real reason why Shakespeare was killed. I originally thought his murder was tied up with his intention to give away the whereabouts of Merlin's tomb. Now that it seems clear it was the bloodline, rather than the tomb itself, that was important, this scenario no longer makes sense. Penelope married a high-ranking courtier named Sir Robert Spencer in 1615, only a few months before Shakespeare died. Perhaps he intended to announce that he was her true father. A common playwright as the father of the Star Child—this would have been something the Rosicrucians would never want to be known."

"Didn't you say Jonson's writings referred to Shakespeare discovering something about the two serpents on Excalibur's hilt, and that was why he was killed?"

Glynn gave some thought before answering. I remembered he had told me he would be giving away Masonic secrets if he revealed any more about Ben Jonson's writings that belonged to his lodge. "Jonson uses the phrase 'as serpents entwine to smother life' when he speaks of Shakespeare's death. As he also refers to a sword, I assumed he was talking about the Excalibur serpents. The sword, though, may have been simply metaphorical. The serpents might actually refer to the caduceus wand, which in Masonic symbolism can represent intermarriage—a mixing of bloodlines. It is clear now that Jonson may have been referring to the fact that Shakespeare died because it was deemed that he tainted the sacred bloodline."

I was still curious to know exactly what Ben Jonson said, but in his usual polite way Glynn refused to tell me any more. "Believe me, it really isn't relevant," he insisted. There was, though, something far more interesting that Glynn had touched upon, and I was determined to have him elaborate.

"You said that the true Star Child's descendant has yet to be crowned," I said. "Who were Penelope's descendants?" Thankfully, this did not seem to have any relevance to Masonic secrets.

"James I made Sir Robert Spencer a baron, and he and Penelope began an aristocratic line of descent that is still important today. Penelope's ninth-great-granddaughter was Princess Diana, and her son Prince William is in line to be the English king after Prince Charles. It may well be that a future king of England will have the blood of Merlin running in his veins."

Prince William descended from Merlin and King Arthur—perhaps even Shakespeare—it was certainly an intriguing thought. "So Penelope was the Star Child and, according to the prophecy, the first of her descendants to be crowned would . . . do what?" I asked.

"According to Studion, he or she would inherit the powers of Christian Rosencreutz—in other words, Merlin."

"Which were?"

"The ability to see the future, the capacity to make the right decisions based of mystic foresight."

"The legendary Merlin may have had the gift of prophecy, but I doubt the historical Merlin, Ambrosius, had any such powers," I said as we parted company that day. "At least I've found no historical evidence for it." Strangely, Glynn did not respond. Instead, he looked deep in thought.

There were still unanswered questions and puzzles. What was the meaning of Inigo Jones's strange windmill and of the weird tower in Rhode Island? Who was the mysterious enemy who went to such lengths to solve the Rosicrucians' code? What did the enigmatic inscription on Manana Island actually say? I was still in the dark as to what Glynn's Freemasons really knew. Nonetheless, my quest to discover the truth about Merlin was a success, and I was certain I had discovered his grave.

Merlin was a historical figure: He united Britain in the last days of the Roman Empire; he traveled to America fifteen centuries before Columbus; and he may have learned the secrets of the ancient Druids. I doubted, though, that he was ever a prophet. However, the night I arrived back from Wales, a phone call from Glynn Davis had me wondering.

"You say you don't think the historical Merlin had the gift of prophecy, that he could see the future," Glynn said over the phone.

"Well, there's no historical evidence for it," I replied.

"Can you answer a question?" he asked enigmatically. "Why do you regard *The Voyage of Maelduin's Boat* as evidence of an early transatlantic voyage?"

"It describes things that could not have been described except by someone who had been on such a voyage: icebergs, the Faroe Isles, the volcanoes of Iceland; details concerning the shores of Greenland and Labrador."

"But why do you regard it as proof that it occurred before Columbus or the Vikings?"

"Because it was written in the eighth century, well before other Europeans are known to have gone there."

Glynn remained silent for a while, as if to let my words sink in. "After you left, I read *The Voyage of Maelduin's Boat,* and I found something else that, by your own logic, proves Merlin could see the future."

I thought through the account in my mind, but had no idea what he meant.

Glynn continued: "The islands the mariners discovered were thought to be the islands of the Otherworld, right? Islands you think are the islands of New England and northeastern America? And one of the Otherworld islands was said to be Avalon?"

"Correct, but they never actually found Avalon. Instead they ended up on Manannan's Island—if I'm right, Manana Island."

"But Merlin has a dream about Avalon when he falls asleep on the voyage?"

"Yes, he dreams of a crystal city."

"Have you read the account of that dream?"

"Yes. I don't see your point."

"Merlin dreams of Avalon as the magical capital of the Otherworld. It's an island full of marvels with a city built from crystal, silver, marble, and bronze. In the dream, when Merlin and his friends arrive there, they are greeted by its giant queen." Glynn read the passage aloud:

> She wore a white mantle, with a circlet of gold in her hair . . . Two sandals she wore on her feet and a silken smock she wore next to her white skin, tied with a brooch . . .

"Doesn't this sound familiar to you? A huge white-skinned woman, wearing sandals, dressed in a robe, tied with a brooch, with a circlet on her head . . ."

"I'm not sure what a circlet is," I said, trying to think what he meant.

"It's a small crown or coronet, a sort of tiara."

"Sorry, I still don't know what you mean."

"A huge woman, she stands next to a crystal city—somewhere on an island off the coast of northeastern America?"

Suddenly I understood. "The Statue of Liberty!"

"Precisely! This is an exact description of something that did not exist until hundreds of years after the account was written. It would seem that someone—Merlin, according to the account—had a prophetic vision of New York as it would one day be."

"It has to be a coincidence," I said.

"You don't think that the similarity between giant floating crystals and icebergs is a coincidence," Glynn replied with a knowing laugh.

I was speechless, for—what could I say? He was right!

NOTES

CHAPTER 1—TWO MERLINS

1. Martin Keatman, Graham Phillips, *King Arthur: The True Story* (London: Random House, 1992); Graham Phillips, *The Chalice of Magdalene* (Rochester, Vt.: Bear & Company, 2004).

2. The oldest manuscript copy of Malory's work *Le Morte Darthur* is known as the *Winchester Manuscript* and is in the British Library.

3. Nennius, *Historia Brittonum*, preserved in the manuscript cataloged as Harlian 3859 in the British Library.

4. There are a number of copies of Gildas's work, of which the oldest manuscript in Britain is cataloged as Cotton Vitellius A. IV in the British Library.

5. *The Black Book of Carmarthen*, preserved in the National Library of Wales, where it is cataloged as Peniarth MS. 1.

6. *The Red Book of Hergest*, preserved in the Bodleian Library, Oxford, where it is cataloged as MS. Jesus 111.

7. The *Welsh Annals*, preserved in the same composite manuscript as Nennius's *Historia Brittonum*—Harlian 3859 in the British Library.

8. Geoffrey of Monmouth, *History of the Kings of Britain*, preserved in the manuscript cataloged as Cotton Nero D.V. in the British Library.

9. The complete text of the poem survives in a thirteenth-century manuscript cataloged as Cotton Vespasian E. 4 in the British Library.

10. "The Dream of Rhonabwy," preserved in *The Red Book of Hergest*.

11. The *Notitia Dignitatum*, or "Register of Dignitaries," was a document produced around 410 A.D. that listed the official posts and military units of the late Roman Empire. It survives in a medieval copy in a manuscript cataloged as MS. Canon. Misc. 378 in the Bodleian Library, Oxford.

12. Martin Keatman, Graham Phillips, *The Shakespeare Conspiracy* (London: Random House, 1994).

CHAPTER 2—A BOY WITH NO FATHER

1. Geoffrey of Monmouth, *The History of the Kings of Britain*, book 6, ch. 17.

2. Ibid., book 6, ch. 19.

3. Ibid.

4. Bede, *The Ecclesiastical History of the English People*, survives in a ninth-century copy, cataloged as Cotton Tiberius CII, in the British Library.

5. Nine varying copies of the *Anglo-Saxon Chronicle* survive. The oldest is an eleventh-century copy, known as the *Parker Chronicle* after its first collector, in the manuscript collection of Corpus Christi College, Cambridge.

6. H. N. Savory, *Excavations at Dinas Emrys 1954–56: Archaeologia Cambrensis* vol. 109, 1960, 13–77.

7. Nennius, *Historia Brittonum*, ch. 40.

8. Ibid., ch. 41–42.

9. Ibid., ch. 42.

10. Ibid.

11. Ibid.

12. Geoffrey of Monmouth, *The History of the Kings of Britain*, book 6, ch. 19.

CHAPTER 3—THE NOTABLE STORM

1. Gildas, *On the Ruin and Conquest of Britain*, trans. by M. Winterbottom (Chichester, U.K.: 1978) ch. 25.

2. Gildas, *De Excidio Brittonum*, trans. John Allan Giles, George Bell and Sons (London: 1891).

3. Nennius, *Historia Brittonum*, trans. John Allan Giles, Henry G. Bohn, (London: 1848).

4. Bede, *The Ecclesiastical History of the English People*, trans. V. D. Scudder (New York: Dutton, 1910).

5. *The Anglo-Saxon Chronicle*, trans. James Ingram (London: Everyman Press, 1912).

6. *The Welsh Annals: History from the Sources*, vol. 8, trans. John Morris (Chichester, U.K.: Phillimore, 1980).

7. Nennius, ch. 40.

8. Ibid., ch. 47.

9. Geoffrey of Monmouth, *The History of the Kings of Britain*, book 6, ch. 17.

10. Ibid., ch. 47.

11. Steven Muhlberger, *The Fifth-Century Chroniclers: Prosper, Hydatius and the Gallic Chronicle of 452* (Leeds, U.K.: Francis Cairns, 1990).

12. Bede, *The Ecclesiastical History*, ch. 21.

13. Nennius, ch. 66.

14. Bede, ch. 16.

15. *The Life of St. Germanus of Auxerre* in *Soldiers of Christ: Saints' Lives from Late Antiquity and the Early Middle Ages*, trans. T. Noble and T. Head (University Park, Pa.: Pennsylvania State University Press, 1994).

16. Gildas, *On the Ruin and Conquest of Britain*, ch. 24.

17. Ibid., ch. 25.

18. M. Darling, *Caister-on-Sea: Excavations by Charles Green 1951–55* (King's Lynn, U.K.: Heritage Marketing & Publications, 2000).

19. E. Evans, ed., *Britannia Monograph Series 19* (London: Society for the Promotion of Roman Studies, 1988), 485.

20. Nennius, ch. 43.

CHAPTER 4—AMBROSIUS EMRYS

1. Gildas, ch. 25.

2. Bede, ch. 16.

3. C. Morino, *Church and State in the Teaching of St. Ambrose* (Washington, D.C.: Catholic University Press, 1969).

4. Nennius, ch. 42.

5. For the full inscription from the Pillar of Eliseg, see Phillips and Keatman, *King Arthur: The True Story*, 92.

6. John Rhys, *Y Cymmrodor*, vol. 21, (London: The Honourable Society of Cymmrodorion, 1908), 48–50.

7. Harold Mytum, Chris Webster, *Studia Celtica*, vol. 35, no. 1 (Cardiff, U.K.: University of Wales Press, 2001), 89–108.

8. Nennius, ch. 66.

CHAPTER 5—THE LADY OF THE LAKE

1. The source of the English translation of the *Red Book* Triads was: J. Rhys and J. G. Evans, *The Text of the Mabinogion and Other Welsh Tales* (Oxford: Evans, 1887).

2. Ibid.

3. Caesar, *The Gallic War*, vol. 6:13.

4. Ibid., ch. 14.

5. Ibid.

6. Cicero, *De Divinatione*, vol. 1, ch. 41., vs 90.

7. Rhys and Evans, *The Text of the Mabinogion and Other Welsh Tales.*

8. Gildas, *On the Ruin and Conquest of Britain*, ch. 20.

9. E. A. Thompson, *A History of Attila and the Huns* (Oxford: Clarendon Press, 1948).

10. *L' Estoire de Merlin*, also referred to as *The Vugate Merlin*, survives in a manuscript cataloged as BM. Additional Manuscript 10293 in the British Museum.

11. Keatman, Phillips, *King Arthur: The True Story*, 39–41.

12. For further research, see R. S. Loomis, *Celtic Myth and the Arthurian Romance* (New York: Columbia University Press, 1927).

13. Caesar, *The Gallic War*, vol. 6:18.

14. Ibid.

15. See also: B. Bender, R. Cailland, *The Archaeology of Brittany, Normandy and the Channel Islands: An Introduction and Guide* (London: Faber, 1986).

CHAPTER 6—EXCALIBUR

1. Geoffrey of Monmouth, *The Life of Merlin*, ch. 2.

2. Ibid.

3. Ibid.

4. Keatman, Phillips, *King Arthur: The True Story*, 74.

5. E. A. Thompson, *A History of Attila and the Huns.*

6. Priscus's account is preserved in the work of a later historian, Jordanes, who wrote in the city of Constantinople in the 550s. The story of Attila's sword is found in chapter 35 of his *Latin De Origine Actibusque Getarum* (The Origin and Deeds of the Goths).

7. Gildas, *On the Ruin and Conquest of England,* ch. 25.

8. A. Birley, *Lives of the Later Caesars* (New York: Penguin, 1976).

9. Gildas, *On the Ruin and Conquest of England,* ch. 25.

10. Ibid, ch. 26.

11. Nennius, *Historia Brittonum,* ch. 56.

12. Caesar, *The Gallic War,* vol. 6:18.

13. The cauldron, currently on display in the Danish National Museum in Copenhagen, is fourteen inches high and twenty-eight inches in diameter, and weighs about twenty pounds.

14. There are a number of Irish manuscripts that include various aspects of the Invasion Cycle, the oldest being the *Lebor na hUidre* (The Book of the Dun Cow), an eleventh-century manuscript in the Royal Irish Academy, Dublin (RIA MS. 23 E. 25); the *Lebhar Laighneach* (The Book of Leinster), a twelfth-century manuscript in the library of Trinity College, Dublin (TCD MS. 1339); the *Leabhar Bhaile an Mhóta* (The Book of Ballymote), a fourteenth-century manuscript in the Royal Irish Academy, Dublin (RIA MS. 23 P. 12).

15. Lludd appears, for example, in tales preserved in *The Red Book of Hergest.*

16. In an Irish story called "The Cattle Raid of Cooley," a legendary hero named Fergus MacRoich finds and briefly possesses Lugh's sword. The story is preserved in the *Leabhar Buidhe Lecain,* "The Yellow Book of Lecan," a fourteenth-century manuscript (cataloged as MS. 1318. H2. 16), now in the library of Trinity College, Dublin.

17. Robert's story is preserved in a manuscript cataloged as MS. Ff.3.11 in Cambridge University Library, England.

18. R. Wheeler, T. Wheeler, *Report on the Excavations of the Prehistoric, Roman and Post-Roman Site in Lydney Park, Gloucestershire* (Oxford: Oxford University Press, 1932).

19. *Three Fortunate Concealments,* a Triad in *The Red Book of Hergest,* trans. by Jenny Bradley.

20. Ibid.

CHAPTER 7—THE SHAKESPEARE ENIGMA

1. Keatman, Phillips, *The Shakespeare Conspiracy.*
2. Ibid., 25–26.
3. Ibid., 25–29.
4. Ibid., 42–44.
5. Ibid., 46.
6. Ibid., 37–41.
7. Ibid., 50–89.
8. A facsimile reproduction of the *First Folio* was published by W. W. Norton, New York, 1968.
9. Keatman, Phillips, *The Shakespeare Conspiracy,* 21–36.
10. Ibid.
11. A. Plowden, *The Elizabethan Secret Service* (New York: Palgrave-Macmillan, 1991).
12. Charles Nicholl, *The Reckoning* (London: Cape, 1992).
13. Keatman, Phillips, *The Shakespeare Conspiracy,* 174–87.
14. Ibid.
15. Ibid., 188–98.

CHAPTER 8—THE ALCHEMICAL WEDDING

1. A modern edition of *The Birth of Merlin* is published by Robson Books, London, 2001.
2. Peter French, *John Dee—The World of an Elizabethan Magus* (London: Routledge, 1972).
3. Frances Yates, *The Rosicrucian Enlightenment* (London: Routledge, 2004), 42–57.
4. Ibid., 63–69.
5. Willard Wallace, *Sir Walter Raleigh* (Princeton: Princeton University Press, 1959), 38–41.
6. Ibid., 52–60.
7. Dee's own diary of the events still survives as a manuscript cataloged as MSS. Sloane 3188 in the British Library.
8. Kepler not only recorded his observations but also commented on the political changes it was thought to herald in his *Da Stella Nova in pede Serpentarii,* published in Prague in 1606.

9. Christopher McIntosh, *The Rosicrucians* (New York: Weiser, 1998), 17–18.

10. Yates, *The Rosicrucian Enlightenment,* 46–48.

11. Ibid., 58–81.

12. Ibid., 1–20.

13. Ibid., 82–95.

14. Ibid., 86–87.

15. The letter survives in Lambeth Palace Library, London, in a collection of state papers cataloged as LP. MS. 650.

CHAPTER 9—INTRIGUE

1. For a discussion regarding *The Tempest* and its Rosicrucian symbolism, see Frances Yates, *Shakespeare's Last Plays: A New Approach* (London: Routledge, 1975), 41–58.

2. For an appraisal of Jonson's masque and its connection with the Rosicrucians, see Frances Yates, *Shakespeare's Last Plays: A New Approach,* 87–105.

3. For a full English translation of the *Fama Fraternitatis,* see Frances Yates, *The Rosicrucian Enlightenment* (New York: Routledge, 2002), 297–312.

4. For the full transcript of the masque, see *The Cambridge Edition of the Works of Ben Jonson* (Cambridge: Cambridge University Press, 2005).

5. For the history of Elizabeth and Frederick, see Carola Oman, *The Winter Queen* (London: Phoenix Press, 2000).

6. An English translation of the *Themis Aurea* is published under the title *Laws of the Fraternity of the Rosie Cross* (Los Angeles: PRS Publishing, 1998).

7. An English translation of the *Atalanta Fugiens* is published under the title *Michael Maier's* Atalanta Fugiens (Berwick, Maine: Nicolas-Hays, 2004).

CHAPTER 10—WHERE WAS AVALON?

1. Keatman, Phillips, *King Arthur: The True Story* (London: Arrow, 1993), 15–18.

2. Phillips, *The Virgin Mary Conspiracy* (Rochester, Vt.: Bear & Company, 2005).

3. *The Song of Llywarch the Old* is published under its Welsh title, *Canu Llywarch Hen,* ed. I. Williams (Cardiff, U.K.: University of Wales Press, 1935).

4. Keatman, Phillips, *King Arthur: The True Story.*

5. Ibid.

6. I. Williams, ed., *Canu Llywarch Hen.*

7. Keatman, Phillips, *King Arthur: The True Story*, 171–75.

8. L. T. Topsfield, *Chrétien de Troyes: A Study of the Arthurian Romances* (Cambridge: Cambridge University Press, 1981).

9. W. Roach, trans., *The Continuations of the Old French Perceval* (Philadelphia: University of Pennsylvania Press, 1983).

10. D. Skeels, *The Romance of Perceval in Prose* (Seattle: University of Washington Press, 1961).

11. W. Nitze, trans., *Perlesvaus* (Chicago: Chicago University Press, 1937).

12. G. Jones, T. Jones, trans., *The Mabinogion* (London: Everyman, 1975).

13. T. Wright, trans., *Fulke le Fitz Waryn* (London: Warton Club, 1855).

14. Phillips, *The Chalice of Magdalene.*

CHAPTER 11—THE VOYAGE OF MAELDUIN

1. For a modern English translation, see P. Joyce, *Old Celtic Romances* (Ware, U.K.: Wordsworth, 2000).

2. *Immram Curaig Maelduin Inso,* ch. 21. English translation from the *Lebor na hUidre* by Tara Connolly.

3. Ibid., ch. 22.

4. Ibid., ch. 26.

5. *The Voyage of Bran* survives in fragmentary form in a number of manuscripts, but the oldest full version is found in an early-tenth-century manuscript cataloged as Harleian 5280 in the British Library. For an English translation, see K. Meyer, *The Voyage of Bran: An Old Irish Saga* (London: David Nutt, 1895).

6. *Immram Curaig Maelduin Inso,* ch. 17.

7. Ibid., ch. 30.

8. The oldest surviving copy of the *Voyage of Saint Brendan* dates from the tenth century and is found in a manuscript cataloged as BN. f. fr. 9759 in the Bibliotech National in Paris. For a modern English translation, see W. Barron, G. Burgess, eds., *The Voyage of St. Brendan: Representative Versions of the Legend in English Translation* (Exeter: The University of Exeter Press, 2002).

9. *Navigatio Sancti Brendani,* ch. 12. English translation: Isabella Persse, *A Book of Saints and Wonders* (Dublin: Dun Emer Press, 1906).

10. Ibid., ch. 16.

11. Tim Severin, *The Brendan Voyage* (London: Arrow, 1978).

12. *Immram Curaig Maelduin Inso,* ch. 22.

13. Ibid., ch. 23.

14. One scholar who made a study of such inscriptions was Barry Fell, an emeritus professor at Harvard University. See Barry Fell, *America B.C.: Ancient Settlers in the New World* (New York: Demeter Press, 1977).

15. I. Traavik, *The Red Ochre People* (Oslo: Aschehoug Forlag, 1999).

CHAPTER 12—MEONIA

1. H. S. Burrage, ed., *Early English and French Voyages* (New York: Charles Scribner and Sons, 1906).

2. For a comprehensive account of Pierre Dugua's life, see Jean-Yves Grenon, *Pierre Dugua De Mons*, (Annapolis Royal, N.S.: Peninsular Press, 1999).

3. D. Simmons, *Henri of Naverre* (London: Blakewell, 1941), 67–78.

4. Ibid., 81–93.

5. The surviving copies of Dugua's pamphlets were later printed in the *Tractatus Apologeticus* [Apologetic Treatise for the Integrity of the Rosicrucians], (Hamburg: Oppenheim, 1617).

6. John A. Goodwin, *The Pilgrim Republic* (Boston: Houghton, 1893), 57–70.

7. E. Arber, *The Story of the Pilgrim Fathers, 1606–1623* (Boston: Houghton, 1897), ch. 3.

8. Dagua's autobiography survives in two volumes in *La vie d'un exploer* [Life of an Explorer] (Paris: Lapérouse, 1626).

9. D. Simmons, *Henri of Naverre,* 103.

10. Dagua, *La vie d'un exploer.*

11. Ibid.

12. Ibid., vol. 2, ch 9.

13. D. Simmons, *Henri of Naverre,* 161–80.

14. C. Oman, *The Winter Queen* (London: Hodder & Stoughton, 1938), ch. 5.

15. Dagua, *La vie d'un exploer,* vol. 2, ch. 9.

16. E. Arber, *The Story of the Pilgrim Fathers,* ch. 5.

17. For an English translation of the *Confessio,* see Frances Yates, *The Rosicrucian Enlightenment* (New York: Routledge, 1972), 312–22.

CHAPTER 13—ISLAND OF THE DEAD

1. British Library: MS. Cotton Vespasian E.4.
2. For further reading, see S. M. Trento, *Field Guide to Mysterious Places of Eastern North America* (New York: Owl Publishing, 1997).
3. L. White, *Mysterious Inscriptions of New England* (New York: Farrar, 1951), ch. 9.
4. R. W. Sewall, *Ancient Voyages to the Western Continent: Three Phases of History on the Coast of Maine* (New York: Knickerbocker Press, 1895).
5. I. S. Proper, *Monhegan: The Cradle of New England* (Portland, Maine: Southworth Press, 1930).

CHAPTER 14—THE FIFTH ELEMENT

1. S. E. Roser, Mayflower *Births and Deaths: From the Files of George Ernest Bowman at the Massachusetts Society of* Mayflower *Descendants* (Baltimore: Genealogical Publishing Co., 1992).
2. D. Bushnell, *Burials of the Algonquian Tribes* (Washington, D. C., Washington Government Printing Office, 1927).
3. This tenth-century manuscript detailing the family trees of important Dark Age chieftains is attached to the manuscript Harleian MS. 3859 in the British Library.
4. For a full discussion concerning this genealogy, see Keatman, Phillips, *King Arthur: The True Story* (London: Arrow, 1993), ch. 17.
5. Genesis, 1:28.
6. The surviving copy of the *Naometria* survives in the *Landesbibliothek* in Stuttgart, cataloged as Cod. Theol. 2, 34.
7. Phillips, *The Chalice of Magdalene*, ch. 12.
8. H. Hammerschmidt-Hummel, *In Search of Shakespeare's Dark Lady* (Darmstadt, Germany: Primus Verlag, 1999).

CHRONOLOGY OF KEY EVENTS

27 B.C.E.	Augustus becomes the first Roman emperor.
43 A.D.	Romans begin conquest of Britain.
161–180	Marcus Aurelius becomes emperor.
325	The Roman Empire adopts Christianity as state religion.
374	St. Ambrose, Bishop of Milan.
397	St. Ambrose dies.
410	Visigoths sack Rome. Roman legions leave Britain.
429	Germanus makes first visit to Britain.
430	Birth of Ambrosius.
435	Vortigern becomes overlord of Britain.
440	Huns attack Roman Empire.
446	Consulship of Quintus Aurelius.
447	Germanus's second visit to Britain. Ambrosius leaves Britain for Armorica. Death of Vortigern.

448	Romans secure temporary peace with the Huns.
451	Huns defeated at the battle of Chalons.
454	Death of Aetius.
459	Ambrosius becomes British leader.
476	Death of Romulus Augustulus, the last Roman emperor.
500	Battle of Badon. Arthur assumes control of Britain.
510	The voyage of Merlin.
545	Gildas writes *On the Ruin and Conquest of Britain*.
575	Battle of Arfderydd.
597	St. Augustine named first British archbishop.
650	*The Song of Llywarch the Old* composed.
731	Bede writes *The Ecclesiastical History of the English People*.
750	Composition of *The Voyage of Maelduin's Boat*.
830	Nennius writes the *Historia Brittonum*.
871	*The Anglo-Saxon Chronicle* is compiled.
927	The Saxon king Athelstan becomes ruler of all England.
930	*The Great Prophecy of Britain* is composed.
950	The *Welsh Annals* are compiled.
1000	Vikings settle a colony in Canada.
1066	Normans invade England.
1100	Adelise Peveril marries Sir Richard Vernon.
1135	Geoffrey of Monmouth writes *The History of the Kings of Britain*.
1150	Geoffrey of Monmouth writes the *Life of Merlin*. The Welsh tale *Peredur* is composed.

1190	Chrétien de Troyes writes *Le Conte del Graal.*
1195	The *First Continuation* is composed.
1200	Robert de Boron's writes *Le Roman du Graal.* The *Didot Perceval* is written.
1220	The *Estoire de Merlin* is composed. *Perlesvaus* is written.
1250	*The Black Book of Carmarthen* is compiled.
1260	*Fulke le Fitz Waryn* is written.
1275	*The Book of Taliesin* is compiled.
1325	*The White Book of Rhydderch* is compiled.
1400	*The Red Book of Hergest* is compiled.
1527	Birth of John Dee.
1553	Mary Tudor, queen of England.
1558	Mary Tudor dies.
1564	Birth of William Shakespeare. John Dee writes the *Monas Hieroglyphica.*
1582	Dee and Kelly leave for France.
1587	Mary Queen of Scots dies.
1588	Assassination of Henry III of France.
1590	In a period of twenty-six years, between 1590 and his death in 1616, Shakespeare writes at least thirty-six plays and dozens of poems.
1594	Henry IV of France is crowned.
1596	The appearance of the star Mira; Princess Elizabeth and Penelope Vernon are born.
1600	Separatist movement founded.

1603	Elizabeth I dies. The voyage of Martin Pring.
1604	The voyage of Pierre Dugua. Merlin's tomb is discovered. A new star appears in the constellation Ophiuchus. Simon Studion writes the *Naometria*.
1608	Separatists move to Leiden.
1610	The *Fama Fraternitatis* is published. Princess Elizabeth has her coming-of-age pageant. French King Henry IV is assassinated.
1613	Princess Elizabeth and Prince Frederick of the Palatinate marry.
1615	Dugua flees France. The *Confessio Fraternitatis* is published.
1616	*The Alchemical Wedding* is published. William Shakespeare dies.
1617	Michael Maier publishes the *Atalanta Fugiens*.
1618	Michael Maier publishes the *Themis Aurea*.
1619	Elizabeth and Frederick become king and queen of Bohemia.
1620	Elizabeth and Frederick are deposed. Rosicrucians hold final meeting in Leiden. The *Mayflower* sets sail.
1632	Inigo Jones builds the Chesterton Windmill.

BIBLIOGRAPHY

Alcock, Leslie. *Arthur's Britain: History and Archaeology A.D. 376–634.* London: Penguin, 1971.

Arber, E. *The Story of the Pilgrim Fathers, 1606–1623.* Boston: Houghton, 1897.

Ashe, Geoffrey. *Avalonian Quest.* London: Fontana, 1984.

———. *Camelot and the Vision of Albion.* London: Heinemann, 1971.

———. *The Discovery of King Arthur.* London: Debrett's Peerage, 1985.

———. *A Guidebook to Arthurian Britain.* Wellingborough, U.K.: Aquarian, 1983.

———. *The Quest for Arthur's Britain.* London: Pall Mall Press, 1968.

Barber, Richard. *King Arthur in Legend and History.* London: Cardinal Books, 1973.

Barron, W., and G. Burgess, eds. *The Voyage of St. Brendan: Representative Versions of the Legend in English Translation.* Exeter, U.K.: University of Exeter Press, 2002.

Bede. *The Ecclesiastical History of the English Nation.* Translated by J. A. Giles. London: Everyman's Library, 1970.

Bender, B., and R. Cailland. *The Archaeology of Brittany, Normandy, and the Channel Islands: An Introduction and Guide.* London: Faber, 1986.

Birley, A. *Lives of the Later Caesars.* New York: Penguin, 1976.

Bland, R., and C. Johns. *The Hoxne Treasure.* London: British Museum Press, 1993.

Burrage, H. S., ed. *Early English and French Voyages.* New York: Charles Scribner and Sons, 1906.

Cavendish, Richard. *King Arthur and the Grail.* London: Weidenfeld and Nicolson, 1978.

Chadwick, Nora. K. *The Age of the Saints in the Early Celtic Church.* London: Oxford University Press, 1981.

———. *Celtic Britain.* New York: Praeger, 1963.

———. *The Celts.* Harmondsworth: Penguin, 1970.

Clancy, Joseph. *Pendragon: Arthur and His Britain.* London: Macmillan, 1971.

Comfort, W. W. *Arthurian Romances.* New York: Dutton, 1914.

Copley, Gordon K. *The Conquest of Wessex in the Sixth Century.* London: Phoenix House, 1954.

Crossley-Holland, Kevin. *British Folk Tales.* London: Orchard Books, 1987.

Darling, M. *Caister-on-Sea: Excavations by Charles Green 1951–55.* King's Lynn, U.K.: Heritage Marketing & Publications, 2000.

Davidson, H. E. *Gods and Myths in Northern Europe.* Harmondsworth, U.K.: Penguin, 1964.

Delaney, Frank. *Legends of the Celts.* London: Hodder & Stoughton, 1989.

Dillon, Myles, and Nora K. Chadwick. *The Celtic Realms.* New York: New American Library, 1967.

Dunning, Robert. *Arthur: King in the West.* London: Alan Sutton, 1988.

Evans, E., ed. *Britannia Monograph Series.* London: Society for the Promotion of Roman Studies, 1988.

Fell, Barry. *America B.C. Ancient Settlers in the New World.* New York: Demeter Press, 1977.

Fife, Graham. *Arthur the King.* London: BBC Enterprises, 1990.

French, Peter. *John Dee: The World of an Elizabethan Magus.* London: Routledge, 1972.

Frere, S. *Britannia.* London: Routledge and Kegan Paul, 1967.

Geoffrey of Monmouth. *History of the Kings of Britain.* Translated by Lewis Thorpe. London: Penguin, 1966.

Gildas. *On the Ruin and Conquest of Britain.* Translated by Michael Winterbottom. Chichester, U.K.: Phillimore, 1978.

Goetinck, Glenys. *Peredur: A Study of Welsh Tradition in the Grail Legends.* Cardiff: University of Wales Press, 1975.

Goodrich, Norma. *Arthur.* New York: Franklin Watts, 1989.

———. *Merlin.* New York: Franklin Watts, 1987.

Goodwin, John, A. *The Pilgrim Republic.* Boston: Houghton, 1893.

Green, Miranda. *The Gods of the Celts.* Gloucester, U.K.: Alan Sutton, 1986.

Grenon, Jean-Yves. *Pierre Dugua De Mons.* Annapolis: Peninsular Press, 1999.

Hodgkin, R. H. *A History of the Anglo-Saxons,* vol. 1. London: Oxford University Press, 1952.

———. *A History of the Anglo-Saxons,* vol. 2. London: Oxford University Press, 1952.

Jarman, A. O. H. *The Legend of Merlin.* Cardiff: University of Wales Press, 1960.

Jarman, A. O. H., and Gwilym Rees Hughes. *A Guide to Welsh Literature.* Swansea, Wales: Davis, 1976.

Jones, A. M. H. *The Decline of the Ancient World.* London: Longman, 1966.

Jones, G., and T. Jones, trans. *The Mabinogion.* London: Everyman, 1975.

Joyce, P. *Old Celtic Romances.* Ware, U.K.: Wordsworth, 2000.

Lacy, Norris, ed. *The Arthurian Encyclopedia.* London: Boydell, 1988.

Loomis, Roger Sherman. *Celtic Myth and the Arthurian Romance.* New York: Columbia University Press, 1927.

———. *Wales and the Arthurian Legend.* Cardiff: University of Wales Press, 1966.

———, ed. *Arthurian Literature in the Middle Ages.* Oxford: Clarendon Press, 1959.

Markale, Jean. *King Arthur: King of Kings.* London: Gordon & Cremonesi, 1977.

McIntosh, Christopher. *The Rosicrucians.* New York: Weiser, 1998.

Meyer, K., trans. *The Voyage of Bran: An Old Irish Saga.* London: David Nutt, 1895.

Morino, C. *Church and State in the Teaching of St. Ambrose.* Washington, D.C.: Catholic University Press, 1969.

Morris, John, ed. *The Age of Arthur,* vol. 1. Chichester, U.K.: Phillimore, 1977.

———. *The Age of Arthur,* vol. 2. Chichester, U.K.: Phillimore, 1977.

———. *The Age of Arthur,* vol. 3. Chichester, U.K.: Phillimore, 1977.

Mytum, Harold, and Chris Webster. *Studia Celtica,* vol. 35. Cardiff: University of Wales Press, 2001.

Nennius. *Historia Brittonum.* Translated by John Morris. Chichester, U.K.: Phillimore, 1980.

Nicholl, Charles. *The Reckoning.* London: Cape, 1992.

Nitze, W., trans. *Parlesvaus.* Chicago: Chicago University Press, 1937.

Noble, T., and T. Head. *Soldiers of Christ: Saints' Lives from Late Antiquity and the Early Middle Ages.* University Park, Pa.: Pennsylvania State University Press, 1994.

Oman, Carola. *The Winter Queen.* London: Phoenix Press, 2000.

Owen, D. D. R. *The Evolution of the Grail Legend.* London: Oliver and Boyd, 1968.

Persse, Isabella. *A Book of Saints and Wonders.* Dublin: Dun Emer Press, 1906.

Phillips, Graham. *The Chalice of Magdalene.* Rochester, VT: Bear & Company, 2004.

————. *The Virgin Mary Conspiracy.* Rochester, VT: Bear & Company, 2005.

Plowden, A. *The Elizabethan Secret Service.* New York: Palgrave-Macmillan, 1991.

Pollard, Alfred. *The Romance of King Arthur.* London: Macmillan, 1979.

Proper, I. S. *Monhegan, The Cradle of New England.* Portland, ME.: Southworth Press, 1930.

Rhys, John. *Y Cymmrodor,* vol. 21. London: The Honourable Society of Cymmrodorion, 1908.

Rhys, J., and J. G. Evans. *The Text of the Mabinogion and Other Welsh Tales.* Oxford: Evans, 1887.

Roach, W., trans. *The Continuations of the Old French Perceval.* Philadelphia: University of Pennsylvania Press, 1983.

Salway, Peter. *The Frontier People of Roman Britain.* Cambridge: Cambridge University Press, 1965.

Severin, Tim. *The Brendan Voyage.* London: Arrow, 1978.

Sewall, R. W. *Ancient Voyages to the Western Continent: Three Phases of History on the Coast of Maine.* New York: Knickerbocker Press, 1895.

Simmons, D. *Henri of Naverre.* London: Blakewell, 1941.

Skeels, D., trans. *The Romance of Perceval in Prose.* Seattle: University of Washington Press, 1961.

Stephens, Meic, ed. *The Oxford Companion to the Literature of Wales.* Oxford: Oxford University Press, 1986.

Thomas, Charles. *Britain and Ireland in Early Christian Times.* London: Thames & Hudson, 1971.

Thompson, E. A. *A History of Attila and the Huns.* Oxford: Clarendon Press, 1948.

Topsfield, L. T. *Chrétien de Troyes: A Study of the Arthurian Romances.* Cambridge: Cambridge University Press, 1981.

Traavik, I. *The Red Ochre People.* Oslo: Aschehoug Forlag, 1999.

Treharne, R. F. *The Glastonbury Legends.* London: Cresset, 1967.

Trento, S. M. *Field Guide to Mysterious Places of Eastern North America*. New York: Owl Publishing, 1997.

Wallace, Willard. *Sir Walter Raleigh*. Princeton, NJ: Princeton Univiversity Press, 1959.

Westwood, Jennifer. *Albion: A Guide to Legendary Britain*. London: Paladin, 1987.

Wheeler, R., and T. Wheeler. *Report on the Excavations of the Prehistoric, Roman and Post-Roman Site in Lydney Park, Gloucestershire*. Oxford: Oxford University Press, 1932.

White, L. *Mysterious Inscriptions of New England*. New York: Farrar, 1951.

Williams, A. H. *An Introduction to the History of Wales*. Cardiff: University of Wales Press, 1962.

Wright, T., trans. *Fulke le Fitz Waryn*. London: Warton Club, 1855.

Yates, Frances. *The Rosicrucian Enlightenment*. London: Routledge, 2004.

———. *Shakespeare's Last Plays: A New Approach*. London: Routledge, 1975.